WE DON'T SPEAK OF FEAR

WE DON'T SPEAK OF FEAR
Large-Group Identity, Societal Conflict, and Collective Trauma

Edited by

Vamık D. Volkan, Regine Scholz, and M. Gerard Fromm

First published in 2023 by
Phoenix Publishing House Ltd
62 Bucknell Road
Bicester
Oxfordshire OX26 2DS

Copyright © 2023 to Vamık D. Volkan, Regine Scholz, and M. Gerard Fromm for the edited collection, and to the individual authors for their contributions.

The rights of the contributors to be identified as the authors of this work have been asserted in accordance with §§ 77 and 78 of the Copyright Design and Patents Act 1988.

All rights reserved. No part of this publication may be reproduced, stored in a retrieval system, or transmitted, in any form or by any means, electronic, mechanical, photocopying, recording, or otherwise, without the prior written permission of the publisher.

British Library Cataloguing in Publication Data

A C.I.P. for this book is available from the British Library

ISBN-13: 978-1-912691-09-8

Typeset by Medlar Publishing Solutions Pvt Ltd, India

www.firingthemind.com

To the IDI family

and

to coworkers in peace building

throughout the world

Contents

Permissions and acknowledgments   xi

About the editors and contributors   xiii

Introduction   xix
M. Gerard Fromm

Part I: Theory

1. Massive traumas, their societal and political consequences, and collective healing   3
   Vamık D. Volkan

2. Dehumanization—the defense that makes evil, cruelty, and murder possible: a psychoanalytic exploration   25
   Lord John Alderdice

3. When time becomes an illusion—collective trauma and memory   39
   Regine Scholz

4. We don't speak of fear: large-group identity and
   chosen trauma   51
   M. Gerard Fromm

5. Braving the new: the struggle from loss to agency   67
   Coline Covington

6. Two facets of the pandemic: stigmatization and
   the psychopolitics of heroization   91
   Deniz Ülke Arıboğan

Part II: Application

7. American identity   119
   Edward R. Shapiro

8. Moral-psychological aspects of ethno-political conflicts
   in Russia and other post-Soviet countries   133
   Alexander V. Obolonsky

9. The German "welcoming culture": some thoughts about
   its psychodynamics   157
   Regine Scholz

10. Identities in flux in a globalized world   181
    Abdülkadir Çevik

11. Cultural exchanges between Turkey and Israel: set for reset 195
    Senem B. Çevik

12. Multiple layers of laws and legal structures: a challenge
    to rendering justice and a source of identity crisis   211
    Hiba Husseini

13. Religious identity and shared trauma: the First Crusade   227
    Ford Rowan

14. IDI thinking in one Georgetown lawyer working in one
    small pocket of the legal community   245
    David G. Fromm

Part III: Methodology

15. International conflict is within individuals: a reflection   255
    Edward R. Shapiro

16. The Sandwich Model: applying the power of small and
    large groups to conflict resolution   263
    Robi Friedman

17. Traveling through time: a group intervention
    in Northern Ireland   273
    M. Gerard Fromm

Index   287

Permissions and acknowledgments

Chapter 2 is based on the 2005 J. S. Grotstein Lecture, given by Lord Alderdice at the J. S. Grotstein Annual Conference, at UCLA, Los Angeles, in February 2005. It was later presented in various forms at other conferences including as the Lionel Monteith Memorial Lecture, at St Thomas's Hospital, London, in April 2005, under the title "Killing for a Cause—The Frightening Phenomenon of Terrorism," and as "Trauma and Terrorism" at the 14th Annual Conference of the International Association for Forensic Psychotherapy at Dublin Castle, in May 2005. A version under the former title was published in 2006 in the *Werkstattschriften Forensische Psychiatrie und Psychotherapie*, Supplement II, pp. 7–22. It is reproduced here with the kind permission of Pabst Publishing.

Chapter 3 is a revised and updated version of a paper delivered in Prague on the occasion of the Prix Irene Conference, December 1, 2012, which was then published in the March 2014 issue of *Agrafa—Journal of Philosophy of Psychoanalysis*, 2: 29–38.

Chapter 4 was originally published as Chapter 11 in *Traveling through Time: How Trauma Plays Itself out in Families, Organizations and Society*, by M. G. Fromm, 2022. It is reproduced here with the kind permission of Phoenix Publishing House.

Chapter 5 was originally published as Chapter 8 in *For Goodness Sake: Bravery, Patriotism and Identity*, by Coline Covington, 2021. It is reproduced here with the kind permission of Phoenix Publishing House.

Chapter 7 was originally published in *Organisational and Social Dynamics*, 3: 121–133, 2003. A revised version was published as Chapter 13 of *Finding a Place to Stand: Developing Self-Reflective Institutions, Leaders and Citizens*, by Edward Shapiro, 2020. It is reproduced here with the kind permission of Phoenix Publishing House.

Chapter 8 is a revised and expanded version of the author's article "Ethnopolitical Conflicts in a Period of Transit as Moral-Psychological Phenomena (Diagnostics and Attempts at Treatment)" published in Russian, in 2020, in the journal *Social Sciences and Contemporary World*.

Chapter 9 was originally published as Chapter 7 in A. Zajenkowska & U. Levin (Eds.), *A Psychoanalytic and Socio-Cultural Exploration of a Continent* (pp. 85–98), 2020. London & New York: Routledge. It is reproduced here with the kind permission of the licensor through PLSclear.

Chapter 10 uses material from "Globalization and Identity," in Sverre Varvin and Vamık Volkan (Eds.), *Violence or Dialogue? Psychoanalytic Insights on Terror and Terrorism* (pp. 85–93), 2003. London: Routledge.

Chapter 17 was originally published as Chapter 13 in *Traveling through Time: How Trauma Plays Itself out in Families, Organizations and Society*, by M. G. Fromm, 2022. It is reproduced here with the kind permission of Phoenix Publishing House.

We are very grateful to Lee Watroba and Jeri Hautzig for their dedicated assistance with this volume and to the whole IDI family for their thoughtful contributions and enthusiastic support for this project.

About the editors and contributors

Lord John Alderdice is a member of the upper house of the British Parliament and former president of Liberal International, the world federation of liberal political parties. As leader of the Alliance Party, he was one of the negotiators of the 1998 Belfast Agreement, first speaker of the new Northern Ireland Assembly, and then one of four international commissioners overseeing security normalization. A psychoanalytic psychiatrist, he works on fundamentalism, radicalization, terrorism, and the problems of indigenous peoples and is currently a senior research fellow at Harris Manchester College, Oxford University, and executive chairman of The Changing Character of War Centre at Pembroke College, Oxford. He is a vice president and cofounder of the International Dialogue Initiative.

Deniz Ülke Arıboğan, PhD, is a political scientist at Istanbul Dogus University. She teaches courses on political psychology and international politics, and received her academic degrees in international relations. In 1995, she finished the Summer School for International Security and Terrorism, at St. Andrews University and between the years 2006 and 2017 she worked at Oxford University as a visiting scholar.

In 2013, she was assigned as a member of the "Wise Man Committee" organized to encourage the Kurdish peace process. She is currently a fellow of the International Dialogue Initiative and a senior fellow at Oxford University's Centre for the Resolution of Intractable Conflict. Her recent book, *The Wall*, was published in English.

Abdülkadir Çevik, M.D.Hfacopsa, is a retired professor of psychiatry. After completing his residency, he was a visiting researcher at the Child and Family Psychiatry Clinic of the University of Virginia Medical School. He served as the chairperson of the Department of Psychiatry at Ankara University Medical School from 2003 to 2013. He advised the Turkish prime minister from 1992 to 1997 while he was the director of the Prime Ministry Political Psychology Center. He taught at various institutions including the NATO COE-DAT and the Turkish Foreign Ministry. Dr. Çevik established the Turkish Political Psychology Association in 2006. He was the chair of the Turkish Group Psychotherapy Association from 2000 to 2021, and is a fellow of the International Dialogue Initiative.

Senem B. Çevik, PhD, is a communication scholar specializing in public diplomacy and a fellow of the International Dialogue Initiative. She taught international studies courses at the University of California, Irvine and UCLA. Her research focuses on the intersection of identity, communication, and psychology with an emphasis on Turkey. She is a member of the Turkey–Israel Civil Society Forum (TICSF) and the American Jewish Committee (AJC) Muslim-Jewish Advisory Council. Dr. Çevik is completed a research project at UC Irvine's Center on Ethics and Morality, and served as the vice president of Light of Anatolia Apricot Tree, a Los Angeles based nonprofit. She is published in *Middle East Critique*, *Caucasus Survey*, and *Southeast European and Black Sea Studies*. She is the founder and executive director of the Nexchange collective and a faculty member at Woodbury University Media Studies Department.

Coline Covington, PhD, is a training analyst and supervisor of the Society of Analytical Psychology and the British Psychotherapy Foundation. She is a fellow of the International Dialogue Initiative (IDI).

Among her publications, Dr. Covington has written a trilogy on morality and the unconscious. The first book of the trilogy is *Everyday Evils: A Psychoanalytic View of Evil and Morality*, published by Routledge, 2017. The second book is *For Goodness Sake: Bravery, Patriotism and Identity*, published by Phoenix Publishing House in 2020. The third book is *Who's to Blame? Collective Guilt on Trial*, to be published by Routledge in May 2023.

Robi Friedman, PhD, is a clinical psychologist and group analyst, past president of the Group Analytic Society (International) of the Israeli Institute of Group Analysis and the Israeli Association for Group Psychotherapy, and is a vice president and cofounder the International Dialogue Initiative. He writes on innovative collective approaches to working with dreams and relational psychopathology, is a teaching group analyst in the Zurich Institute for Group Analysis, and works regularly with institutes in Denmark, Germany, Italy, Russia, and China. He uses the "Sandwich Model," a combined small/large group model applied in conflict dialogues with Palestinians and in other settings, including the ongoing conferences of "Voices after Auschwitz."

David G. Fromm, JD, has practiced civil litigation and dispute resolution in U.S. state and federal courts since 1998. He holds a Juris Doctor degree from Georgetown University Law Center and degrees in international relations from the Central European University (MA, 1995) and the Fletcher School of Law and Diplomacy (LLM, 2011). He is also an author of a sports memoir entitled *Expatriate Games* and a novel entitled *The Duration*. He is a fellow of the International Dialogue Initiative.

M. Gerard Fromm, PhD, is a fellow of the American Board and Academy of Psychoanalysis and a distinguished faculty member and former director of the Erikson Institute of the Austen Riggs Center. He has taught at and consulted to various educational and health organizations across the US, including several psychoanalytic institutes. He is a past president of the International Society for the Psychoanalytic Study of Organizations and the Center for the Study of Groups and Social Systems, and the current president of the International Dialogue

Initiative. His most recent book is *Traveling through Time: How Trauma Plays Itself out in Families, Organizations and Society.*

Hiba Husseini, JD, MA, MSc, is the managing partner of the law firm Husseini and Husseini, in Palestine. The firm serves domestic and international clients. Formerly, she practiced law in Washington, DC. Ms. Husseini chairs the Legal Committee to Final Status Negotiations between the Palestinians and Israelis. She has served as legal advisor to the peace process negotiations since 1994. She serves on the boards of various professional organizations, both in Palestine and internationally, and speaks three languages. She is a fellow of the International Dialogue Initiative.

Alexander V. Obolonsky, Doctor of Science, is a Russian multidisciplinary social scholar, currently professor in the Research University-Higher School of Economics (Moscow). His fields of professional interest cover many different social and humanitarian problems, including historical dynamics of Russia, comparative political analysis of governance, liberalism, the psychology of inter-ethnic and inter-cultural conflicts and the theory of bureaucracy. His publications of recent years are devoted to the problems of liberalism, psychology of conflicts, general crisis of bureaucratic governance, pathologies of bureaucratic consciousness and its negative consequences, critiques of geopolitical approaches as a wrong and dangerous form of consciousness, political street protests, and moral aspects of public policy and politics, both in comparative and domestic respects. He is a fellow of the International Dialogue Initiative. His most important books are: *The Drama of Russian Political History: System against Individuality* (Texas A&M University Press (in English), 2003) and *The Ethics of Public Sphere and the Realities of Political Life* (M. Publishing (in Russian), 2016).

Ford Rowan, JD, DPA, chairs the National Center for Critical Incident Analysis and coauthored *Weathering the Storm: Leading Your Organization Through a Pandemic* (2006). His doctorate in public administration from the University of Southern California focused on preparedness for health crises. He is on the advisory board of the Bioethics Institute at Johns Hopkins University where earlier he earned a degree in applied behavioral science. At Harvard, he studied the roots of religious violence. A cofounder and fellow of the International Dialogue Initiative, he is a former news reporter for NBC News, who covered the Watergate trials, combat in the Mideast, and race relations in the US.

Regine Scholz, Dr. Phil., is training director and a fellow of the International Dialogue Initiative, and a group analyst. Since 1987, she has worked in private practice, specializing in individual and collective trauma. As board member (2010–2017) of the Group Analytic Society International (GASI) she organized its international summer schools (Belgrade 2013, Prague 2015, Athens 2016). She also is the co-organizer of five conferences so far on the heritage of Auschwitz, "Voices after Auschwitz." A founding member of the German Society for Group Analysis and Group Psychotherapy (D3G), Dr. Scholz is a supervisor and training analyst of D3G and member of the editorial board of the journal *Group Analysis*.

Edward R. Shapiro, MD, is the author of *Finding a Place to Stand: Developing Self-Reflective Institutions, Leaders, and Citizens*. He was clinical professor at the Yale Child Study Center and a medical director/CEO at Austen Riggs Center. He received the Deutsch Scientific Award from the Boston Psychoanalytic Society, the Research Prize from the Society for Family Therapy and Research, the Philip Isenberg Teaching Award from McLean Hospital, and was named Outstanding Psychiatrist for Advancement of the Profession by the Massachusetts Psychiatric Association and as one of US News & World Report's *Top Doctors*. He is a cofounder and fellow of the International Dialogue Initiative.

Vamık D. Volkan, MD, DLFAPA, is an emeritus professor of psychiatry at the University of Virginia; an emeritus training and supervising analyst at the Washington Baltimore Center for Psychoanalysis; an emeritus Senior Erik Erikson Scholar at the Erikson Institute of the Austen Riggs Center; the emeritus president and founding member of the International Dialogue Initiative; and a former president of the Turkish-American Neuropsychiatric Society, the International Society of Political Psychology, the Virginia Psychoanalytic Society, and the American College of Psychoanalysts. Dr. Volkan is the author, coauthor, editor, or coeditor of sixty-two psychoanalytic and psychopolitical books.

* * *

We wish to acknowledge other IDI members, whose thinking and colleagueship have contributed immensely to the work in this book: Donna Elmendorf, PhD, Massachusetts-based psychologist and director of the Austen Riggs Center's therapeutic community program; Anatoly Golubovsky, PhD, sociologist and museum expert in Moscow; Bijan Khajehpour, PhD, Iranian-born managing partner of EUNEPA, a consulting firm in Vienna; Reuven Merhav, former senior member of the Israeli intelligence community and former director general of the Israeli Ministry of Foreign Affairs; Farrokh Negahdar, Iranian-born political analyst, living in London; and Frank Ochberg, MD, Florida-based psychiatrist, founding member and Lifetime Achievement Award recipient, International Society for Traumatic Stress Studies.

Introduction

M. Gerard Fromm

A few years ago, three International Dialogue Initiative colleagues—two from Israel and one from Palestine—met informally with a senior diplomat working with the Israel–Palestine negotiating team. At some point in the conversation, one colleague asked the official what happened in the formal negotiating discussion when people on either side talked about their fears. This very experienced diplomat seemed surprised. "We don't speak of fear," he said, later adding that he could see the potential usefulness of trying to address fear during negotiations, but that the team did not know how to do this. As we shall see throughout this volume, powerful emotions, like fear, and powerful defenses against these emotions are at the heart of intractable conflicts. The IDI, in its practice and now in this volume, works toward a framework for understanding these intense feelings, so that they can be brought into speech. Some of the concepts behind that understanding and some of the "know how" for talking are to be found in the pages that follow.

The IDI was founded by Dr. Vamık Volkan in 2007. Dr. Volkan is a psychiatrist and psychoanalyst whose study of societal conflict was galvanized by two moments: the first when his friend was killed in the civil war in Cyprus; the second when Anwar Sadat, then president of Egypt, said that the trouble between Arabs and Israelis was "seventy percent psychological." Volkan, in the midst of a career in clinical practice, immersed himself in learning and in projects related to international conflict, over many years working closely with Turks and Kurds, Israelis and Arabs, Estonians and Russians, and a number of other groups in conflict. At the University of Virginia, where he held a medical school professorship, he founded the Center for the Study of Mind and Human Interaction, through which to organize this work and share the learning from it. That learning came to include a theory of large-group identity, of the intergenerational transmission of trauma and of societal regression. It also included a methodology called the Tree Model, which maps out the back-and-forth dynamics of working with enemy groups, the outcome of which prepares the ground for future negotiations.

When Dr. Volkan retired from the university, he joined Edward Shapiro, the medical director of the Austen Riggs Center, and me at Riggs' Erikson Institute in Stockbridge, Massachusetts. Austen Riggs is a psychiatric hospital, devoted to the in-depth psychotherapeutic treatment of seriously troubled people in an open therapeutic community setting. The clinical data from this work—the generational stories of trauma, the intimate struggles and risks within the treatment relationship, the unlocking of creative potential—is unusually rich, and sadly all too rare in today's mental health world. We felt it was essential that we bring this data into conversation with others. So we founded the Erikson Institute, which I directed for many years (Fromm, 2022) and which included, among other things, a program of Scholars-in-Residence, one of whom was Dr. Volkan.

Erik Erikson, for whom the institute was named, was one of the most important psychoanalysts of the mid-twentieth century. His own history, as the illegitimate child of a German Jewish woman and a Danish gentile father, whom he never knew, had predisposed this sensitive young man to the silent fault lines in a person's identity and to a restless search to know his true origins. Trained in psychoanalysis—with only a high school degree—Erikson contributed enormously to our understanding of developmental crises throughout the life cycle, to our knowledge about the effect of social context on how that development unfolds, and, perhaps most importantly, to a recognition of the power of identity disturbance in the young adult.

Here is Erikson sixty years ago speaking to us today. For example, about radicalization:

> Such vindictive choices of a negative identity represent ... a desperate attempt at [the adolescent's] regaining some mastery in a situation in which the available positive identity elements cancel each other out ... [I]t is easier to derive a sense of identity out of a *total* identification with that which one is *least* supposed to be than to struggle for a feeling of reality in acceptable roles which are unattainable ... Many a late adolescent, if faced with continuing [identity] diffusion, would rather be *nobody*, or *somebody bad*, or *indeed dead*—and this totally and by free choice—than not quite somebody. (1959, p. 132)

Or about destructive polarization: "Where the human being despairs of an essential wholeness, he restructures himself and the world ... an absolute boundary is emphasized ... nothing that belongs inside must be left outside, nothing that must be outside should be tolerated inside" (1959, p. 133).

When I spoke with Erik, late in his life, about what he hoped for from the Erikson Scholar program, his response was characteristically humble, but also stunning from such an accomplished man: "Only that a promising person gets a real chance: the one that I had when I came to Riggs." Erikson was not interested in our enshrining his theory but rather in our holding to his stance, a stance in which he kept one foot, so to speak, securely in the clinical situation: the situation of disturbed relationships, of overwhelming feelings and ingrained defenses, of trauma and identity crisis, with its potential for resolution in creative and destructive directions. But Erikson placed the other foot in anthropology, history, or some other field to see what might be learned in that boundary area. In a notoriously isolationist profession, Erikson made psychoanalysis interdisciplinary, as though agreeing with the observation of his friend—the theologian Reinhold Niebuhr—that "Nothing worth doing can be accomplished alone."

In mid-career, Vamık Volkan took the chance to step into the field of societal conflict and attempt to contribute to its understanding and resolution. He brought people from various disciplines together to work at this, and many of his concepts—like the way in which a society's "chosen trauma" gets organized as part of a compelling, but deeply defensive, large-group identity (Volkan, 2013, 2020)—are extremely important successors to Erikson's. He was a perfect choice to be our Senior Erikson Scholar, and for several years, Vamık spent snowy winters in Stockbridge, writing a book every year. With the help of a seed grant from the Dart Foundation, he also created the IDI, which, at first, was a project of the Erikson Institute. While Volkan had long since fulfilled his promise as a clinician, theoretician, and practitioner in the fields of clinical work and international conflict, his taking up again the leadership of an organization studying societal dynamics gave a new generation the chance he had—and used so well—back in Virginia.

The IDI is now an independent group of about twenty members from various parts of the world and various professions whose task it is to develop psychological understandings of international events and conflicts, and to consider possible interventions. It's actually a network of support, learning, and consultation for the work that individual members carry out, whether that be Dr. Volkan's teaching, or Lord John Alderdice's consultations to governments, or Robi Friedman's and Regine Scholz's large-group interventions in areas of conflict. We meet at least yearly to share reflections and develop our thinking, summaries of which are available on our website at www.internationaldialogueinitiative.com.

At our annual meetings, we also try to learn about and contribute to whatever issues our host city is dealing with. In Berlin, we heard from NGO and clinical leaders about their efforts to bring mental health assistance to refugees. We took up a related topic in Vienna and also heard about and consulted to informal dialogues between professionals whose Middle Eastern countries were in serious conflict. We developed a Volkan Scholar award to recognize the next generation of psychologically informed societal conflict workers, and joined them in the study, for example, of the process of radicalization and of the traumatic legacy of World War II in Eastern Europe. Throughout our work, we pay attention to the particular emotional obstacles to a society's progressive movement, especially in its dealings with "enemy" groups. We hold to a "How are they right?" stance—that is, from what sociohistorical context might a given phenomenon be understood?—while "listening with a third ear," so to speak, to the particular emotional urgency beneath the surface.

We also try to use the process of our discussions—during which each of us functions inevitably as an informal representative of our own nations—to generate hypotheses. I recall a discussion in which members from Iran and the US became increasingly stuck in a heated and repetitive argument about Iran's nuclear program. No one else intervened, or even participated at all, until a female professor from the UAE said with feeling to the man from Iran, "Don't you realize that in a nuclear conflict we would be collateral damage?" This plaintive comment unlocked the dialogue and seemed to permit other representatives from Middle Eastern countries—all men—to say, "Yes, we would be too." Finally, what felt like a defensive silence among the "brotherhood" had broken, allowing more personal speech, including expressions of guilt from Israeli members for their country's role in the conflict. Quietly, the US faded out of its regressive inter-group role as the "big man" and necessary enemy.

That it took a woman to break this dynamic—and a guest at that—was striking, which led to a hypothesis about the role of gender in negotiating this regional conflict. This idea gained some support when a female professor from Istanbul said passionately, "Who gave us this name, 'Middle East,' anyway? That's not how I see Turkey." This second protest by a woman, now about the traditional role of being named by someone else, joined that first plea to profoundly shift the dynamic and to open a dialogue that had seemed closed off behind the silence among the men. How to understand that silence and how to understand the role of women in breaking it were next level questions.

This use of group dynamics to develop societal hypotheses comes in part from work in what are called group relations conferences, first developed at the Tavistock Institute in London. In my experience, these conferences function, among other things, as societal MRIs, illuminating, in a given moment and at a visceral level, the currently prevailing dynamics within that society. I recall conferences in which, for example, Northern Europe's turn toward nationalism was suddenly evident, or in which Israel's struggle with irreconcilable identity elements was right there in front of us. More importantly, these dynamics were available for examination because they had been allowed to come into a learning environment, in which a sturdy and trustworthy framework made intimate, even risky, conversation possible. The IDI includes learning environments of a similar sort among its interventions.

In recent years, the IDI has begun a training program, initially at the request of an experienced negotiator who felt that something "clinical" was missing from his own training. To the degree that past trauma plays an active role in current conflict, embattled groups could indeed be said to be "ill" with intense feelings and irrational reactions, even though the individual participants, of course, are not. It's this "illness" that needs "clinical" understanding, without which negotiations and other interventions may go terribly awry or simply lead to exhaustion and futility. Participants in conflict resolution work inevitably and largely unconsciously bring these troubles with them, with some degree of hope that they will be acknowledged, contained, and understood. This is the focus we bring to our training workshops, one of which uses a case conference model to illuminate societal dynamics. We include in each workshop the three basic elements of psychoanalytic training: didactic lectures, application to cases, and self-reflection groups, the last of these extremely important for members' visceral understanding of large-group identity in their own lives and in the lives of those they work with.

Indeed, the understanding of large-group identity at a personal level is a core aspect of the IDI's regular meetings as well. Its members have come to know each other over the years. We have spent informal time together, adapted to local customs, encountered the unforeseen in the various places we've met, been exposed to each other's personal and national histories, and visited each other's families. Our dialogues have deepened our learning about who we are to ourselves and to others. And we have inevitably learned to face our reactions toward the "otherness" within our own group—toward not only our members' differing values and points of view but also to the language and habits of thinking that are as much a result of the group's interdisciplinarity as its internationality. The chapters that follow were mostly written by those of us involved, broadly speaking, in psychology, but others were written by IDI members whose expertise includes political science, sociology, history, journalism, and the law. It's our hope that the challenge this may present to the reader will be offset by the exposure to new information, new perspectives, and the opportunity to explore some of the ways that psychological concepts are being brought to an understanding of real world conflicts.

One of those horrific conflicts has erupted since this book was written: the brutal invasion of Ukraine by Russia. It is not at all clear when and how this destruction will end, but it is all too clear that its pain will be deep and lasting. There will be lessons to be learned—including, once again, the way that historical trauma plays out in the life of a people and its leaders—and disturbed relationships to be slowly, painstakingly rebuilt. That is for a future we have not yet reached. For now, many of us are doing what we can to support Ukrainian clinicians in their work with traumatized patients and in their efforts to prevent trauma with vulnerable children.

A few years ago, an IDI intervention in Northern Ireland began with an informal communication from one of the participants, who told us, during a coffee break, of a tattoo she had seen on the shoulder of one of her clients, a young girl whose father had been shot during the Troubles: "Bullets don't just travel through skin and bone. They travel through time." The reader will learn more about this intervention in a later chapter. For now, we will simply note that this wrenching, volatile, but also binding truth—this core statement of the "clinical" trouble—is something we in the International Dialogue Initiative think about a great deal. That thinking is the core of this book. The truth in that young woman's tattoo is a truth about traumatic experiences that happen to a family, but also to a society and to the large-group identity that has shaped that society unconsciously over long periods of time. It's also a truth about the way that trauma plays out between generations and between countries, and, in one way or another and in one place or the other, it's a truth that animates all of the chapters to follow.

References

Erikson, E. H. (1959). *Identity and the Life Cycle*. In: G. S. Klein (Ed.), *Psychological Issues* (pp. 1–171). New York: International Universities Press.

Fromm, M. G. (2022). *Traveling through Time: How Trauma Plays Itself out in Families, Organizations and Society*. Bicester, UK: Phoenix.

Volkan, V. D. (2013). *Enemies on the Couch: A Psychopolitical Journey through War and Peace*. Durham, NC: Pitchstone.

Volkan, V. D. (2020). *Large-Group Psychology: Racism, Societal Division, Narcissistic Leaders and Who We Are Now*. Bicester, UK: Phoenix.

Part I

Theory

CHAPTER 1

Massive traumas, their societal and political consequences, and collective healing

Vamık D. Volkan

This chapter focuses on massive traumas at the hand of the Other such as enemies or opponents. Societal/political consequences of such traumas always include shared losses, from losing persons and physical properties to losing self-esteem and prestige, and induce societal mourning. Complications in societal mourning and how they lead to transgenerational transmission of the undigested images of massive trauma to the generations that follow, and how some of such images turn into large-group identity markers, are described. My term "large group" refers to thousands or millions of individuals who share a sense of belonging, even though most of these people never cross paths personally. In our daily life, we might reference these identities using shared ethnic, national, religious, or idealistic terminology, such as when we say we are Catalan, Lithuanian Jews, French, Sunni Muslims, communists, or American white supremacists. The need to protect and maintain large-group identities contaminates political, economic, legal, military, and other real-world issues in relationships and conflicts between large groups. Lastly, this chapter examines psychoanalytically informed interventions that support collective healing as well as peaceful coexistence between enemy large groups.

Types of massive traumas

Massive traumas vary in type. Some spring from natural causes, such as earthquakes, tropical storms, tsunamis, floods, forest fires, or volcanic eruptions. Some are accidentally or deliberately man-made. An example of an accidental disaster is the 1986 Chernobyl explosion which contaminated the atmosphere with tons of radioactive dust. Society may also respond traumatically to the murder or sudden death of a person who functioned as a symbol that unconsciously stood for a parent figure and/or was perceived as a representative of a large-group identity. Assassinations of John F. Kennedy (Wolfenstein & Kliman, 1965) and Martin Luther King, Jr. in the United States, Yitzhak Rabin in Israel (Erlich, 1998; Moses-Hrushovski, 2000; Raviv et al., 2000), Prime Minister Olof Palme in Sweden, the National Democratic Party leader Giorgi Chanturia in the Republic of Georgia, former Prime Minister Rafik Hariri in Lebanon, or the deaths of the American astronauts, especially teacher Christa McAuliffe, in the 1986 space shuttle Challenger explosion (Volkan, 1997) and Diana, Princess of Wales, in a car accident in 1997 (Shapiro, 2020), all led to responses that were experienced as shared trauma.

Other massive traumas such as terrorist attacks, wars, and genocide can be ascribed to the *deliberate actions* of an enemy, an outsider. It might spring from a territorial conflict between two neighboring countries that results in mass atrocities, such as the territorial conflict between India and Pakistan in Kashmir that has led to the disappearance of more than 8,000 people since 1989 along with thousands of extra-judicial killings, torture, rape and Kashmiri Muslims' fear of losing their culture (Haq, 2021). As this book was sent to the publisher, we are witnessing massive traumas due to inhumane acts and a huge refugee crisis as the result of the invasion of Ukraine by Russia.

Such deliberate catastrophes can also occur within a national boundary when there is chronic mistreatment or oppression of a smaller racial or ethnic group by the dominant Other. One of the best-known examples of this is the history of slavery in the United States and discrimination toward black Americans.

When nature shows its fury and people suffer, victims tend ultimately to accept the event as fate or as the will of God (Lifton

& Olson, 1976), but after man-made accidental disasters, survivors blame a small number of individuals or governmental organizations for their neglect or carelessness. Obviously, those suffering severe loss, like the death of a relative, will feel the impact of a trauma more than the people in the same large group who are removed from a catastrophic forest fire or an erupting volcano. Such natural or man-made disasters can also evoke societal responses within the traumatized large group, mostly within the communities near the tragedy. If the backbone of the community is not broken, however, the society recovers. Here is a classic example of "biological regeneration": In October 1966, a hill of coal waste collapsed, sending around 300,000 cubic yards of coal slurry onto the Welsh village of Aberfan, killing 144 people, among them 116 children. For five years following this tragedy, there was a significant increase in the birthrate among women who had not themselves lost a child. The "loss" and the "gain" in the number of children were balanced. The community recovered in a process of "biosocial regeneration" (Williams & Parks, 1975, p. 304). On the other hand, there may be biosocial degeneration such as after the Chernobyl accident when women in Belarus, due to their exposure to radiation, feared having handicapped children. Thus, the birthrate declined and there was no biosocial regeneration during the initial years following this man-made disaster.

Occasionally a natural or man-made accidental trauma is reflected in the traumatized large group's political relationship with a neighboring large group. Here I make references to two huge earthquakes after which one increased and the other decreased political tension. Between 25,000 and 50,000 were killed and up to 130,000 injured in the Armenian earthquake of December 1988, a time when a hot Armenian–Azeri conflict was present. Most injured Armenians refused to accept blood donated by Azerbaijanis after the earthquake. This illustrated resistance to "mixing blood" with the enemy. There was also a massive earthquake in Turkey in August, 1999 that killed an estimated 20,000 people. Only a few years before the quake, Turkey and Greece had almost gone to war in a dispute over some rocks (Kardak/Imia) near the Turkish coast (Volkan, 1997) and there remained high tension between the two countries. After the earthquake, rescue workers from many nations rushed to Turkey to help, among them Greeks. By publishing pictures and stories of Greek rescue workers, Turkish newspapers helped to "humanize" the Greeks as a large group. The Turkish disaster and the earthquake in Greece the following month actually initiated a new relationship between the two nations. Many people in diplomatic circles at that time used the term "earthquake diplomacy" to characterize this positive outcome.

If a political leader or public figure is killed (not by Others but by an individual belonging to the same large group as that of the leader), rage focuses on that killer and, if it exists, against the political organization the killer represents. Although this tragedy does not initiate an international conflict, it may sometimes inflame political tension within the same country.

When a massive trauma results from deliberate oppression or widespread torture by the Other who has a different large-group identity, narcissistic investment in large-group identity, its symbols, and its undigested historical images become inflamed. The heavy shadow of large-group identity falls upon individual identities.

My background in studying massive traumas

Before focusing on massive traumas at the hand of the Other that inflame large-group identity issues, I will briefly outline how I collected information about this subject. As a psychiatrist and psychoanalyst, my involvement in political and societal conflicts started after Egyptian president Anwar Sadat visited Israel in 1977. During this historic visit to the Knesset, Sadat referred to a psychological "wall" between the Israelis and the Arabs—a wall that he stated accounted for 70 percent of the problems between them. The American Psychiatric Association's Committee on Psychiatry and Foreign Affairs, of which I was a member, responded by bringing influential Egyptians and Israelis together for unofficial dialogues once or twice a year for six years to find out if this "wall" could be made permeable. Palestinian representatives joined us during the last three years.

In 1988, at the University of Virginia School of Medicine, I opened the Center for the Study of Mind and Human Interaction (CSMHI) with a faculty of psychoanalysts, other mental health professionals, former diplomats, political scientists, historians, an environmentalist, and a linguist. This interdisciplinary team and I visited many areas of the world where international conflicts existed and brought together representatives of opposing large groups, such as Soviets and Americans, Russians and Estonians, Croats and Bosnians, Georgians and South Ossetians, Turks and Greeks, for years-long unofficial dialogues. CSMHI was closed in 2004 after my retirement. These dialogues involved many discussions about massive traumas, undigested pasts, and ancestors' histories. During my involvement in this work in different countries I also interviewed, often assisted by a translator, many people about their large group's remembered traumatic times and images of past events. We met people on the streets, in parks, elementary schools, cemeteries, or ruins, and while moving about in taxis or trains.

My observations on the impact of massive trauma began even before I opened the CSMHI. I observed firsthand the ethnic conflict in Cyprus, which began in the early 1960s (Volkan, 1979). In 1990, I spent one week in an orphanage in Tunis with Palestinian children who had lost their parents to violence. In the 1990s, I also visited Kuwait twice and talked with adults and youngsters who were adjusting to life following the withdrawal of Saddam Hussein's forces from their country. I also interviewed Romanians and Albanians who had been tortured during the dictatorial regimes of Nicolae Ceauşescu and Enver Hoxha respectively. In the late 1990s and early 2000s, I visited internally displaced ethnic groups in the Republic of Georgia and South Ossetia following ethnic conflicts in this part of the world (Volkan, 1997, 2004, 2006, 2013). Most recently, I went to Colombia and Malaysia. In Colombia, I learned a great deal about the impact that "war" between the government of Colombia, paramilitary groups, communist guerrillas, and crime syndicates has had on individuals. In Malaysia, I observed concerns about the possibility of escalation of tensions between the Malay people and Chinese and Indian ethnic populations living there, as well as negative outcomes due to the influence of fundamentalist Islam from abroad. Here I must add that human beings anywhere in the world have the same psychological makeup. Under different circumstances, as individuals and as large groups, people can potentially become "bad" and carry out inhumane actions.

Individual and large-group identities

Unlike the terms "character" and "personality," which are observed and perceived by mental health clinicians, *individual identity* refers to a person's inner working model—he or she, not an outsider, senses and experiences it. Erik Erikson (1956) described this as "a persistent sameness within oneself … [and] a persistent sharing of some kind of essential character with others" (p. 57). Individual identity is interconnected with *large-group identity*. Using an analogy of a large canvas tent helps explain large-group identity. Think in terms of learning to wear two layers of clothing from the time we are children. The first layer, the individual layer, fits each of us snugly. It is one's personal identity. The second layer is the canvas of the tent which is loose fitting, but allows a person to share a sense of sameness with others under a common large-group tent. The canvas of the tent refers to one's core large-group identity. Some common threads, such as identifications with intimate others in one's environment including their prejudices toward Others, are used in the construction of the two layers, the individual garment as well as the canvas of the tent (Volkan, 1988, 1997, 2004, 2020). While it is the tent pole—the leader—that holds the tent erect or shakes the tent, the tent's canvas (large-group identity) protects the psychological state of both the leader and the group. In this chapter, I will not focus on large-group leaders and the psychological two-way street between them and their followers. Elsewhere I studied in depth the importance of the tent's pole in steadying the tent canvas (Volkan, 1997, 2020).

Worldwide, large-group identities develop in childhood and then become fixed after the individual goes through the adolescence passage. Under a huge large-group tent, there are subgroups and subgroup identities, such as professional identities. A person can change a subgroup identity without much anxiety, but, for practical purposes, an individual cannot change his or her core large-group identity. I am referring to general and typical situations here and not considering unusual individuals in a society, such as those who may be products of parents from different ethnic groups, or voluntary immigrants, especially in childhood. Think of a man—let's say he is French—who is an amateur photographer. If he decides to stop practicing photography and take up carpentry, he may call himself a carpenter instead of a photographer, but he cannot stop being French and become German. While a large group's identity may become modified by major historical events, its evolving a new large-group identity is rare, such as when a substantial group of South Slavs became Bosniaks while under the rule of the Ottoman Empire.

Sometimes new large-group identities develop in adulthood. We see this especially in certain religious cults such as Aum Shinrikyo and the Branch Davidians, guerrilla or terrorist organizations such as Fuerzas Armadas Revolucionarias de Colombia (the Revolutionary Armed Forces of Colombia, FARC) and the so-called Islamic State of Iraq and the Levant (ISIL), and organizations with extreme political aims such as white supremacists and neo-Nazis in the United States (Suistola & Volkan, 2017; Volkan, 2020). Members of such large groups exaggerate selected aspects of their childhood large-group identities by holding on to a restricted special nationalistic, religious, or political belief. Sometimes they become believers in ideas that were not available in their childhood environments. In short, they give up sharing overall sentiments with people who had the same childhood large-group identity but who have not made such specific new selections.

Initial reactions to massive trauma at the hand of the Other

In this chapter, from now on I will focus *only* on human Others who cause massive atrocities and traumas and the shared reactions to them. I will start by giving two examples of *initial reactions* to a trauma caused by the human Other, one from Cyprus and the other from Kuwait. The first one illustrates a kind of biosocial regeneration and the second one a biosocial degeneration.

Following a deadly ethnic conflict with Cypriot Greeks that started in 1963, Cypriot Turks were forced to live in enclaves within 3% of the island for eleven years under subhuman conditions until the Turkish army came to the island in 1974 and divided Cyprus into northern Turkish and southern Greek areas. During the first five years of living surrounded by their enemy, until 1968, the Cypriot Turks could not even leave their enclaves. Because they maintained hope that Turkey would save them, their backbone was not broken, and they became involved in a form of regeneration using shared symbols and displacement. During this time, they developed a hobby of raising thousands of parakeets. The caged birds represented their imprisoned selves. As long as they could care for the parakeets and as long as the parakeets survived, produced babies, and sang, the Cypriot Turks could tolerate their inhumane conditions (Volkan, 1979).

Saddam Hussein's Iraqi forces' occupation of Kuwait started in October 1990 and lasted for seven months. The invading Iraqi soldiers opened the doors of the cages in the Kuwait City zoo, and they also reportedly raped Kuwaiti women and locked up one or two of them naked in these emptied cages. Whether this story was true or not did not matter. What mattered was the Kuwaitis' belief that such degrading events took place. Our team's interviews illuminated that young Kuwaiti men generalized the idea of the raped women incidents and thus, for some time, wanted to postpone marriage in the (mostly unconscious) belief that the women they would marry might also have been raped (Volkan, 1997). The reader will notice how this societal response to the Other in Kuwait brings to our minds the biological degeneration phase in Belarus following the Chernobyl accident.

Besides telling the story of an initial response to a specific massive trauma, it is more important to study the *usual* initial responses when any large group's conflict with an opposing large group becomes inflamed. At such times, the relationships between people in each large group become governed by two obligatory principles: 1) keeping the large-group identity separate from the identity of the enemy; 2) maintaining a *psychological border* between the two large groups at any cost (Volkan, 1988, 1997, 2006).

When people perceive that two large groups are not the same, each side can externalize its own unwanted aspects and project unacceptable thoughts and affects more effectively onto the enemy—sometimes unfortunately escalating to the "*dehumanizing*" of that enemy to varying degrees. Keeping a psychological border between the two large groups is important for controlling the externalizations and projections from returning. Whether the victimization becomes chronic or not, after the acute phase of the catastrophe ends, these two principles may remain operational for years or decades to come. Anything that disturbs them brings massive anxiety, and large groups may feel entitled to do anything to preserve the principles of absolute differentiation, which, in turn, protects their large-group identity. Thus, hostile interactions are perpetuated. *Minor differences* between opposing groups, such as dialect differences between Croats and Serbs—the Croat *mlijeko* (milk) versus the Serb *mleko*—assume attention. Minor differences become major ones in order to maintain the distinctions between the two large groups and the psychological border between them. Sinhalese mobs in the Sri Lankan riots of 1958, for example, relied on a variety of subtle indicators—such as the presence of earring holes in the ear or the manner in which a shirt is worn—to identify their enemy Tamils, whom they then attacked or killed (Horowitz, 1985).

Complications in mourning, transgenerational transmissions, chosen traumas, and entitlement ideologies

A massive trauma at the hand of the Other is connected with various types of losses, such as losing family members and friends, home, economic resources, pride, and self-esteem. Whether a person is fully aware of it or not, every significant loss is mourned. We need to differentiate the mourning process from the acute grief reaction when a mourner is in shock and, in a sense, beats his or her head against a wall and cries until reaching a deep recognition that the lost person or thing will not return. We have a mental representation, a "mental double," of people and things that are important to us. Mourning means being preoccupied and having a relationship with the mental double of a lost person or thing in our minds until this mental double becomes "futureless" (Tähkä, 1984).

For example, when a man reaches the practical end of mourning, he no longer remains preoccupied with associated emotions, for instance with the image of a lover he has lost, and no longer fantasizes having sex with her. The nature of the *actual* relationship with a person or thing before they were lost determines if the mourning process will last a year or so or much longer. Sometimes people may become perennial mourners (Volkan, 1981; Volkan & Zintl, 1993).

Losses after a massive trauma at the hand of the Other are linked to other psychological pressures such as humiliation, helplessness, inability to be assertive, "survivor guilt" (Niederland, 1968), and sometimes unwanted unconscious identifications with the oppressor (Šebek, 1996).

Shifa Haq (2021) noted that decades after the disappearance of their loved ones, Kashmiri survivors-mourners continued to have fantasies that the disappeared individuals might one day return. This prevented them from bringing their mourning process to a practical end.

When members of an affected large group cannot mourn the group's losses or reverse its feelings of helplessness and humiliation, often they psychologically *deposit* their traumatized self-images, accompanied by the mental doubles of Others who played a role in the trauma, into the developing selves of children in their care. By the term "depositing," I refer to the creation of a kind of "psychological DNA" within the child, a transgenerational element of the foundation for identity formation. This situation is known as "transgenerational transmission" or by other names such as "transgenerational transposition" (Kestenberg, 1982) or "the telescoping of generations" (Faimberg, 1993). Psychoanalytic knowledge of transgenerational transmissions of trauma from one generation to the next primarily came from studies of Jewish Holocaust survivors and their offspring. The literature on transgenerational transmission is vast. (For references to such studies, see: Bollas, 1987; Brenner, 2019; Fromm, 2012; Kogan, 1995; Schützenberger, 1998; Volkan, Ast, & Greer, 2002.) I have detailed clinical examples to illustrate that without paying attention to their ancestors' traumas, we cannot fully understand some individuals' interpersonal relationships, symptoms, and the nature of their adjustment to life (Volkan, 2015, 2019).

A child who is a reservoir of depositing is given a *psychological gene* that influences his or her individual and large-group identity. Those in the next generation—when they are not successful in dealing with the psychological tasks given to them—in turn will hand down such images with their associated tasks to a newer generation. Through the decades, tasks carried forward, generation after generation, may *"change function"* (Waelder, 1936). For example, an attempt to reverse humiliation may become an attempt to humiliate the Other. Descendants of victimizers too may experience similar processes, such as difficulty or inability to mourn, as was observed among Germans after the Nazi era (Mitscherlich & Mitscherlich, 1975). Among the descendants of perpetrators, there is more preoccupation with consequences of shared feelings of guilt than preoccupation with the shared feeling of humiliation.

As decades pass and images and tasks included in the transgenerational transmission of massive trauma reference the same historical event, the mental representation of the event links all the individuals in the large group. The mental representation of the event may then emerge as a *chosen trauma* (Volkan, 1991, 2013, 2020). A large group does not choose to be victimized. Its choice is to make the shared representation of the ancestors' massive trauma at the hand of the enemy a most significant large-group identity marker.

In open or in dormant fashion, or in both alternately, chosen traumas can continue to exist for centuries. In "normal" times, the chosen traumas can be ritualistically recalled at the anniversary of the original event. Greeks link themselves when they share the "memory" of the fall of Constantinople (Istanbul) to the Turks in 1453; Russians recall the "memory" of the centuries-past Tatar-Mongol invasion; Czechs commemorate the battle of Bila Hora in 1620 that led to their subjugation under the Hapsburg Empire for nearly 300 years; Scots keep alive the story of the battle of Culloden in 1746 and the failure of Bonnie Prince Charlie to restore a Stuart to the British throne; the Dakota Indians of the United States recall the anniversary of their decimation at Wounded Knee in 1890. Some chosen traumas are difficult to detect because they are not simply connected to one well-recognized historical event. For example, the Estonians' chosen trauma is not related to one specific event, but to their ongoing, almost constant dominance by Others for thousands of years.

When my team from the Center for the Study of Mind and Human Interaction and I were bringing together influential delegates of opposing large groups for years-long unofficial dialogues, we would inevitably see inflammation of chosen traumas. For example, when in the 1990s we worked with people representing Estonians, Russians, and Russian-speakers who were living in Estonia in order to help Estonia develop its new independent identity in a peaceful fashion, we had to deal with the Russian chosen trauma known as "Mongol-Tatar Yoke." The Russian delegates went back to a thirteenth-century massive trauma and, through a *time collapse*, linked emotions connected to this chosen trauma to problems with the Estonians after the collapse of the Soviet Union. When Greek and Turkish representatives were involved in a series of talks, inevitably the Greeks evoked the image of the Ottoman Turks' capture of Constantinople in 1453.

The inflammation of a chosen trauma that raises obstacles against finding peaceful solutions for a present-day conflict is due to a chosen trauma's link to an *entitlement ideology*. For example, the Greeks' chosen trauma is linked to the Greek entitlement ideology known as *Megali Idea* (Great Idea). It refers to a shared wish to recapture land under the rule of "Others" that is considered lost Greek land (Herzfeld, 1986; Markides, 1977; Volkan & Itzkowitz, 1994). A reactivated chosen trauma and the entitlement ideology linked to it increase the large group's narcissistic investment in large-group identity. Then, peculiarly, peace is perceived as a process of withdrawal of such narcissistic investment.

In order to illustrate why we need to pay great attention to chosen traumas and entitlement ideologies, I examined and wrote about the story of the inflammation of the Serbian chosen trauma by Slobodan Milošević and his advisors (Volkan, 1996, 2004). The Serbian chosen trauma is the shared mental representation of the June 28, 1389 Battle of Kosovo. The entitlement ideology connected with it is called *Christoslavism* (Sells, 2002). According to the myth that developed among the Serbs some seventy years after the Battle of Kosovo, the event and the Serbian characters of this battle—especially the Serbian leader Prince Lazar, who was killed during the battle—mingled with elements and characters of Christianity. As decades passed, Prince Lazar became associated with Jesus Christ, and icons showing Lazar's representation in fact decorated many Serbian churches throughout the six centuries following the battle. Even during the communist period, when the government discouraged hero worship, Serbs were able to drink (introject) a popular red wine called "Prince Lazar."

During the year preceding the 600th anniversary of the Battle of Kosovo, an elaborate ritual took place with the full permission and encouragement of Milošević. Lazar's 600-year-old remains, most likely some bones, which had been kept north of Belgrade, were placed in a coffin and taken to almost every Serb village and town, where they were received by huge crowds of mourners dressed in black. Over and over, Lazar's remains were ritualistically buried and reincarnated, until they were given a final resting place at the original battleground in Kosovo where a huge monument made of red stone symbolizing blood had been built. It was June 28, 1989, the 600th anniversary of the battle. In the mythology, Prince Lazar had chosen the Kingdom of Heaven over the Kingdom of Earth. By design, Milošević arrived by descending from a helicopter, representing Prince Lazar coming to earth to found a new kingdom, a Greater Serbia. Thus, Milošević and his associates, by activating the mental representations of Lazar and the Battle of Kosovo, along with the peak emotions they generated, first encouraged a shared sense of victimization followed by a shared sense of entitlement for revenge. This led to new massive traumas in Europe at the end of the twentieth century. Even present-day conflicts that continue in this region cannot be fully understood without paying attention to the Serbian chosen trauma.

A chosen trauma is not an image of a relatively recent historical event. Only over many generations, when an individual, that person's parents, grandparents, other relatives, and friends have no actual memory of the ancestors' trauma, it may become a chosen trauma. Not every major trauma at the hand of the Other evolves as a chosen trauma centuries later. Vladimir Putin, unlike Slobodan Milošević, did not focus on a chosen trauma, in the invasion of Ukraine, but on an undigested trauma from the World War II period (Volkan & Javakhishvili, 2022).

Undigested past

The Holocaust that links all Jewish people, whether they were directly affected by Nazis or not, is not a chosen trauma. Survivors and their descendants still possess photographs and some belongings from that time, and their stories are still "alive." Those affected by the Holocaust and their offspring are still dealing with their *undigested past*. A large group's preoccupation with an undigested trauma, directly or indirectly, is related to continuing difficulties related to large-group mourning. Visiting Yad Vashem in Jerusalem, for example, still induces strong feelings in Jewish people, and indeed in all those who allow themselves to feel the impact of the Holocaust. Yad Vashem is not associated with keeping the wounds caused by the Holocaust alive in the hope of recovering what has been lost; it is not associated with a sense of revenge.

Sometimes the emergence of entitlement ideologies is stimulated by undigested past. I live in Charlottesville, Virginia. On August 11 and 12, 2017, a white supremacist and neo-Nazi rally was conducted in my beautiful city. Marchers who came from other locations in the United States chanted racist and anti-Semitic slogans and carried Nazi and neo-Nazi symbols as they opposed removing a statue of Robert E. Lee, the commanding general of the Confederate States Army during the American Civil War, from a park in the city's historical downtown. During the demonstration, a white supremacist deliberately rammed his car into a gathering of counter-protestors, killing a thirty-two-year-old woman and injuring others. The tragic event in my city and other similar events in the United States are linked to American white supremacists and neo-Nazis who belong to large groups with a shared entitlement ideology of establishing a country populated and controlled by pure descendants of selected white Europeans. Their illusionary entitlement ideology is related to their undigested past or perhaps already a chosen trauma: their losing slavery and racial segregation (Volkan, 2020). We also observed the impact of stimulated and shared "entitlement ideology" that led to the January 6, 2021 attack on the U.S. Capitol by a pro-Trump mob. Meanwhile, African Americans' undigested past/chosen trauma is not recalled by a single event; a huge collection of images of tragic events is stitched on the canvas of their large-group identity tent.

Covid-19

We can consider Covid-19 yet another kind of massive trauma that threatens everyone, regardless of their large-group identities. Elsewhere, I have presented sixteen analysands' shared and individualized responses to this pandemic during its first nine months (Volkan, 2021). I also noted that, since every large group needs to protect itself, preoccupation with physical borders and border closings after the Covid-19 pandemic were expected and realistic. These developments became linked to political themes, leader-follower relationships, and border psychology. By looking back at deadly plagues throughout history, such as the Black Death peaking in Europe and causing the deaths of 75–200 million people in Eurasia and North Africa in the fourteenth century, some scholars expect huge social, economic, and technological changes after the Covid-19 pandemic is over. We will have to wait to evaluate from a psychological point of view how this "enemy" will influence large-group psychology and international relationships.

On healing

Countless methods have been applied in the effort to achieve collective healing of undigested pasts as well as the continuing impact of chosen traumas. Some of them, such as the Truth and Reconciliation Commission's work in South Africa under the leadership of Desmond Tutu, are well known. Others, even when they bring some interesting ideas to consider, do not lead to changes in societies and do not significantly help to improve peaceful coexistence between opposing large groups. During the last three years, I was present at two series of meetings in the United States attended by both white and black Americans, people with high-level religious positions, historians, political scientists, former diplomats, and mental health professionals. It was moving to hear stories related to slavery and racism. Sharing such experiences made all participants feel close to one another, and ideas about what could be done emerged. For example, during one meeting, an African American participant demanded that whenever a black person is on trial, at least three African Americans should be on the jury. In another meeting, participants agreed that erecting a monument in Washington, DC symbolizing both the black and white Americans' traumas during the American Civil War would be helpful in bringing the races together. Such demands or suggestions, even though they may be thoughtful and positive, remained within the conference room. To actually change racist circumstances in a specific area, such dialogues should be followed by some actual, concrete activity.

In November 2006, at Cape Town University in South Africa, I was honored to give the opening speech for the celebration of Archbishop Desmond Tutu's seventy-fifth birthday and the tenth anniversary of the Truth and Reconciliation Commission's founding. The work of South Africa's Truth and Reconciliation Commission (TRC) began in the 1990s as a way to deal with atrocities committed during apartheid. It involved victims telling their stories and "forgiving" their victimizers, who apologized for their deeds. During the 2006 anniversary gathering, I observed some hostility between individual victims and perpetrators who had appeared at the Commission's meetings. I became convinced that the success of the TRC was due to its helping the societal mourning process in South Africa and evolving to serve as a monument that absorbs painful affects (Volkan, 2009). I had met Desmond Tutu earlier at the Carter Center after I was invited to join the International Negotiation Network (INN) under the leadership of former United States President Jimmy Carter in the late 1980s. Instead of seeing an angry man, I saw in Archbishop Tutu a man full of goodness. He was for me a living symbol of human dignity, and his personality organization helped South Africans go through a mourning process.

After the South African Truth and Reconciliation Commission's work, the practice of "apology and forgiveness" that exists in many religions began to be promoted also as a diplomatic/political practice for healing massive traumas and finding solutions for large-group conflicts. The problems faced by those attempting to recreate the TRC's work, and their failures, suggest that a closer examination of when and how reliance on apology and forgiveness is useful, and when it is not, would be of value. Furthermore, my observations of dialogue series between representatives of "enemy" large groups in the presence of a psychologically informed neutral third party show that parties in conflict cannot reach an agreement on making an apology, accepting it, and forgiving the Other without controversy; mostly, they cannot reach such an agreement at all.

Attempts in different locations following the example set by the TRC in South Africa did not end in success. A few years ago, when I was in Colombia, the selection of members for a Colombian truth and reconciliation commission was taking place. I sent a message recommending that a Colombian person with extensive knowledge of individual and large-group psychology be included as a member of this future commission. My suggestion fell on deaf ears. Here we should remember once more the importance of the personality organizations of political and community leaders: Do they support societal healing and have the capacity to feel empathy for others, or do they focus on personal narcissistic gains?

Members of the Center for the Study of Mind and Human Interaction and I developed a methodology for helping to develop peaceful coexistence between opposing large groups in conflict. We named it the *Tree Model*. The title of this methodology reflects the slow process of an unofficial diplomatic activity that grows like a tree and develops many branches. It is a psychoanalytically informed, interdisciplinary methodology for finding peaceful coexistence between enemy groups, and it has *three basic phases*:

(1) *Psychopolitical diagnosis of the situation between the enemy large groups:* This phase includes the facilitating team's in-depth psychoanalytically informed interviews with a wide range of members of the large groups involved. This leads to an understanding of the main conscious and unconscious dynamics of the situation that need to be addressed. Sometimes understanding unconscious shared processes in a large group requires months.
(2) *Psychopolitical dialogues between the influential representatives of opposing large groups:* When the same influential delegates representing "enemies" come together for a series of dialogues for unofficial negotiations, usually meeting for four days every three months over some years, they evolve as spokespersons of their large group's shared sentiments. The facilitators do not offer advice or their own strategies for conflict resolution, but they utilize ideas stemming from psychoanalytic technique in conducting the psychopolitical dialogues. It will be sufficient to state that during the psychopolitical dialogues, the facilitating team pays full attention to large-group identity issues mentioned earlier in this chapter. It takes into consideration the importance of threats against large-group identity, it notices the importance of the shared mental representations of the large groups' histories, and includes the impact of transgenerational transmission of trauma, images of past historical events, as well as time collapse.

One crucial aim of the psychopolitical dialogues is to establish a "time expansion" between more recent problems and past ones belonging to the ancestors so that more realistic negotiations about current issues can take place. This is done by not forgetting or denying ancestors' traumas, but by understanding and feeling how the mental representations of such traumas have become large-group identity markers. Eventually, the opposing large-group participants go through mourning processes and more realistic communications between the representatives of enemy large groups take place.

Earlier I discussed concepts of apology and forgiveness. These concepts are related to what I have named an "accordion phenomenon" (Volkan, 1988, 1997, 1999, 2020), which appears during the second phase of the Tree Model. This refers to opposing participants suddenly experiencing a rapprochement that is followed by a sudden withdrawal from one another. This phenomenon resembles the playing of an accordion, as the groups "squeeze" together and then pull apart.

Derivatives of aggression within the participants from the opposing groups, even when they may be denied, underlie this phenomenon. Initial distancing is thus a defensive maneuver to keep aggressive attitudes and feelings in check, since, if the opponents were to come close, they may harm one another—at least in fantasy—or in turn become targets of retaliation. When opposing parties are confined together in a meeting room with a third "neutral" team and are sharing conscious efforts for a civilized negotiation, they tend to deny their aggressive feelings as they press together in a kind of illusory union. After a while, this closeness threatens each side's large-group identity. The closeness then induces anxiety; it feels dangerous, and as a result, a distancing occurs. It is during times of squeezing together that participants become directly interested in ideas or feelings that can be related to concepts of apology and forgiveness. But, as I stated, when the accordion phenomenon is at work in the dialogue process, giving and accepting apology and forgiveness are illusory. When the accordion pulls apart, preoccupations with such efforts disappear. Realistic negotiations can be carried out when the alternating between distance and togetherness (the accordion action) is no longer extreme and everyone can easily hold on to their group identity. It is at such times that forgiveness and apology also can be considered realistically. However, on their own, they have no magical powers; they are useful only when they are part of a multilevel effort toward reconciliation.

(3) *Collaborative political/societal actions and governmental and societal institutions that grow out of the dialogue process:* In order for the newly gained insights to have an impact on policy makers, as well as on the populace at large, the final third phase of the Tree Model, which also lasts for some years, requires the collaborative

development of concrete actions and institutions approved directly or indirectly by central governments and regional authorities. In Estonia, we were able to build model coexistence projects in two villages where the population is half Estonian and half Russian. We also created a model to promote integration among Estonian and Russian schoolchildren, and influenced the language examination required for Russians to become Estonian citizens. Two persons from our Estonia team ran for the presidency of Estonia, and one of them, Arnold Rüütel, became president of Estonia from 2001 to 2006.

A detailed description of the application of the Tree Model is beyond the scope of this chapter, but such details are published elsewhere (see Volkan, 1999, 2006, 2013, 2020). There are limitations to this model. First, it requires that psychoanalysts and other clinicians develop expertise in international relations and collaborate with diplomats, political scientists, historians, and others. Building an interdisciplinary team has its own psychodynamic challenges. Second, the tree needs water (funds) and it can be difficult to find sponsors for a process that will take many years before the fruits of the tree can be observed by everyone. Nevertheless, as the world changes, there is an increasing need to find serious new methods for preventing conflicts, reducing tensions between opposing groups, and helping with collective healing.

International dialogue initiative

Due to astounding world changes—advances in communication technologies, the evolution of a new type of globalization, massive voluntary and forced migrations, terrorism and related world events, and now the Covid-19 pandemic and the invasion of Ukraine—old official diplomatic methods often may not be enough or even applicable to many current international problems. An understanding of the influence of the psychology of large groups has become a necessity for examining psychological obstacles getting in the way of a peaceful world. We should continue to search for ways to achieve collective healing and a peaceful world.

In order to increase our knowledge about the collective behavior of large groups, in 2007, with the help of Lord John Alderdice in the United Kingdom and other scholars and friends from other locations, I established the International Dialogue Initiative (IDI), which brings together psychoanalysts, diplomats, political scientists, and other professionals from eight countries several times a year. For me, the IDI has become a symbol illustrating how human beings with different large-group identities and historical backgrounds can continue to speak with one another, and coexist peacefully.

References

Bollas, C. (1987). *The Shadow of the Object*. London: Free Association.
Brenner, I. (Ed.) (2019). *The Handbook of Psychoanalytic Holocaust Studies: International Perspectives*. New York: Routledge.
Erikson, E. H. (1956). The problem of ego identity. *Journal of the American Psychoanalytic Association*, 4: 56–121.
Erlich, H. S. (1998). Adolescents' reactions to Rabin's assassination: A case of patricide? In: A. Esman (Ed.), *Adolescent Psychiatry: Developmental and Clinical Studies* (pp. 189–205). London: Analytic Press.
Faimberg, H. (1993). *The Telescoping of Generations. Listening to the Narcissistic Links between Generations*. London: Routledge, 2005.
Fromm, M. G. (Ed.) (2012). *Lost in Transmission: Studies of Trauma Across Generations*. London: Karnac.
Haq, S. (2021). *In Search of Return: Mourning the Disappearances in Kashmir*. Lanham, MD: Lexington.
Herzfeld, M. (1986). *Ours Once More: Folklore, Ideology, and the Making of Modern Greece*. New York: Pella.
Horowitz, D. L. (1985). *Ethnic Groups in Conflict*. Berkeley, CA: University of California Press.
Kestenberg, J. S. (1982). A psychological assessment based on analysis of a survivor's child. In: M. S. Bergmann & M. E. Jucovy (Eds.), *Generations of the Holocaust* (pp. 158–177). New York: Columbia University Press.
Kogan, I. (1995). *The Cry of Mute Children: A Psychoanalytic Perspective of the Second Generation of the Holocaust*. London: Free Association.
Lifton, R. J., & Olson, E. (1976). The human meaning of total disaster: The Buffalo Creek experience. *Psychiatry*, 39: 1–18.
Markides, K. C. (1977). *The Rise and Fall of the Cyprus Republic*. New Haven, CT: Yale University Press.
Mitscherlich, A., & Mitscherlich, M. (1975). *The Inability to Mourn: Principles of Collective Behavior*. New York: Grove.

Moses-Hrushovski, R. (2000). *Grief and Grievance: The Assassination of Yitzhak Rabin.* London: Minerva.

Niederland, W. C. (1968). Clinical observations of the "survivor syndrome." *International Journal of Psychoanalysis, 49*: 313–315.

Raviv, A., Sadeh, A., Raviv, A., Silberstein, O., & Diver, O. (2000). Young Israelis' reactions to national trauma: The Rabin assassination and terror attacks. *Political Psychology, 21*: 299–322.

Schützenberger, A. A. (1998). *The Ancestor Syndrome: Transgenerational Psychotherapy and the Hidden Links in the Family Tree.* New York: Routledge.

Šebek, M. (1996). The fate of the totalitarian object. *International Forum of Psychoanalysis, 5*: 289–294.

Sells, M. A. (2002). The construction of Islam in Serbian religious mythology and its consequences. In: M. Schatzmiller (Ed.), *Islam and Bosnia* (pp. 56–85). Montreal, Canada: McGill University Press.

Shapiro, E. (2020). *Finding a Place to Stand: Developing Self-Reflective Institutions, Leaders and Citizens.* Bicester, UK: Phoenix.

Suistola, J., & Volkan, V. D. (2017). *Religious Knives: Historical and Psychological Dimensions of International Terrorism.* Durham, NC: Pitchstone.

Tähkä, V. (1984). Dealing with object loss. *Scandinavian Psychoanalytic Review, 7*: 13–33.

Volkan, V. D. (1979). *Cyprus—War and Adaptation: A Psychoanalytic History of Two Ethnic Groups in Conflict.* Charlottesville, VA: University Press of Virginia.

Volkan, V. D. (1981). *Linking Objects and Linking Phenomena: A Study of the Forms, Symptoms, Metapsychology and Therapy of Complicated Mourning.* New York: International Universities Press.

Volkan, V. D. (1988). *The Need to Have Enemies and Allies: From Clinical Practice to International Relationships.* Northvale, NJ: Jason Aronson.

Volkan, V. D. (1991). On "Chosen Trauma." *Mind and Human Interaction, 3*: 13.

Volkan, V. D. (1996). Bosnia-Herzegovina: Ancient fuel of a modern inferno. *Mind and Human Interaction, 7*: 110–127.

Volkan, V. D. (1997). *Bloodlines: From Ethnic Pride to Ethnic Terrorism.* New York: Farrar, Straus & Giroux.

Volkan, V. D. (1999). The tree model: A comprehensive psychopolitical approach to unofficial diplomacy and the reduction of ethnic tension. *Mind and Human Interaction, 3*: 142–210.

Volkan, V. D. (2004). *Blind Trust: Large Groups and Leaders in Times of Crisis and Terror.* Charlottesville, VA: Pitchstone.

Volkan, V. D. (2006). *Killing in the Name of Identity: Stories of Bloody Conflicts*. Charlottesville, VA: Pitchstone.

Volkan, V. D. (2009). The next chapter: Consequences of social trauma. In: P. Gobodo-Madikizela & C. Van Der Merwe (Eds.), *Memory, Narrative and Forgiveness: Perspectives on the Unfinished Journeys of the Past* (pp. 1–26). Newcastle upon Tyne, UK: Cambridge Scholars Publishing.

Volkan, V. D. (2013). *Enemies on the Couch: A Psychopolitical Journey Through War and Peace*. Durham, NC: Pitchstone.

Volkan, V. D. (2015). *A Nazi Legacy: A Study of Depositing, Transgenerational Transmission, Dissociation and Remembering Through Action*. London: Karnac.

Volkan, V. D. (2019). *Ghosts in the Human Psyche: The Story of a Muslim Armenian*. Bicester, UK: Phoenix.

Volkan, V. D. (2020). *Large-Group Psychology: Racism, Societal Divisions, Narcissistic Leaders and Who We Are Now*. Bicester, UK: Phoenix.

Volkan, V. D. (2021). Sixteen analysands' and large groups' reactions to the COVID-19 pandemic. *Journal for Applied Psychoanalytic Studies*, 18(2): 159–168.

Volkan, V. D., Ast, G., & Greer, W. (2002). *The Third Reich in the Unconscious: Transgenerational Transmission and Its Consequences*. New York: Brunner-Routledge.

Volkan, V. D., & Itzkowitz, N. (1994). *Turks and Greeks: Neighbours in Conflict*. Huntingdon, UK: Eothen.

Volkan, V. D., & Javakhishvili, J. D. (2022). Invasion of Ukraine: Observations on leader-followers relationships. *American Journal of Psychoanalysis*, 82: 1–21.

Volkan, V. D., & Zintl, E. (1993). *Life after Loss: Lessons of Grief*. New York: Charles Scribner's Sons.

Waelder, R. (1936). The principle of multiple function: Observations on overdetermination. *Psychoanalytic Quarterly*, 5: 45–62.

Williams, R. M., & Parkes, C. M. (1975). Psychosocial effects of disaster: Birth rate in Aberfan. *British Medical Journal*, 2: 303–304.

Wolfenstein, M., & Kliman, G. (Eds.) (1965). *Children and the Death of a President: Multi-disciplinary Studies*. Garden City, NY: Doubleday.

CHAPTER 2

Dehumanization—the defense that makes evil, cruelty, and murder possible: a psychoanalytic exploration

Lord John Alderdice

I still remember, as a trainee in psychotherapy back in February 1985, hearing Nina Coltart deliver a paper entitled "Slouching towards Bethlehem ... or thinking the unthinkable in psychoanalysis." She spoke in the paper of the importance of being able to have faith in the psychoanalytic process, which can help us through the necessary experience of not knowing, especially when dealing with things which cannot as yet be thought by us or our patients, much less put into words. The title of her paper came from the last line of "The Second Coming," a short poem by the Irishman, W. B. Yeats (1920), in which the lines express optimism that something of hope may be emerging,

> *And what rough beast, its hour come round at last,*
> *Slouches towards Bethlehem to be born?*

The poem, however, starts with a stanza that, especially given Yeats's Irishness, I often felt during the Northern Ireland "Troubles" expressed my own experience.

> *Turning and turning in the widening gyre*
> *The falcon cannot hear the falconer;*
> *Things fall apart; the centre cannot hold;*
> *Mere anarchy is loosed upon the world,*
> *The blood-dimmed tide is loosed, and everywhere*
> *The ceremony of innocence is drowned;*
> *The best lack all conviction, while the worst*
> *Are full of passionate intensity.*

In these difficult and dangerous times, many people around the world may feel it expresses their feelings of profound anxiety too. The new millennium started with many opportunities and challenges, but the events of September 11, 2001 ensured that terror, visited upon people by other people, was top of our list of concerns. At that time, we were also becoming increasingly troubled by the unpredictable forces of nature, represented in the deaths of more than 150,000 people in the 2004 Asian tsunami, not to mention the storms and hurricanes that were battering many countries. However, despite the fact that we sometimes refer to these as "acts of God," few of us see them as intentional occurrences with a malign or angry purpose at their source. Indeed, our gathering concern even then was that climate change was an existential threat to which we as humanity have made the key direct, albeit not intentional, contribution. Those who use terrorism to promote their causes are also spreading fear, not as an unfortunate side effect of their activities but as a purposeful tactic that impresses and frightens us. That this planned use of the tactic of terror is carried through with passionate intensity adds to our fear, but also propels us into serious thought and reflection. How can it be that, as W. B. Yeats puts it, "twenty centuries" after the life of the Jew who proclaimed the new possibilities of better relationships, the region of his birth is such a focus of violence and instability? The tradition from which Jesus emerged (and incidentally from which psychoanalysis emerged) has brought us the three great Abrahamic faiths, but despite their transcendent visions, it is their inability to find ways of living together that is currently contributing to some of the most dangerous divisions in our world. Their relationships with each other are not only less than transcendent but often less than human.

My own interest in these problems comes from a much more local experience of inter-communal violence where religious identity is significant. I grew up in Northern Ireland during the period of what is euphemistically known as "the Troubles." As analysts, we try to develop a context in which we can observe and explore what lies at the back of our patients' internal conflicts in order to help them become free of them. Using this model, I set myself to apply a similar approach to the conflict in my own community, treating the community as a patient. This is not the place to describe how I developed this approach save to say that as I got to know those who represented the different strands of life in Ireland, North and South, I was struck by the powerful and universal wish to be treated with respect. Listening through the process of our "Talks" to their different stories and the reasons which they identified as the most significant causes of the violence, it was experiences of disrespect and humiliation which seemed most salient. In individuals and in communities, the toxic impact of humiliation results in harm to oneself and a wish to do harm to those who have caused such deep disrespect. Personal and communal memories of such times when one's continued existence is threatened provoke deep fears and create a capacity for responses at least as violent as those which have been experienced. I set out to explore whether this dynamic of humiliation and its relationship to the outbreak of terrorism was particular to Northern Ireland, and to that end I visited and examined a number of other countries which had also experienced violent insurgencies.

My attention was drawn to Peru by Moisés Lemlij, a psychoanalyst who returned to his native country and tried to assist his people to explore the roots of the Maoist insurgency they had experienced there in the 1980s and 1990s. The main terrorist organization, Sendero Luminoso, or "Shining Path," began among students in Ayacucho, a university town in the mountains. Their claim that native people were not receiving fair attention to their needs was indisputable. Centuries after the Spanish conquered the region, the minority of Spanish descendents still control all the main elements of wealth and governance. However, this picture of a minority ruling elite is not a merely Spanish phenomenon, for they had defeated and replaced the Incas who had occupied a similar position. It was not difficult to appreciate that the Quechua-speaking Indian people and others like them had not been accorded any respect. This lack of recognition and respect was borne in on me as I participated in a ceremony when the remains of seven of the tens of thousands of the "disappeared" were returned to their families. As I walked with the families through the streets of Ayacucho, following the coffins, few people paid any attention. They just went about their business, ignoring this multiple funeral. These grieving people and their dead relatives seemed to be of no import. What was striking about the Maoist strategy, whether conducted there or elsewhere, was that despite its angry and profoundly violent promotion of the cause of these oppressed people, their treatment of these same people was appalling. The lack of humanity in the treatment of those in whose cause they fought was remarkable.

The same abuse of a downtrodden group was evident to me in Nepal, another mountainous country, but one whose background was not quite the same. Nepal has no colonial past. Even at the height of the British Raj in India, Nepal remained independent, and prior to the establishment of the republic in 2008, it was the world's last remaining Hindu kingdom. The country is a poor one, but it seemed to me that the problems which led to the violent Maoist insurgency were not so much economic deprivation but the caste system and its results. Power in the country was held by those who came from the upper castes. Soldiers of the army, in particular the officers who supported the monarchy at the time, were largely drawn from an upper-caste background and were extraordinarily dismissive of those of lower caste, who were not treated as deserving of any regard. The failure of a brief attempt at democracy to enable the lower-caste population and their representatives to play a proper role in the country led to a withdrawal into violence, which eventually resulted in the overthrow of the monarchy, and Nepal is now the only multi-party, fully democratic state in the world currently ruled by a communist party.

Although the situations in Northern Ireland, Peru, and Nepal are widely divergent when assessed on economic grounds, and the history, politics, and forms of government are also different, all three experienced violent internal insurgencies characterized by the use of terrorism. I would argue that in all three cases these insurgencies stem from the long-standing sense of humiliation and disrespect felt by a significant section of the population. Similar remarks could also be made about South Africa and Israel/Palestine but these are more complex, both in their origins and presentation, and they deserve further exploration on their own. In particular, it is clear that when humiliation was visited on the local indigenous population by the incomers, it had elements of a repetition of the abuse that they (that is to say, the Afrikaaners and the Jews) had themselves experienced in their own places of origin, and so their behavior toward the indigenous people was characterized by what we would call "identification with the aggressor."

In short, when the question is asked "Why do people engage in the dreadful violence we call terrorism?" it seems likely that experiences of humiliation play an important role. The main intention of this chapter is to engage with a different but equally common question: "How can people engage in the dreadful violence we call terrorism?" This is not a technical inquiry as to the ways and means of a terrorist insurgency, but an expression of astonishment and distress that human beings can do such terrible things to each other.

In discussing my observations about the importance of humiliation in the origins of terrorist violence with Dr. Estela Welldon many years ago, she drew my attention to the work of James Gilligan (1996) with individuals who had committed very serious violent crimes and were incarcerated in institutions for the criminally insane in the United States. He had made observations about what he called "shaming" in the experience of patients who had committed very violent crimes against other persons. This was similar to what I was noting as "humiliation" in the origins of the terrorism of the IRA. When working with the patients, he became aware that despite the awfulness of their crimes, they believed themselves to be justified. It became apparent that they saw themselves as righting some terrible wrong, some humiliation, a deep disrespect that had been done them. This is similar to those who engage in terrorism. While the rest of the world may see them as evil, they believe that theirs is a moral and courageous activity motivated not by personal material gain but by principle. The question remains, however, how is it possible for one human being to do such a thing to others?

In the closing scientific presentation on the theme of "Aggression" delivered at the 27th International Psycho-analytical Congress in 1971, Anna Freud made two observations about aggression in young children (1982a). She noted that toddlers are not easy to control because they are extremely aggressive to each other, not only in order to have what they want—sweets, toys, attention—but sometimes for no very obvious reason they will bite, scratch, hit out, and kick. The toddler who is attacked may be unable to defend him- or herself and may just as easily be the aggressor or have been an aggressor shortly before or after. She took from this that the direct expression of aggression is an earlier stage in development than the use of aggression for the purposes of defense.

The second observation she made concerned the attitude to the hurt being inflicted. She noted that the toddlers were, at least initially, oblivious of the damage they were doing, which had to be drawn to their attention. In other words, the basic purpose of aggression is not to inflict hurt, though of course subsequently it can be marshalled to this effect. Though it was not the term she used, another way of putting this could be that the appreciation of the effect of one's aggression on the Other is partway along a developmental line to humanization. Becoming a human being is a developmental task or process—the "rough beast ... slouching ... to be born." To lose this capacity of being aware of the effect of one's aggression on the Other would then be a slipping back or reversal in the process. Not only would one be treating the Other as less than human, one would also be losing some of one's own capacity for being human—that is, dehumanization not only affects how one treats the Other, it also affects oneself.

Miss Freud's observations came at the end of a very cautious discussion about the source, aim, object of, and defenses against aggression, in which she advised against simply applying the understanding we have gained from work on libidinal development. She took the view that much more observation was required, and subsequently in "The Study Guide to Freud's Writings" (1982b) she encouraged the view that observation and application of psychoanalysis should include the social and cultural as well as that which emerged and may be applied in the treatment of patients. Thus encouraged, I will continue to explore the question of aggression, combining our clinical understandings with other observations.

Returning to the work of Gilligan, it seems clear that while his patients may well have regressed into psychosis, they do not fail to appreciate that their victims are suffering. They have not simply fallen back to a point in childhood development where they do not understand the damaging nature of their actions. Their violence is, after all, retributive. There may be a condensation of the internal object representations of their victim with the aggressor from the past, but the intention is still to exact primitive justice. One explanation of the regression into psychosis would then be that it occurs because the aggressive drive, which has been given enormous added power arising from the experience of humiliation, comes into conflict with more advanced components of the superego that appreciate the human-ness of the Other, which situation can only be satisfied by a dissolution of the ego and a regression into primary process thinking. Neurotic defense or compromise formation in this situation is inadequate to prevent a descent into psychotic illness. Precisely why humiliation should be so profoundly toxic, and whether the strengthening of the power of aggression is related to some primitive superego component is not clear to me, but the result with these patients was an unthinkable rage, which burst out with tragic consequences.

Is something similar at work with those involved in terrorism? That there is a venomous resentment cannot be doubted, and that it has been strengthened by communal and individual experiences of various kinds is also a matter of observation by anyone who takes seriously the thinking of those involved in acts of terrorism. Often thoughtful and articulate young people, they may try to protect themselves from the enormity of the injuries which they inflict on Others. Activists in some places may take alcohol before going out on an operation, and some have noted that they make a point of not watching the news of their atrocities. Others strengthen themselves with words from a piece of their movement's literature, a team talk or other encouraging or displacement activity. There is, however, no evidence of individual psychosis; on the contrary, vulnerable people are carefully weeded out by handlers within the organizations, but there is often a "fundamentalism" in the beliefs held. This is not just a matter of the content of their beliefs but is represented by a more primitive mode of thinking, and one which is difficult to engage in rational debate or argument. It does seem that there is a denial in word and action of the individual humanity of those who are about to suffer. The perception of the people who they intended would die in the Twin Towers or a bomb in Belfast or Tel Aviv is that they are Americans, or Protestants or Jews, and that this is all that is to be said. That they may not share the position of their government or state, or even have campaigned for the cause espoused by those who will now kill them, is shut out from thinking. They are set aside as the "unfortunate collateral damage of war." Even in using such language we become aware that such a defense is no different for those involved in official armed forces than in terrorist groups. The need to set aside the humanity of the enemy is a necessary and common defense for the soldier or the bomber pilot as much as for the terrorist.

As I have tried to understand the psychology of those who employ the tactic of terrorism, I have found myself examining their arguments, and asking whether there is any element of veracity in them. Those defenses are the stoutest which can marshal an element of reality to assist them in protecting against the underlying anxiety. When terrorists and others attack the United States, therefore, I have to ask myself, does this come solely out of envy, or is there something about the way that the USA conducts itself which adds force to their resentment, and if so, what is the origin of the defensive structure of the USA? This thought has led me to look at the history of the United States, just as I have tried to look at my own and at other communities' histories, on the model of the reconstruction of the individual story in psychoanalysis. The collective myth in the States seems to run something like this.

After the discovery of the New World by Columbus, North America received attention not alone from the imperial powers of Spain, France, and Britain, but also from adventurers and fugitives from famine and persecution. These different groups struggled with each other and eventually the malign influence of the old imperial powers was seen off and a new progressive nation founded out of many nations, and now leads the world.

There is little in this story about the fact that many indigenous people already lived in North America. What happened to them? I have followed this story a little way, enough to meet some of these "first nations" people and hear the terrible history of broken treaties, dishonesty, disregard for the law, and the brutal use of force. An extraordinary number of these people were killed off, not only by disease but through massacres and atrocities such as the "Trail of Tears" when the Cherokees were driven from their homes in North Carolina and thousands died on the way to Oklahoma. This set me to recalling my own memories of "Cowboys and Indians" films. The cowboys had personalities and stories. They had names and relationships, wishes, personal lives, and children, and they were heroically protected with their own guns and arrival of the US Cavalry. The Indians were portrayed as brutal, dishonest savages whose lives had little value, and whose destruction and defeat was a cause for celebration. An examination of the rhetoric of the time, and indeed of much later, makes clear that it was not just that their humanity was shut out from thinking as if, under the anxiety of their precarious lives, the colonists had regressed to the stage of the toddlers to which I referred earlier. A much more active mental step was taken. Arguments were constructed that these were not human beings to be considered in the same way as the colonists. This was a process beyond denial; it was dehumanization. It was not just applied to Native Americans but later also to slaves brought against their will from Africa, and to their descendants.

Only with the use of the powerful defense mechanism of dehumanization would it be possible for someone to perceive another person and yet intentionally treat them so ill, while still satisfying the requirements of a superego. "I am not doing harm, for this is not really a human being." Indeed, under the pressure of the superego, the perceived dehumanized person may further become a representation of evil, and therefore it is not just permissible to do damage to them, it may even be given a moral imprimatur. Is it possible that some of this historical construction of the personality of the United States has not yet been fully addressed and processed and that when America spreads its civilizing influence around the world, it does so with an unconscious negative underlying flavor drawn from this history of not so long ago? Is it possible that this is detected and responded to with great negativity? So, paradoxically, "US Cavalry" help is seen as an attack, and the US embarks on attacks because it believes that this is how to help.

Whatever the truth or otherwise of this speculation, the observation about the sometimes brutal origins of the United States makes it clear that dehumanization is not a mechanism that we can locate only in those people and places where terrorist activity takes place. It is rather a protective device which maintains the integrity of the self when the pressures of aggressive demands bring conflict with other aspects of the self. While it may therefore protect to some degree the integrity of the self, it removes important restrictions on the permissibility of inhuman behavior. The profoundly disturbing degree to which this can develop was described in detail in R. J. Lifton's remarkable study, *The Nazi Doctors* (1986). In it he charts the various psychological elements in the process of dehumanization, from the German experiences of humiliation in the peace settlement of the First World War through the process by which powerful feelings of aggression are given expression in a community and the appreciation of reality gradually distorted for a whole body of people, while an increasingly harsh superego comes into the service of instinctual expression and killing becomes the mechanism for healing of the nation.

Two things seem to me to emerge from his work. First, dehumanization may be less a mechanism than a group of mechanisms. Second, it has a profoundly infectious and paradoxical nature. Those who invoke dehumanization in their assault on the Other, or in order to make such an assault possible, rapidly find themselves dehumanized, and this dehumanized self can then be used to attack the Other. Here we return to the question of terrorism and in particular the form in which it has presented itself in the 9/11 attacks and since then in the suicide bombings in Israel/Palestine. In these terrorist attacks, the dehumanization of the self is a prerequisite for the attack. 9/11 was not the first demonstration of such a mechanism. The Tamil Tigers had used it much earlier, and arguably something of this mechanism was at play in Japanese pilots flying suicide missions in World War II. In Northern Ireland, we all observed this mechanism during the Hunger Strike in 1981. The failure of the IRA's terrorist campaign in the 1970s to bring about a withdrawal of British forces led to a rethink by the prisoners whose struggle with the authorities resulted in a cycle of regressive self-abuse and dehumanization. Firstly they refused to wear prison clothes, since these would identify them as criminals rather than prisoners of war. When this resulted in the prisoners being refused leave from their cells for calls of nature, they responded by taking feces from their slop buckets and smearing themselves and their cell walls.

The inhumanity of the circumstances for them and their jailers brought by this so-called "dirty protest" was responded to by the prison authorities with power hosing and disinfection of the cells and inevitably physical abuse and fights. The cold, unswerving, and punitive approach taken by the highly symbolic woman prime minister, Margaret Thatcher, was reacted to with a decision to go on hunger strike. When the first of these hunger strikes ended with recriminations and accusations by the prisoners of bad faith by her and her officials, the stage was set for a climactic starvation to death of ten men. The tensions heightened when the leader of the hunger strike, Bobby Sands, was elected an MP at Westminster. He continued his fast and was, as he had planned, the first to die. This progressive and profoundly inhuman treatment of themselves brought few obvious short-term benefits in that they died and the process was abandoned without concessions when the families, especially the mothers, began to intervene after the later participants in the hunger strike fell unconscious. They successfully requested resuscitative measures to be employed on the unconscious hunger strikers—good mothers who cared deeply, in contrast to the symbolic bad mother in 10 Downing Street who allowed her MP colleague, as well as sworn enemy, Bobby Sands, to die.

The result was that the hunger strikers became martyrs, in a remarkable and possibly conscious repetition of the executions of the leaders of the 1916 Easter Rising. Their deaths were regarded as blood sacrifices and became the basis for the political rise of Sinn Fein. The party moved over a number of years from being a politically marginal minority to being the main representatives of the Catholic nationalist community in Northern Ireland, even while they were still involved in violent criminal activity, though not (especially after 9/11) overt terrorist tactics. The dehumanization continued for some time with control of their own people and terrain by the use of punitive attacks on their young people, involving destroying the elbows or knees and breaking other bones by savage beatings and shootings.

In the Middle East, suicide bombings also created a generation of martyrs by conscious, voluntary blood sacrifice. By treating themselves in a less than human fashion, they become glorified. While their enemies in Israel responded with a superficial behavioral notion that punishment would stop the bad behavior, Islamists have grasped the transcendence and paradox on the other side of dehumanization.

René Girard (1977) wrote extensively and with considerable insight about these connections between violence, sacrifice, law, religion, culture, and the scapegoat mechanism. Freud realized that while the evidence of the clinic had led him to valuable insights into the vicissitudes of the libidinal drive, the inescapable tragedies of World War I required him to reevaluate his understanding of the aggression. Girard draws attention to the reference in *Group Psychology and the Analysis of the Ego* (1921c) where Freud points up the inevitable conflict arising from identification in the relationship between the boy and his father. The inevitable emergence of hostility when the boy imitates the desire of his father in relation to his mother leads to the Oedipus complex, but as Freud notes in the book, "Identification, in fact, is ambivalent from the very first ... " Girard's complaint is that Freud does not then follow this insight through to what he believed was its logical conclusion—the relational and imitative nature of aggression and its outcome in violence. Girard himself went on to explore the ways in which the mechanism which we call identification and which he refers to as "mimesis" leads inevitably to violence unless the social boundaries of religion, law, and culture are respected.

The implication of this approach is that it is not religion that is the cause of violence, but the breakdown of the boundaries established by religion that results in the release of violence. This argument has some force for those of us who recognize that the breakdown of the horrible but stabilizing boundary of the Cold War has not led to a new and peaceful world order but rather that globalization, with its freedom to trade, travel, and communicate was perceived as a threat, and the current regression to fundamentalist ways of thinking in the East and West is a flight from and defense against this modernity. The Islamists made this clear when they proclaimed that the solution was for the great evil which is America to leave their part of the world, that is to say for a new East/West boundary to be established.

I wonder if it was some recognition of just such problems or limits in Sigmund Freud's theorizing along with clinical experience that led Anna Freud to warn about the limits of what can be done analytically (1936, p. 65). "In analysis," she said,

> we always reassure the patient who is afraid of admitting his id impulses into consciousness by telling him that once they are conscious they are less dangerous and more amenable to control than when they are unconscious. The only situation in which

this promise may prove to be illusory is that in which the defense has been undertaken because the patient dreads the strength of his instincts. All that the ego asks for in such a conflict is to be reinforced. Insofar as analysis can strengthen it by bringing the unconscious id contents into consciousness, it has a therapeutic effect here also. But insofar as the bringing of the unconscious activities of the ego into consciousness has the effect of disclosing the defensive processes and rendering them inoperative, the result of analysis is to weaken the ego still further and to advance the pathological process.

Girard would, I think, concur with the implication that aggression is not always reduced by the removal of boundaries and defenses—on the contrary. In other words, the power of unspeakable rage may not inevitably be weakened by thinking about the unthinkable, which brings us back to Nina Coltart.

In her paper, she described her struggle with a male patient who became increasingly silent, brooding, and depressed. This state proved refractory to the application of all her analytical skill, insight, and patience. Its origin was clearly in a profoundly inhibited aggression toward his mother and the freedom of the psychoanalytical sessions led to a downward spiral as the power of those aggressive feelings was able to be experienced. It was eventually broken, not by a finely toned interpretation, not even one which was repeated time and again, but rather by a single outbreak of genuine emotion from her in which she angrily refused to be destroyed by his aggression. Her humanity broke through and did not allow her to be held in an inhumane relationship with the patient or in an inhuman straightjacket of analytic dogma. Instead of condemning the patient to continue with his punitive behavior, she set down a boundary to it. Herein is the intellectual and emotional struggle: When to say, "No!" Where are the boundaries of freedom? We work, as do artists and lawyers, at the boundaries. Where are we then without them? Only with boundaries is there the possibility of transcendence of the boundaries. Is transcendence then a necessity for freedom? When Yeats refers in the poem, "The Second Coming" (1920) to the "ceremony of innocence," we are reminded of the religious ritual with which he would have been most familiar, the Eucharist. The centerpiece is the symbolic representation of a killing which was healing, a scapegoat mechanism in which one individual was sacrificed for all. Have we, as a human race, got beyond the need for the scapegoat mechanism? Certainly, as René Girard suggested, it is hard to be convinced that the strength of the intellect alone can yet enable us to master the power of our instincts without the boundaries, arbitrary and symbolic as they often appear, of religion, culture, and law. Without them we are vulnerable to the violence and dehumanization which makes evil, cruelty, and murder possible.

References

Freud, A. (1982a). Comments on aggression. In: *Psychoanalytic Psychology of Normal Development*. London: Hogarth, 1981.
Freud, A. (1982b). The study guide to Freud's writings. In: *Psychoanalytic Psychology of Normal Development*. London: Hogarth, 1981.
Freud, A. (1936). *The Ego and The Mechanisms of Defence*. London: Hogarth, 1986 [revised edition].
Freud, S. (1921c). *Group Psychology and the Analysis of the Ego*. In: *S. E.*, 18: 67–147. London: Hogarth.
Gilligan, J. (1996). *Violence: Our Deadly Epidemic and Its Causes*. New York: Putnam.
Girard, R. (1977). *Violence and the Sacred*. Baltimore, MD: Johns Hopkins University Press.
Lifton, R. J. (1986). *The Nazi Doctors*. London: Macmillan.
Yeats, W. B. (1920). The Second Coming. In: *Michael Robartes and the Dancer*. Dundrum, Ireland: Chuala.

CHAPTER 3

When time becomes an illusion—collective trauma and memory

Regine Scholz

Trauma in general and collective traumata especially have a tendency to be experienced as being somehow unaffected by time, as being in a way timeless—making us forget that the events referred to happened at a certain time and a given place. Nowadays it's not debated anymore that important parts of a trauma's heritage are unconscious. Therefore one might connect this "timelessness" to Freud's notion that the unconscious does not know about time. Nevertheless, this line of thought is not sufficient to explain the intergenerational transmission of trauma. This chapter tries to explore the special relation of collective trauma to time—in a first step discriminating different types of trauma and then connecting these with different types of memories and different emotional tasks. Emphasis is laid on the adaptive function of emotions and the change of a trauma's function over time. Some conclusions are made about what types of actions might be helpful or necessary depending on the specific character and stage of a collective trauma.

Though Freud claimed that the unconscious does not know about time (Freud, 1915e), we nowadays know that traumata leave an unconscious heritage passed on to the following generations (e.g., Kogan,

1995; Leuzinger-Bohleber, 2003; Wardi, 1992). To understand these processes of tradition, a reconsideration of the correlation of time and unconscious processes is needed (Scholz, 2004)—and this article tries to work further on that topic.

Initially I want to give a short outline of what to expect when reading further:

- First, different types of collective trauma are differentiated
- Then these different types of trauma are connected to various types of memory, with an emphasis on the diverse emotional tasks connected to the different memory types
- And finally there is a focus on the consequences—security needs—that are to be considered, if working in the field.

Thus I hope to convince you that these classifications are not just an academic toy but of high practical value.

Collective trauma: some specifications

First let us have a closer look at the term "collective trauma." The term has been criticized for being too vague, covering over concrete political circumstances and obfuscating the difference between victims and perpetrators (Becker, 2006; Hillebrandt, 2004). But as it refers and gives a name to a field of violent experiences in which many people are involved—each person at a different position in this field—I do not have a better expression. One proposal to overcome the disadvantages of the term was to specify mass traumatization and to differentiate between different types of collective trauma (Kühner, 2007). In my opinion, further differentiation is needed, since under the shared name "collective trauma" a multitude of phenomena is described, from a concrete mass trauma to the "making up" of a trauma narration (Kühner, 2008).

To develop these ideas, I want as a first step to make a clear distinction between *mass traumata and group traumata*. **Mass trauma** means first of all that many people are affected by an event (e.g., a flood disaster) or a field of connected events (genocide, war). Not all individuals experience the same thing, but many experience similar, terrible things and all these experiences can be classified within and refer to the same context. Not all those affected will develop trauma symptoms in a narrower sense or connected mental illnesses, such as depressions or anxieties (Heuft, 2008), and yet the mental organization of the survivors—victims as well as perpetrators—will to a large extent remain affected by the events.

For a mass trauma to develop into a **group trauma** it needs not only a certain geographical distance and/or historical delay—which nevertheless can be reduced significantly in the media age. It definitely *presupposes a group* that is "hurt." Emphasis is laid on the aspect of the group as an already existing community of interaction and communication, of which the individuals are a part.

A group trauma thus includes, on a first level, those who were directly exposed to a terrible event, and second those that feel connected to those directly involved via identification with a previously defined social group. In this sense, 9/11 can be defined as a collective trauma or group trauma that not only affected the people in the World Trade Center and their relatives, but via the immediately distributed pictures, first all Americans and beyond them the "whole free world" (Kühner, 2007; Wirth, 2004). The example of 9/11 also shows clearly that the number of traumatized people—though a certain amount is needed—is not necessarily the crucial momentum for the characterization of a disastrous event as a collective trauma. In 2008, for example, about 10 million people were made homeless by floods in Northern India, Nepal, and Bangladesh; more than 2,000 died. Without doubt, millions of people were traumatized, but nothing indicates that these people see themselves as a group or that the state, or religious or ethnic groups, of which these people are members, regarded the events as relevant to the way they perceive themselves.

A mass trauma can be considered a group trauma, when the event is relevant for the self-understanding and the self-definition of a group and thus the psychic life of group members.

This perspective allows a new approach to what is called chosen trauma (Volkan, 1999), which can be considered as a—possibly the most important—special case of a group trauma, because very often it is connected to an ideology of entitlement. With the term "chosen trauma," Vamık Volkan describes large-scale traumatic events that are unconsciously being chosen by a given group for their self-definition. What happened lies back so far in time (the fall of Constantinople, the destruction of the second temple in Jerusalem, the Polish separations) that no personal or even family memory can exist. Nevertheless, to participate in the mental representation of these events—to feel certain feelings, to think certain thoughts—is what defines group membership. Here again it is the identification with the social group that allows us to speak of a collective trauma, but in this case the trauma is highly condensed and transferred over generations.

Memories

This brings us to the idea that the different types of trauma are organized along a dimension of space and time from the original traumatic events and raises the question of how they are "stored," and how they are communicated and transferred. In a very rough manner, one might say that mass trauma (or direct trauma) is remembered mainly without words, by body memory and by acting out unconsciously traumatic scenes. Additionally—and later, because in the beginning there are no words—speaking becomes relevant. And by telling our family members and the members of our community what happened, how it was, we are at the beginning of a group trauma. This mainly oral tradition constitutes what Harald Welzer calls the communicative memory (Welzer, 2002). It includes people not directly involved and creates a memorizing community—limited to the close and intimate context of a family and near community. While the body memories definitely die with the traumatized individual's death, the communicative memory can have a span of perhaps 80 to 100 years—the life span of those family and community members who knew the traumatized person.

Chosen trauma usually dates back much further in time. In fact, what "really" happened fades over the generations, because oral and/or family transferal here cannot secure the transmission of the story. What remains is a highly condensed version of historic events, which become part of what Aleida Assmann (1999) and Jan Assmann (1992) call the cultural memory. Contents of the cultural memory have to be set down and externalized in hallowed books and in memorials; they have to be revived in ceremonies and rituals in order to bring them to mind over and over again, so that they can become part of the mental representation of each group member and thus of the "we"-feeling (Bosse, 2005) of the group, through the process of participation and memorization. For example, the killing of eighty-two Swedish nobles in 1520 in the "Stockholm Bloodbath"—the chosen trauma and thus the founding myth of the Swedish nation—is revived every year by the "Vasalopped," an 89 km cross-country ski race with thousands of participants (en.wikipedia.org/wiki/Stockholm Bloodbath).

Time collapse as memory-disorder

Volkan (1999) describes "chosen trauma" as the result of an intergenerational transfer in which the narrative of a humiliating event is being established over many generations and thus becomes an integral part of the psychic life of each group member. Though there was originally a certain ambiguity in Volkan's thinking—defining chosen trauma as long-passed events, of which no personal memory exists but illustrating his theory with examples that date only one or two generations back in time—he later closed this gap by introducing the category of a "hot" trauma "to describe traumatized individuals and their offspring who are still involved in attempting to make sense of what has happened, mourning their losses, and memorializing the tragedy. For example, I consider the Holocaust to still be a 'hot' trauma on its way toward becoming a chosen trauma" (http://vamikvolkan.com/Massive-Trauma%3A-The-Political-Ideology-of-Entitlement-and-Violence.php).

A differentiation between communicative and cultural memory might be helpful here. Thus we can better understand the processes in which an event is transferred from personal pain to family narrations (or family silence) to the schoolbooks to the museums and the memorial days. As the immediacy of personal recollection fades, and people who were directly affected die, books, libraries, exhibitions, and memorials become important.

Large-group cohesion and thus identity always need some kind of shared memories. And since recollection is less a matter of the past than one of personal and group orientation in the present, in order to gain some orientation for the future (Welzer, 2008) the fight about what should be part of the collective memory and how certain facts have to be interpreted is always a part of these widely unconscious processes. The outcome of these fights depends on the power distribution between the collective actors involved—and can be revisited when power constellations change. As these changes usually do not happen peacefully, they are accompanied by intense emotions. Among other things, each individual as part of a given group has to redefine his or her own identity, which is part of the large-group identity. In times of threat, stress, and anxieties, these memories—more exactly, narrations about past traumata—are likely to be reactivated and, in a regressive move, can be experienced as if the humiliation had just happened.

Volkan summed up these phenomena under the term time collapse. The "chosen trauma is then experienced as if it has happened only yesterday: feelings, perceptions, and expectations associated with the past heavily contaminate those connected to current events and current enemies. Leading to irrational political decision-making and destructive behavior" (Volkan, 2006, p. 50). The past replaces the present and is even projected into the future, where it can be fought out again. The familiar order of time collapses. In other words: chosen trauma causes something like a collective memory-disorder.

The difference between the collective memory-disorder and Freud's original concept of timelessness is that, with the collective disorder, events that happened at a distinct time and a distinct place are transformed into a myth, which means that they are being treated *as if* they were timeless; they are *made* timeless. That is how *they can contaminate any interaction; they can ground all emotions and every behavior on conscious but above all unconscious levels.*

For individuals, the narcissistic gain in classifying and reevaluating collective traumata as a chosen trauma lies in being able to defend against feelings of impotence and the implied shame, and in feeling and presenting oneself as a "savior" by investing various experiences of impotence—which may actually result from totally different sources (see Erdheim, 1982)—and the narcissistic rage originating from them, into a reestablishing of "dignity" (e.g., "this is not about me but about my country").

"Creating" a chosen trauma serves several functions: The individual's group membership is emphasized, the aggressions which stem from frustration within the group find legitimate addressees outside, and pain—feelings of helplessness and insignificance—are not to be felt any more. From the group perspective, this constellation acts as a powerful bond for intensifying the group's cohesion, or it can even play a crucial role when a group is born. Very often this constellation is exploited; the chosen trauma is the (ab)used trauma, which then becomes a source of new violent conflicts, leading again to mass traumata and becoming again part of the collective memory.

Some conclusions

Let me return to the differentiations made earlier in this chapter, where I tentatively tried to connect the different types of collective traumata with various forms of memory. Mass traumata correlate with body memory and scenic actions, group traumata with communicative memory, and chosen traumata with cultural memory. From this very rough scheme, some different emotional tasks, and therefore varied needs for action on various personal and social levels, can be derived. In cases of mass traumatization, the emotional task for traumatized persons is to learn to live with their unbearable memories; on the individual level, psychotherapy here can have its place in bringing some relief. The task of the collective is to rebuild elementary general living conditions and prevent further traumatization, which often is difficult enough if not impossible.

In the case of group traumata, the above also holds true for those directly traumatized, but beyond this we enter into the area of the identifications that build up our identities. No individual and no group can do without identifications, but if they become too tight, if only one identity is allowed, group members can be severely harmed. Therefore, it is a task of the community to keep communication channels open for overlapping identities and different interpretations of traumatic events and allow for deviating versions. That implies the guarantee of the security of (deviating) individuals and preventing their expulsion from the group. Carefully constructed experiential groups can do a great job here.

Perhaps the best-known work in this field is that by Dan Bar On, who brought together descendants of Holocaust survivors and perpetrators of the second generation for intense encounters (Bar On, 1998). Being together, witnessing "the other's" feelings—pain, rage, despair, shame, and guilt—can bring back (or allow people to find for the first time) the words, mitigate the projections, and allow personal growth, which had been stuck in too tight identifications. What is needed is a conductor who can function as a good container: helping the group and its members overcome regressive group processes, like splitting and scapegoating, and allowing free expression of thoughts and feelings, which may have been neither expected nor allowed by part of one's own or the other's identity. A well-conducted group in the end allows differences as well as similarities between the subgroups as well as between all its members.

A sad example of regressive group processes on a larger scale was given by a colleague, Martin Mahler, in a conference paper (Prix Irene Conference 2012 in Prague), where he describes the Slansky process. In the heated (regressed) atmosphere of the Cold War, a person like Slansky—being a communist, a Czech citizen, and a Jew—had to be eliminated, because the public was frightened by his different affiliations/identities and their complexities. They needed clearly monolithic identities and a scapegoat. In cases like that, a democratic press (which at that time didn't exist anymore in Czechoslovakia) is needed and can fulfill, with a wider range of influence, the function of offering different viewpoints.

All of the above actions related to post-trauma emotional tasks are necessary yet insufficient in the area of chosen trauma. Since in that case we are dealing with a transformation of collective identity on a great scale, additionally the "invention" of new rituals, museums, and memorials is called for. To bring these huge changes in mentality forward, a society will always need protagonists—at best, transformative leaders. As the transformation of large group-identities affects every single individual of the group in its core, enormous emotions are set free. What is then needed is to safeguard a culture by guaranteeing the physical protection of "dissenters," who in this context are easily called "traitors." The killings of Martin Luther King, John F. Kennedy, Yitzhak Rabin, Anwar el-Sadat (just to name a few) and the concern colleagues in the US had for the physical safety of president Barack Obama make this point clearly and probably are only the tip of an iceberg. Creating and maintaining such a culture of openness and safety demands, among other things, a multifaceted civil society and a wise government. If, however, we are dealing with a nonexistent or a criminal state, things will go bad for a long time.

The arguments outlined above imply that group analysis can contribute a lot to the understanding of these processes, even if its direct possibilities to influence them are limited.

It is obvious that the time rhythms of the above-mentioned processes and the dimensions of the groups involved imply emotional forces of such magnitude that their containment cannot be achieved by one group conductor alone (or with a coleader). Moreover, the societal process needs time in itself. The treatment of trauma always means "reclaiming space and time" (Schlapobersky, 2000), which, in effect, is the abolishment of time collapse. It's about leaving the past or, for the first time, assigning the past its worth in order to live the present and meet the challenges of the future. One could also call it the task of discontinuing or at least mitigating the repetition compulsion. That again is a collective task, in which persons, small groups, and all sorts of social groups and institutions take part, because cultures and their foundation matrices exist only in and through them.

References

Assmann, A. (1999). *Erinnerungsräume—Formen und Wandlungen des kulturellen Gedächtnisses* (*Spaces of Memory—Shapes and Changes of the Cultural Memory*). Munich, Germany: C. H. Beck.

Assmann, J. (1992). *Das kulturelle Gedächtnis—Schrift, Erinnerung und Identität in frühen Hochkulturen* (*Cultural Memory and Early Civilization: Writing, Remembrance, and Political Imagination*). Munich, Germany: C. H. Beck.

Bar On, D. (1998). *The Indescribable and the Undiscussible: Reconstructing Human Discourse After Trauma*. Budapest, Hungary: Central European University Press.

Becker, D. (2006). *Die Erfindung des Traumas. Verflochtene Geschichten* (*The Invention of Trauma: Intertwined Stories*). Berlin: Edition Freitag.

Bosse, H. (2005). Die Bedeutung des Wir in der Gruppenanalyse (The significance of the "we" in group analysis). *Gruppenanalyse*, 15/1: 13–40.

Erdheim, M. (1982). *Die gesellschaftliche Produktion von Unbewusstheit. Eine Einführung in den ethnopsychoanalytischen Prozess* (*The Collective Production of Unconsciousness: An Introduction to the Ethnopsychoanalytical Process*). Frankfurt am Main, Germany: Suhrkamp.

Freud, S. (1915e). Das Unbewusste. *G. W., 10*: 264–303. Frankfurt am Main: S. Fischer (The unconscious. *S. E., 14*: 159–190). London: Hogarth.

Heuft, G. (2008). Individuelles und kollektives Gedächtnis—Kindheiten im Zweiten Weltkrieg im psychoanalytischen Dialog (Individual and collective memory—childhood during WWII in psychoanalytical dialogue). In: *Arbeitshefte Gruppenanalyse* (Hg): 45–55. Psychosozial 111. Giessen, Germany: Psychosozial.

Hillebrandt, R. (2004). *Das Trauma in der Psychoanalyse—Eine psychologische und politische Kritik an der psychoanalytischen Traumatheorie (The Trauma in Psychoanalysis—A Psychological and Political Critic of the Psychoanalytical Theory of Trauma)*. Giessen, Germany: Psychosozial.

Kogan, I. (1995). *Der stumme Schrei der Kinder—Die zweite Generation der Holocaust-Opfer (The Cry of Mute Children: A Psychoanalytic Perspective of the Second Generation of the Holocaust)*. Frankfurt am Main, Germany: S. Fischer, 1998.

Kühner, A. (2007). *Kollektive Traumata—Konzepte, Argumente, Perspektiven (Collective Trauma—Concepts, Arguments, Perspectives)*. Giessen, Germany: Psychosozial.

Kühner, A. (2008). *Wessen Trauma? Eine theoretische Perspektive auf "kollektive Traumen" (Whose Trauma? A Theoretical Perspective on "Collective Trauma")*. Giessen, Germany: Psychosozial.

Leuzinger-Bohleber, M. (2003). Transgenerative Weitergabe von Traumatisierungen (Transgenerational tradition of traumatization). In: M. Leuzinger-Bohleber & R. Zwiebel (Eds.), *Trauma, Beziehung und soziale Realität* (pp. 107–137). Tübingen, Germany: Edition diskord.

Schlapobersky, J. (2000). Die Rückforderung von Raum und Zeit (The reclamation of space and time). In: *Arbeitshefte Gruppenanalyse* (pp. 61–86). Munster, Germany: Votum.

Scholz, R. (2004). Das Unbewusste kennt keine Zeit! Das Unbewusste kennt keine Zeit? (The unconscious does not know about time! The unconscious does not know about time?). *Gruppenanalyse, 2*(4): 147–154.

Volkan, V. D. (1999). The Tree Model: A comprehensive approach to unofficial diplomacy and the reduction of ethnic tension. *Mind and Human Interaction, 10*: 142–206.

Volkan, V. D. (2006). *Killing in the Name of Identity: A Study of Bloody Conflicts*. Charlottesville, VA: Pitchstone.

Wardi, D. (1992). *Memorial Candles: Children of the Holocaust.* London: Routledge.

Welzer, H. (2002). *Das kommunikative Gedächtnis—Eine Theorie der Erinnerung (The Communicative Memory—A Theory of Remembering).* Munich, Germany: C. H. Beck, 2005 [revised and enlarged edition].

Welzer, H. (2008). Warum Menschen sich erinnern können und warum sie Geschichte haben. (Why humans can remember and why they have history.) In: *Arbeitshefte Gruppenanalyse* (Hg.): 57–68. Psychosozial 111, Giessen, Germany: Psychosozial.

Wirth, H.-J. (2004). *9/11 as a Collective Trauma.* Giessen, Germany: Psychozial.

CHAPTER 4

We don't speak of fear: large-group identity and chosen trauma

M. Gerard Fromm

As mentioned in the Introduction, a few years ago three International Dialogue Initiative colleagues, two from Israel and one from Palestine, met informally with a senior diplomat who was working with the Israel–Palestine negotiating team. One colleague asked the official what happened in the formal negotiating conversation when people on either side talked about their fears. The diplomat seemed surprised. "We don't speak of fear," he said, later adding that he could see the sense in trying to address fear during negotiations, but that the team did not know how to do this.

How might we understand the absence of discussion about fear during these conversations, beyond the negotiating team's inability to lead it? After all, fear is one of the emotions at the heart of the conflict: fear for one's survival as a group, fear of the mortal harm another group wants to inflict on one's own group, fear that disasters from the past will happen again. One answer to this question is tactical: the concern that the acknowledgment of fear weakens one's bargaining position. From this perspective, a posture of strength, or even machismo, may seem to promise better results.

One consequence of such fear-denying posturing, however, is that the other group is likely to mirror it. In a group context where acknowledging fear is considered a weakness, "toughness" becomes an attractive fallback position. The risk, of course, to the enactment of what my colleague, Robi Friedman calls the "soldier's matrix" (2019a) is of escalation: tit-for-tat positions, each in response to the other side. There are other consequences as well; this type of posturing, and also its embeddedness in the soldier's matrix, conflates fear with weakness, as though the two are the same. It thereby closes the opportunity to connect with the fear of others at a more human level—indeed as a shared and sensible emotion in a context of danger.

Chosen trauma

Peace talks between Israeli and Palestinian leaders seem forever stuck in limbo, effectively leaving the Israeli and Palestinian people, and generations to come, in limbo as well. Considering events as of this writing in late 2020—especially the specter of Israeli annexation of parts of the West Bank—stalled or broken-off talks seem like a tragedy waiting to happen. Young people may succumb to apathy temporarily but a return to rage is always a possibility, in part as a vitalizing alternative to helplessness or despair. Among other topics, the IDI examines mounting tensions in Israel and Palestine, in the hope of contributing to an understanding of, and a way of working differently with, this and other intractable conflicts. Central to that understanding is that emotions—like fear—are at the heart of such conflicts and learning how to speak about them safely prepares the ground for future negotiation (Rifkind, 2019).

Israelis and Palestinians have suffered enormous trauma. The Holocaust for Israelis and the Nakba for Palestinians condense into two words a multitude of horrific experiences suffered by millions of people. They constitute an unimaginable level of trauma for those who suffered them directly and also for their descendants. Beyond the reality of such trauma, we might also consider them in terms of what Volkan (2013, 2020) calls "chosen trauma." Chosen traumas are traumatic experiences that over time have come to represent and to organize the collective identities of the large groups who suffered the historical trauma. They become part of what characterizes and distinguishes each group of people as who they are, and they sometimes anchor those identities in a definition of the Other as the enemy.

The historical catastrophes behind the Israeli–Palestinian conflict are still within living memory, and so not yet what Volkan means by chosen trauma. But negotiations that do not speak about fear may well reflect large-group identities that have been hardened by the collective memory of emotional trauma, and, in a basic sense, constructed by it as well. "Never again" constructs Israeli identity at some level. "Never surrender" does the same for Palestinian identity. Both sides know who they are, both sides feel their membership in something larger, and both sides do so through knowing who the Other is. In crises, leaders may perpetuate mutually antagonistic narratives and, consciously or unconsciously, use them to build identity cohesion and garner popular support. Large-group identity (Volkan, 2013, 2020) becomes a key factor in intractable conflicts.

Large-group identity is not a conscious, thought-through process. Nor does it begin in the late adolescent phase of identity formation—crucial as that phase is to the individual's development and to his embracing or differentiating from his large group. Rather, large-group identity is an emotional phenomenon beginning in early life, when a toddler is, both excitedly and fearfully, experimenting with leaving the home base of mother to explore his brand new world. In the course of this exploration, the child quickly takes in messages of "Here, with me, is safe. There is dangerous." And "here" soon generalizes from mother to family to home to village to religion to nationality and so on. It also generalizes from safety to pride and morality. Things that belong "here" are good. Things that belong "there" are dirty or bad. "There" generalizes too, especially as the child takes in messages about the Other. Erikson (1959) noted "the subtler methods by which children are induced to accept … prototypes of good and evil" (p. 27); the way that "minute displays of emotion … transmit to the human child the outlines of what really counts" (p. 28). "Every neurosis," he says, is a "*shared* panic" (p. 28).

Large-group identity has meanings related to one's own group—of sameness, safety, goodness and belonging—and meanings related to those outside the group as well. If group anxiety is low, those meanings may include curiosity, generosity, and other emotions. But if group anxiety is high, for one reason or another, latent meanings of the other group as alien, threatening, or dirty may become prominent. And fear of the Other may be expressed in different forms, for example, as scorn or entitlement or a lack of curiosity. Large-group identity is fundamentally about security, and history may be read as a story of large-group insecurity, based on collective trauma, leading to that group's traumatizing another group.

The concept of "chosen trauma" refers to a powerful psychological process shared by members of a large societal group and taking place over many years. Devastating events at the hands of an Other in the history of any group must be mentally and emotionally processed over time. When members of the victimized group are unable to bear the humiliation, reverse their helplessness, or mourn their losses, they pass on to their children powerful, emotionally charged images of their injured selves. In the process, they bind the next generation to them, and pass along psychologically restorative tasks that the next generation is implicitly charged with taking up—for example, avenging humiliation, restoring pride, honoring the dead, and grieving their loss.

All these images and tasks contain references to the same historical event, and as decades pass, the representation of this event in the minds of thousands of people links them together, emerging virulently in times of crisis. A chosen trauma, in a sense, reflects the infection of a group's mourning process—an interference with efforts to come to terms with, and move beyond, the actual trauma. Its reactivation in times of crisis links group members to a shared, endangered sense of identity, which can be used by political leadership to promote new large-group movements, some of which may turn deadly. Fear—along with grievance and rage—can be mobilized in the service of polarizing "Who we are" and "Who they are."

Who are we?

Nation-states are born differently. Israel is what the historian-psychoanalyst Peter Loewenberg (1995) calls a "synthetic nation." Jewish people with different experiences, different investments in religion, and from different places—Europe, the Americas, the Middle East, Russia, and Africa—came to Israel to live in relative peace and freedom from persecution. To do so, they needed to create a synthesis of their disparate influences. But the effort to unify distinct groups inevitably involves great internal strain, and differences within such a group can begin to feel persecutory to the group as a whole. For Israel, the major internal tension, though by no means the only one, is between religious and secular groups. These internal tensions tend to increase a group's need to externalize problematic narratives and project unacceptable ideas and feelings onto the Other. The word "unacceptable" has a double meaning here: not only may one Israeli group find the other Israeli group unacceptable in, for example, their particular religious practices, but they also may find their animosity toward that group unacceptable because it threatens a more secure societal integration.

At a level that may not be at all conscious, Palestine is not only the Other Israel hates, but also the Other it needs as a target for these animosities, so that some semblance of internal peace can be maintained. The same holds true for Palestine, which has become a flag bearer for the suffering of Arab peoples. Palestine not only has its own terrible problems to deal with—for example, the internal tension between Hamas and Fatah—but it also has problems that *stand for* something to Palestinians and others. Such an identity—for example, as a victimized people or a dishonored people or an occupied people—is not "wanted" by the members of a society. Nor do Israelis want to think of themselves as either victims or aggressors. But dialogues with the other group—necessary as they may be to work toward peaceful solutions—can also feel like threats to the broadly shared sense of who each group is. Struggle coheres and supports identity. In recent years, it has seemed that, when the world's eyes are diverted to other crises—for example, to ISIS—conflict erupts in Jerusalem or is provoked along the Gaza border. Attention once again returns to the Israel–Palestine conflict, which, among other things, has the effect of reinforcing both groups' fundamental understanding of who they are.

A societal MRI

A methodology called group relations is generally used to offer powerful experiential learning about authority, leadership, group and inter-group dynamics, and other important issues. At the heart of this work is the task of speaking to what is being experienced in the moment. Thus, they are one way to learn how to speak about fear and about other emotions as well. They also function, in my experience, as societal MRIs. They tend to capture what the membership has taken in of national anxiety and to show, in the microcosm of the conference, how large-group identity plays out among members and staff. Here is an example from an international conference held in Israel.

One of the events in these conferences is something called the Institutional Event, the task of which has to do with members using their authority to decide which aspects of the conference they want to study further (e.g., how leadership is being enacted in the conference) and with what other groups they want to engage in that study (for example, a group studying leadership may want to engage the staff about their leadership, or may want to engage a group studying gender differences about the interrelatedness of gender and leadership). After the task of the IE is spelled out and questions are responded to, the director leaves, and two staff members stay behind to consult to how the group is taking up its task. Generally, because this large group is unnerved about being left on its own, a relatively tumultuous period follows, as this now unguided group works through phases of confusion, excitement, frustration, and whatever else. Eventually, after a few fits and starts, emergent leaders persuade enough members to join them to study a given topic, and off they go to one of the rooms the staff has made available.

In the Israel conference, however, within five minutes of the director's setting out the task, the large-group room was empty. People fled the public space as though a bomb were going to explode, as they indeed had during the Intifada. The only other time in my experience the opening session of the IE played out this way was at a conference four months after 9/11. Seemingly driven by pervasive fearfulness, small groups in the Israel conference formed impulsively without a sense of identity or purpose. Then, quite startlingly, members of these nascent groups came to the staff to request two things: a room, even though rooms had already been made available to them, and a consultant, even though they had not yet met as a group, didn't know who they were, and didn't know what they wanted consultation about. But want one they did, with an insistence that betrayed the intensity of the anxiety they were carrying. On reflection, it seemed to the staff that this was Israel in a microcosm, desperate for territory of its own and for the security of being with whoever was identified as in authority.

Once these smaller groups actually got to their spaces, they preferred not to speak to other groups. Or, if they had to carry out the second part of their task—which was relating to other groups in the service of learning (for example about leadership and gender)—perhaps they could do it without ever having to leave what they came to call "home." When they eventually did venture out for inter-group work, tensions erupted as members encountered conflicting aspects of Israeli identity. For example, a group who came to identify itself as "chosen"—and who in their "home" group explored that part of what they felt deeply to be their large-group identity—found it unbearable to sustain a meeting with a group who saw themselves as representing "vulnerability." Passions intensified, dialogue ceased, and participants fled the room. In retrospect, the actual explosion people feared in the opening of the IE seemed to have everything to do with parts of the Israeli psyche that were extremely difficult to integrate. These two groups felt powerfully the impossibility of containing Israel's dream and its nightmare within the same room.

In the closing plenary of a similar conference, a member reported a dream. *There was a hospital that looked like a lighthouse. Ariel Sharon, gravely ill, was being wheeled in on a gurney. But the treatment in this hospital was unusual. People were hung upside down for a while, and that seemed to help them get better.* The group's work on this dream—taken up for its potential collective meaning (Friedman, 2019b; Fromm, 2000; Lawrence, 1991)—quickly led to a startling understanding. The conference had turned members' understanding of their home organizations, and in some instances their home identities, upside down. They had seen through to core dysfunction and hugely problematic dynamics. While this learning was potentially transformative for their personal, organizational, and political lives, they now had the problem of reentry. What were they to do with what they had learned? How dangerous would it be to bring this new learning back to their home groups? They were going back to the so-called right-side-up world and they were frightened! As were the members of the Israel conference.

Leaders

The Israeli leader in this dream was very ill, and his treatment attempted to show him something from a perspective diametrically opposed to his own. But seeing things from the other side, so to speak, can be dangerous. Many years ago, two things happened in the life of the psychoanalyst, Vamık Volkan, which brought him to the study of international relations. The first was the death of his medical school roommate in the civil war between Greek and Turkish Cypriots. The second occurred when Anwar Sadat, the president of Egypt, took the extraordinary step of speaking to the Israeli Knesset and said that 70 percent of the trouble between Arabs and Israelis was psychological (Volkan, 2013, p. 23). These two events launched Volkan into a second career; while continuing his clinical psychoanalytic practice, he took up the task of trying to understand the psychological dimension of international conflicts. As we saw in Chapter 1, the Center for the Study of Mind and Human Interaction carried out that work for many years. The International Dialogue Initiative represents his most recent effort in that direction.

Anwar Sadat and his later Israeli counterpart, Yitzhak Rabin, were both assassinated *by their own people*. Their challenge to both sides' large-group identities—and the vested interests that accrue in relation to them—led to their deaths. Their societies, faced with external danger, internal fragmentation, and a context of massive historical trauma, were too vulnerable to allow real negotiation with the Other to occur. Erik Erikson described this regressive process as one in which "an absolute boundary is emphasized. Nothing that belongs inside must be left outside; nothing that must be outside should be tolerated inside" (1959, p. 133). Both Sadat and Rabin had created holes in that boundary at their own peril. The basic idea of talking with and hearing from the other side—and potentially of compromise, which is essential to the self-government of a diverse democracy—had taken on the risk of contamination. In the regressive mindset (Volkan, 2004), to compromise is to be compromised, in the sense of being dishonored and debased.

In psychological terms, this is an extreme splitting dynamic, in which all good is here, all bad is there, and no mixing of these absolutes can occur. Within this mindset, which the psychoanalyst Melanie Klein (1946) called the "paranoid–schizoid" position, any questioning of one's own virtue and the other's vices—a questioning that would actually reflect a mature capacity to own one's shortcomings and to see the actions of both sides as making sense somehow—is unacceptable. (The term "paranoid–schizoid" and the terms below are in no way meant as psychiatric diagnoses; rather they refer to emotionally charged phases of normal human development.) For Erikson, a group's "tak[ing] refuge in totalism" has to do with their "despair of an essential wholeness" (1959, p. 133). He thus linked the splitting/purification dynamic to a longing for wholeness, as well as to defensive refuge-taking and to despair. Societal trauma may well lead to profound despair about a group's "essential wholeness," because so many people have been irreparably lost in one way or another to the conflict. Large-group identity may be felt to be deeply damaged, weakened, helpless, humiliated, and grief-struck. Despair implies hopelessness about ever being made whole again.

In this context, it is no surprise that a society would want, and be vulnerable to, a leader who promises to restore collective self-esteem, a leader who could, in a sense, "treat" profound narcissistic injury. The narcissistic leader's projection of power and pride will be taken in by his people, who feel a kind of quickening that all might not be lost and who look to the leader as a savior (Volkan, 2004). A mirroring dynamic ensues between leader and follower, each thriving on the image the other offers to them. This is analogous to the fundamental mirroring a parent offers a child (Kohut, 1971), part of a healthy process in which the child comes to feel a positive sense of self and a belief that he can thrive in the world. But, at a societal level, the narcissistic leader is dealing with a deeply damaged large group, damaged not only by massive losses but by profound humiliation (Alderdice, 2012, and Chapter 2, this volume) as well. The regressed society's efforts toward repair too often attempt to bypass the losses in favor of reversing the humiliation.

Essential as some version of narcissistic repair is to the restoration of the group's identity, it is profoundly risky. The mirroring dynamic between leader and followers creates collective illusions about both sides, which have a life apart from reality. One's own side is idealized and the other denigrated. Intense emotions are catalyzed and acted out upon the group seen as causing the damage. Retaliatory violence seems to promise relief from despair, as though this crude form of justice will bring back all who have been lost. Even within societies, this kind of mirroring and splitting dynamic takes place, leading to the polarization we saw in the United States under President Trump.

The psychoanalyst Jacques Lacan (1977) studied the mirroring process, which at its heart begins with the loving gaze of mother to child. Lacan argued that what the child sees in his mother's eyes, and later in the mirror, offers an illusory sense of wholeness, which offsets, but only to a degree, the child's everyday feelings of incompetence and frustration, which simply have to do with being new to the world. For Lacan, the mirror and the gaze were a seduction, a partial truth that vulnerable people wanted to believe as the whole truth. The mirroring dynamic defines what he called the "imaginary order," in which narcissistic needs are indeed gratified, but simultaneously an inevitable paranoia develops. Deep down, people know that the image in the mirror—or in the adulatory gaze of followers—is not the whole truth; indeed they know that the truth, whatever it might be, cannot be seen in the mirror. For the wishful-thinking narcissist, seeing is believing. For the paranoid, what is *not seen* is believed. And for Lacan, they are two sides of the same person. Again, witness the conspiracy theories of Trump's followers.

Narcissistic leaders, and the mirroring dynamic they mobilize, present a major risk to the societal self-esteem they are meant to restore. Mirroring is an imaginary process—one involving people's emotionally driven, wishful fantasies about themselves and their leaders. It thereby denies the truths it doesn't want to see and increasingly separates itself from reality. Illusions become more like delusions. The process of restoring a traumatized society takes a paranoid turn toward purification, as what is not seen threatens to invade what is seen. One need not look further than Hitler's Germany to see this process in its most extreme form—from its beginnings in an outraged effort to overcome deep humiliation and massive loss to a paranoid megalomania about purity (Volkan et al., 2002).

The psychological alternative to the paranoid–schizoid position is what Klein (1946) called the "depressive position," from which the whole problem—in the case of politicians, the whole country, its actions, and its history—is taken in as one's own to deal with. It implies seeing the other as a person, rather than a stereotype, and being able to take responsibility for one's own aggression. Finding the other in oneself and vice versa is the psychological difficulty of the work, and, as we have seen, it is dangerous in the context of societal trauma. Barack Obama might be described as an example of a "depressive position" president: that is, a president hoping to lead the whole country from an ethic of bipartisanship while taking responsibility for American aggression. His childhood experience of being the only child of a black-white, American-African marriage may well have given him both the aspiration and the capacity to bridge seemingly unbridgeable differences.

In 2016, Obama became the first sitting US president to visit the Hiroshima Peace Memorial. While recognizing both sides' aggression, his capacity for empathy exemplified the depressive position. Listen to President Obama's words in Hiroshima: "Why do we come to this place? … To force ourselves to imagine the moment when the bomb fell … to feel the dread of children … [to] listen to a silent cry … [to] remember all the innocents killed … to mourn the dead … Their souls speak to us" (Obama, 2016). After his address, he embraced survivors of the bomb—the bomb his country had dropped—one of whom wept in his arms. This is the work of mourning that depressive-position leaders can help societies achieve. Crucially, it includes the leader's being willing to bear guilt and shame, associated with aggression, on behalf of his own group, no matter how justified that aggression might have been.

The Japanese man who wept in President Obama's arms survived because, as an eight-year-old boy walking to school on August 6, 1945, the force of the blast blew him into the river, where he escaped the firestorm. So many of his friends and family simply disappeared in that moment, and for decades, Japan has worked hard to include all of their names in the Peace Memorial. This survivor, however, Mr. Shigeaki Mori, devoted himself to finding the names of the American airmen— prisoners of war in Hiroshima—who had also disappeared that day at the hands of their own countrymen. Both governments seemed content to keep those names among the disappeared, but Mr. Mori persisted and in 2009, sixty-four years after the bomb, those names too were added to the Peace Memorial (Soble, 2016). A "cut out" history (Davoine & Gaudillière, 2004) had been restored by a man who, like President Obama, was willing and able to feel for both sides. This is the great task of leadership.

Who are we now?

The kind and degree of anxiety suffered by some societies, including Israel and Palestine, reaches the level of what the psychoanalyst Donald Winnicott (1974) called a *"primitive agony"*: for example, a group's fear of "disappearing from the face of the earth." Such levels of anxiety make it extremely difficult for people and their leadership to think clearly and contain emotional reactions. But a leader's answering the "Who are we?" question with that society's "chosen trauma" neglects another, at times more pressing, question: "Who are we now?" There is evidence that the next generation on both sides of the Israel–Palestine conflict struggles with this question and does not fully buy into prevailing narratives, even the "chosen trauma" scenario.

Palestinian youth feel stuck in an endless present and alienated from their own leadership. As in other parts of the Arab world, a young person's wish to work to his potential, especially for those well educated, comes up against the enforced dependency and consequent corruption so common in the patriarchal cultures of the Middle East. But identity based on dependency seems no longer sustainable without unbearable humiliation within one's own society. In one IDI meeting, the word most used to describe this phenomenon was "awakening," as though huge groups of people are no longer satisfied living passively in their dream lives and are ready to face reality. "They think they can have an impact," one person said.

Israeli youth struggle with disgust at the excesses, disparities, and corruptions of capitalism as it is playing out in their country; during the Arab Spring, their mantra was "Walk like an Egyptian," a formerly unthinkable identification with the other side. Added to this is resentment about political concessions to the ultra-orthodox minority, which impinge on their ordinary lives. And over all of this hovers the most critical "Who are we now?" question: If Israel annexes Palestine and suddenly has millions more Arab citizens, how can it remain simultaneously a Jewish state and a democratic state? Will it be a country that denies a huge number of Israeli Arab citizens the right to vote? Will it allow that vote and risk its disappearance as a Jewish state? Will it have to go on thinking of itself as an occupier or as living out a de facto apartheid? This is a large-group identity crisis in the making.

All of this is amplified by social media on both sides. The technological revolution has flattened the vertical hierarchy and broadened horizontal connections. Everyone has more information available than was formerly handed down to them from above. They are no longer dependent on government to understand the world. At the same time, they can communicate with colleagues and other groups instantly and take confidence from the sheer numbers they can mobilize. In Western Europe, the Reformation followed the invention of the printing press; are we seeing a correspondingly immense social movement facilitated by the invention of smart phones? And like the decades of religious wars that followed the Reformation, how much social turbulence and destructiveness will be encountered in this new journey toward a different relation to authority?

For the endless time being, however, Prime Minister Netanyahu's stance promises security and territory—the two things the members of that Group Relations Conference were so desperate for—and so even progressive youth movements succumb to inertia. At an IDI meeting in Israel, a visiting Israeli official quipped, "Once I was young and promising. Now I'm just promising." Time has indeed passed, and undelivered promises have left the younger generation in both groups floundering. In response to this malaise, the potential for action, neither focused nor coherent but desperate for some sense of agency and catharsis, is real.

More fear

Meanwhile, both sides' relentless insistence on making sure that history does not repeat itself gravitates frighteningly in that direction. Mutual fear stimulates mutual hatred, which makes retributive justice appear reasonable. In July 2015, a few young ultra-orthodox settlers, in retaliation for a shooting that killed a settler, fire-bombed a random Palestinian home in the West Bank village of Duma. Two adults and their eighteen-month-old baby burned to death, as the attackers watched from a distance. About this carefully planned assault, the group's leader explained why they took the risk of stealthily making their way through an olive grove and bypassing several Palestinian homes on the outskirts of Duma: "When the attack is in the heart of the village, there is more fear."

By all reports, people on both sides of the conflict were "horrified" by this attack, and certainly the image of a burning baby is cause for horror. But perhaps something else too. As many have noted, we either remember or repeat history. The idea that a person whose society's history and large-group identity is fundamentally shaped by the Holocaust would plan and carry out a holocaust-in-microcosm is unthinkable. And yet it happened, with this repetition of history now reversing the roles of victim and aggressor. "Never again," a grief- and love-driven determination we can all understand in our bones, became, in this instance, "Actually, yes, it will happen again, but to them and at our hands." Cause for horror indeed! Fortunately an Israeli court recently ruled that, in the words of the chief prosecutor, "terrorism is terrorism regardless of the identity of the perpetrators" (Halbfinger & Rasgon, 2020).

"We don't speak of fear," and yet creating "more fear" was one goal of this attack. Powerful emotions drive group action but, for various reasons, are excluded from the conversations in which these groups are represented. The capacity to speak feelings—a deceptively simple but actually quite difficult task—remains undeveloped, even as both groups struggle with a range of intense feelings. As human beings, we face many choices in life. A basic one, raised to a critical level in the midst of group conflict, is to speak or to act. At the very least, as the diplomat we met at the beginning of this article suggested, it would be good to know how to do the former.

References

Alderdice, J. (2012, September 13). Speech to the United Nations General Assembly. New York.
Davoine, F., & Gaudillière, J. M. (2004). *History beyond Trauma*. New York: Other Press.
Erikson, E. H. (1959). Identity and the life cycle. In: G. S. Klein (Ed.), *Psychological Issues* (pp. 1–171). New York: International Universities Press.
Friedman, R. (2019a). *Beyond the Soldier's Matrix*. London: Routledge.
Friedman, R. (2019b). *Dreamtelling, Relations and Large Groups*. London: Routledge.
Fromm, M. G. (2000). The other in dreams. *Journal of Applied Psychoanalytic Studies, 2*: 287–298.

Halbfinger, D., & Rasgon, A. (2020, May 18). Israeli settler found guilty of murdering Palestinian family in 2015 arson attack. *The New York Times*.

Klein, M. (1946). Notes on some schizoid mechanisms. *International Journal of Psycho-Analysis, 27*: 99–110.

Kohut, H. (1971). *The Analysis of the Self.* New York: International Universities Press.

Lacan, J. (1977). *Écrits*. New York: W. W. Norton.

Lawrence, W. G. (1991). Won from the void and formless infinite: Experiences of social dreaming. *Free Associations, 2*: 259–294.

Loewenberg, P. (1995). *Fantasy and Reality in History*. New York: Oxford University Press.

Obama, B. (2016, May 28). Excerpts from "The memory of the morning of August 6, 1945, must never fade." *The New York Times*.

Rifkind, G. (2019). Preparing the psychological space for peacemaking. *New England Journal of Public Policy, 31*(1), Article 7.

Soble, J. (2016, May 28). An embrace for a survivor who studied the bombing. *The New York Times*.

Volkan, V. D. (2004). *Blind Trust: Large Groups and Their Leaders in Times of Crisis and Terror*. Charlottesville, VA: Pitchstone.

Volkan, V. D. (2013). *Enemies on the Couch: A Psychopolitical Journey through War and Peace*. Durham, NC: Pitchstone.

Volkan, V. D. (2020). *Large-Group Psychology: Racism, Societal Division, Narcissistic Leaders and Who We Are Now*. Bicester, UK: Phoenix.

Volkan, V. D., Ast, G., & Greer, W. (2002). *The Third Reich in the Unconscious: Transgenerational Transmission and Its Consequences*. New York: Brunner-Routledge.

Winnicott, D. W. (1974). Fear of breakdown. *International Review of Psycho-Analysis, 1*: 103–107.

CHAPTER 5

Braving the new: the struggle from loss to agency

Coline Covington

> … *as the Odyssey knows, to live well in the world, nostalgia must be resisted: you must stay with your ship, stay tied to the present, remain mobile, keep adjusting the rig, work with the swells, watch for a wind-shift, watch as the boom swings over, engage, in other words, with the muddle and duplicity and difficulty of life. Don't be tempted into the lovely simplicities that the heroic past seems to offer.*
>
> —Nicolson, A., *The Mighty Dead*, 2014, p. 6

Our lives are marked by loss from the moment of birth until our death. It is also our experience of loss that enables us to let go of what is familiar and to be open to new experiences and to change. In his study of Homer's *Odyssey*, Adam Nicolson (2014) describes the nostalgic lure of the Sirens' song that promises to restore Odysseus's heroic past as an escape from the pain and losses of the present. Odysseus's crew know that he cannot resist and tie Odysseus to the mast, ensuring that they continue their voyage as they face an unknown future. The lure of an imaginary, idealized past is something we all know and becomes especially powerful at times of change and loss. The current rise of populism around the world is underpinned by just such nostalgic fantasies of a secure past, untouched by loss. This is often a turning point in psychoanalysis when a person becomes aware, for example, that distorted beliefs and images of the past can no longer be sustained and need to be shed. Stepping out of familiar behavior patterns and venturing into new ways of relating—to oneself and others—may feel as frightening as entering a foreign country with no common language. This is the ordinary challenge of living for us all but for those who have been living in isolated or severe conditions or those who face extreme loss, it is a challenge that requires bravery—a bravery that is often unseen but nevertheless palpable.

Exile and starting again

In his first meeting with me, Harry, a tall gaunt man in his early forties, exiled from his country of origin for political crimes, said, "It has taken me a year to contact you. I have had your number the whole time but I was too frightened. Everything has been taken away from me, everything has changed in my life and I am frightened that I will have to change, that I won't know who I will be, that I will become a foreigner to myself." Harry was clenching his fists, not in anger, but from trying to control his pain and his tears. He began to tell me his story, a story of a glorious past in his country where he was a well-known and much revered dissident, fighting for justice and democratic values. He was the leader whom everyone turned to for help and the "fixer" during a crisis. He had adopted this role since childhood when at a young age he became the family "hero." His successful father, a man of mature years, was often away on business and Harry readily stepped into the shoes of being the man of the house, helping his mother, who was bedridden with depression for long periods of Harry's childhood. As the eldest, Harry took care of his four younger siblings, three girls and a boy, making sure they went to school, did their schoolwork, went to bed at the right time at night, and did not get into scrapes with their friends. Although there were nannies looking after the children, Harry made the important decisions about his siblings and looked after them as a surrogate father. His favorite make-believe game was to play the king with his siblings as his courtiers and vassals, coming to him with their problems to solve. Harry created a magical kingdom of justice and plenty in which there was no hunger or poverty, everything was shared equally, and, because of this, there was no crime or suffering. Harry's parents praised their little king, his father glad that Harry was taking over for him during his many trips away and his mother glad that Harry took care not only of his siblings but of her when she felt too depressed to do anything but sleep. For Harry too this was an ideal solution as he was admired and loved as the hero-king and he did not have to be aware of both his absent parents who failed to care for their children.

Harry's empire seemed to grow from strength to strength. He was a natural leader and, even when he came to the UK for his university education, he quickly established his own following on political issues. On returning to his own country, having qualified as a lawyer, Harry resumed his political activities in the face of a government that was rapidly turning into an autocracy. Nevertheless, Harry was an able politician, was known for his diplomacy in dealing with his opponents, and held a respected ministerial position in the government that allowed him certain limited influence and privileges. As Harry accrued a larger power base, many "power-hungry" women, as he called them, began to pursue him. It was Harry's strengths as a leader that became his downfall in his personal life. Harry's face had become ashen as he referred to his downfall and he sat silently facing me with a pleading look on his face. I commented that Harry had experienced a lot of tragedy in his life and we were both left in suspension until our next meeting.

Harry arrived a few days later for his session and asked if he could lie on my couch, explaining, "I'm exhausted; I don't think I can even manage to sit up today." He started to describe the past year as a time when he been so broken that all he could do was stay in his little flat and sleep, like his mother had done throughout his childhood. Harry told me, "The morning when I decided to contact you, I woke up and thought, 'No, I am not going to turn into my mother, I am not going to be defeated by this.'" At the same time, Harry said he felt lost when there was no one to help and the only thing to fix was himself. He also said that he had lost his trust in his own judgment and this was the most difficult and disorienting problem in his life. Harry then went on to explain that he had gotten involved with a very beautiful woman from a rich family who had earmarked him as her future husband. She was intelligent and seductive and was the first person who had expressed a desire to care for him and who, it seemed, was making no demands of him. However, as the relationship developed, Harry began to feel increasingly claustrophobic. Maria wanted to know where he was at any given time of day and was constantly trying to anticipate his needs; she was also anxious to be married and have a child. Before the end of the year, Harry had broken their engagement and, in retaliation, Maria had spread various false political stories about him among his opponents who then leaked these to the national press. With a civil war looming, Harry was forced to escape from his country or face indefinite internment and possibly torture. Harry curled up on the couch and began to sob, "What have I done? I have tried so hard to help others, to be just and loving, to do what is right and what is it for? I have only once said 'no' to someone, to Maria, and now I am being punished." I reflected, "It isn't fair that life has not honored the deal you made with it." Harry replied, "No, that's just the problem, it wasn't meant to turn out like this and now I'm really on my own. The deal has been broken and I don't know how to live or who to be."

Over the next few months Harry's disillusion took on devastating proportions—everything he had believed and worked for had been swept away and destroyed, no one could be trusted and at the same time he berated himself for being so foolish as to allow himself to be vulnerable to this poisonous woman. Harry's fury and confusion when his world toppled around him was like a toddler's rage when he becomes painfully aware that he cannot control the world around him and is not always at the center of it. In the case of the toddler, this experience of impotence is normally mitigated by a mother who can comfort her child. Through this action, the mother demonstrates her child's impact on her and helps to restore some sense of self-agency to the child. In his analysis, I thought Harry needed to use me as a mother who could understand his fall from grace and help him to recover, not only through venting his rage but through experimenting with his limits in his new life. Like learning to walk, this proved to be both exciting and frightening.

A large part of the reason that Harry experienced his fall from grace as overwhelming was because it wasn't only his present but his past that had unraveled. Harry's loss of his kingly status confronted him with the reality that he had used this persona to mask the fact that there were effectively no parents in his home. As Harry exclaimed, "It would have been better if we had been orphans—at least that would have been real. Instead, we all held on to the belief that everything was fine because our parents were there, even when we weren't actually there in their minds. I've been living this charade most of my life. It makes me think that maybe the deal for me was that if I played my part as best as I could, they would then play their parts. But they didn't. That was not the deal for them ... When S came into power in my country at first I thought, 'Good, he will be a real father to his people, he will tell everyone what they need to do and in return he will look after everyone.' But now I can see that this is the father I had been trying to be to my siblings and later on to my colleagues. This kind of deal means that the king is the only one with power because no one has to take responsibility for himself, no one can develop or grow up. It's only now that I'm away, that I can see some of my sisters and my brother beginning to figure some things out for themselves and to wise up to their reality—both in our family and in our country."

Giving up his position as hero-king was a painful process for Harry; he likened himself to a snake shedding its skin for the first time. For several weeks, Harry fluctuated in his thoughts about the future. One day he would tell me excitedly about his plans to resurrect his empire by transplanting it to the UK and how he would essentially set up an alternative government here, where he could once again be the shadow leader. He explained that this setback had taught him a lot and he could be even stronger now with more resources than ever before to help his oppressed countrymen. These manic episodes made Harry feel hopeful but they also made him feel precarious as he could not completely deny that things had changed radically in his life and it might not be so easy to recreate his lost kingdom. During this time Harry dreamt that he was back with his family and his closest colleagues at his family house but they were all under house arrest and couldn't leave without severe consequences. Harry thought the dream was telling him that this was in fact what would happen if he tried to return to his past, he would be imprisoned by it. He then became despondent, recognizing that he was also desperately trying to retrieve a sense of belonging somewhere. Hoping to find a foothold, Harry announced that he thought he would train as a psychotherapist. I understood Harry's wish as primarily his attempt to be accepted and belong to a group rather than a wish to identify with me specifically. He was knocking on doors where he hoped to be allowed in.

These highs were followed predictably by Harry telling me about his despair and fear for the future—he had lost everything in his life and he could see no way forward. At one especially low point, I voiced my concern that Harry's despair might tempt him to kill himself. He paused for a long time and then admitted, "I've been thinking of suicide for weeks now—every time I wake up in the morning I have this idea that at least I can do myself in, at least that is the power I have left in my life when I have no other power." I compared Harry's thoughts of suicide to an internal revolution he was planning, "It's a bit like a coup that you're planning, an assassination of the leader who has failed you and who doesn't listen to you either, who just keeps harping on about the past and how great it was. When you can't get the leader to change, the only way to have any power is to kill him. Is the problem that you're angry with this stubborn, short-sighted, omnipotent leader and really want to do him in? This could be S [the autocrat], your father, or the you who wants to remain king? They've all had their day." Harry suddenly sat up and said, "I'm not going to allow these tyrants to win! If I killed myself, I'd be just as omnipotent as they are—and just as pathetic. It's a bit like the snake deciding to kill itself rather than to change into a new skin."

This realization turned out to be the turning point for Harry. He had only overtly asked for help twice in his life. In the first instance Harry sought help from a wealthy uncle living in the UK to help him secure residency. The second instance was when he contacted me for treatment, fearful of becoming like his mother trapped in a lifetime depression. Without his old skin, Harry was acutely aware of his vulnerability and a deep sense of shame caused by years of denying his need to be cared for by others. He had received care by using others as proxies for himself while starving inside. His old way of relating was no longer sustainable and materially, the funds he had managed to exist on were running out. He was beginning to feel that he might create a new future for himself but was also frightened that he would lose his connections to his past and become uprooted. Faced with having to find a way of continuing to survive in his adopted country, Harry decided he would go back to his university law degree to qualify as a lawyer and approach his uncle for a loan to tide him over. Harry explained, "I'm not going to be king anymore, but I can still work to help others and I can take care of myself better now. I can't go back to my country anymore. I will always miss it and my family and friends but I can't stand still—I want my own family and maybe all these changes that I have been so afraid of are also because I've been afraid of being myself—of discovering what I really feel and what I can and cannot do. I haven't lost my principles but I have to find a different way of living by them."

Identity and the rise of populism

Harry's actual physical and political dislocation triggered a psychic dislocation that fundamentally challenged his ideal image of himself and stripped him of his social identity. This cataclysmic loss initially fueled an impulse to regress to his past self in order to mend the rupture that had occurred in his life and to create even greater defenses against future threats. When this strategy failed, Harry's rage about the loss of the better world he had expected nearly provoked him to take his life. When he realized that such an act would only imitate the destruction of what he valued most, he had to think hard about how to survive his losses and how to forge a different identity that was nevertheless true to the basic values by which he had lived.

Harry's struggle to make sense of the losses in his life provides a kind of microcosm of what we can see happening on a global scale in the wave of populism occurring in countries across the world as local economies, boundaries, and the concept of the nation-state are under threat. Populist groups are characterized by anti-establishment and nationalistic attitudes and tend to favor authoritarian governance. Liberal democracy is in decline if not under outright attack and we are seeing the resurgence of the nation-state with the rise of strong-man leaders, such as Trump, Putin, Erdoğan, Orbán, Duterte, Modi, Xi, and Johnson in the UK. This is no coincidence but clearly the result of globalization's growing threat to national power bases and national identity, with inequality and immigration on the rise and international corporations increasingly owning massive amounts of wealth, even greater than individual nations. In response to the erosion of national political authority, there is a backlash of "apocalyptic nationalism" that has come into vogue, characterized by "machismo" leadership, xenophobia and wall-building, theories of racial purity, and, above all, spectacular promises to restore these nations' glorified pasts—often pasts that were never that glorious or, like the British Empire, ended well over fifty years ago (Dasgupta, 2018). The waves of nostalgia for a time representing a secure powerful identity echo Harry's longing to turn the clock back to the time when in hindsight he had felt loved and powerful, although he admits that in reality his position was always precarious. As the identity of nation-states, and therefore their survival, is increasingly under threat, uncertainty and fear about the future take hold, leaving citizens vulnerable to emotional manipulation and false promises.

Preying on these fears, politicians at both conservative and liberal extremes present themselves as the true defenders of their country by maintaining safe borders that will keep the "enemy" out, cultivating an us and them mentality. As we have seen in the impeachment proceedings, Trump does not hesitate to declare his opponents "treasonous" and "un-American." A similar divisive antagonism against the "elites" is also promoted, as evident in slogans adopted by the liberal left, for example, Bernie Sanders in the US and Jeremy Corbyn in the UK, advocating "for the many, not the few." In writing about Cold War liberalism, Jan-Werner Muller warns us that the narrative of the Other has been dangerously extended. Muller (2018) observes:

> In a speech he gave in Warsaw, Trump's rhetorical question—"Do we have the confidence in our values to defend them at any cost?"—could be mistaken for a soundbite from the height of the cold war, but tellingly, he followed it with another: "Do we have enough respect for our citizens to protect our borders?" With this, he conjured a world in which real Americans are constantly threatened by caravans of Middle Eastern terrorists and people from Latin America who can pass for citizens but might be enemies within.

Trump's message also raises the question as to who qualifies as a citizen and how do we identify a "real American," questions that hark back to Nazi Germany's concerns with racial purity.

On the liberal end, Muller also points to "Hillary Clinton's cynical call for Europe to stop aiding refugees, since, in her view, the migration issue just helps populists. Her underlying idea appears to be that one can defeat one's political adversaries by imitating them" (ibid.). The fallback position at both ends of the political spectrum seems to be to win votes by fostering mass paranoia and populist fantasies of a future protected by isolationism. Change is perceived as dilution of identity and ultimately a threat to survival. Retreat is the safest line of defense.

In writing about the use of xenophobia as a means of bolstering nationalism, Martin Wolf points out that a citizen's passport has become emblematic of identity; it confers belonging and membership, it signifies national characteristics, and, most importantly, it stands for sovereignty of the group. Wolf (2018) comments:

> The more economic outcomes diverge within a nation state, the more easily cynical politicians can persuade anxious citizens that their interests are being sacrificed to those of a "globalist"—that is, treacherous—elite and its foreign associates and servants. The view that those who think globally are traitors is not surprising. It is a natural result of national feeling. Since the middle of the twentieth century, nationalism has gone global. In China, for example, we see the creation, for the first time in its history, of a Chinese nation state. It is no surprise, then, that it cannot deal well with its minority communities. In highly complex societies, such as India, creation of an overarching national identity is even harder. Today, we are witnessing the resurgence of malign nationalism across the west and, most significantly, in the US.

Like pouring money into a bankrupt business to save it, the immediate solution to waning nationalism has been to reinforce nationalist values and to protect the nation-state from invasion. The surge of fake news and interference with the press serve both to enhance the power of the state, while diminishing that of foreign states, and at the same time to increase paranoia. In this way, populist politicians become even more powerful as they can readily capitalize on what people want to believe is true, what politicians want their constituencies to believe, and the illusion that the nation state is largely self-sufficient or, in the case of

Trump's stance in the US, can call the shots on international trade and cooperation. In order to save nationalism, paradoxically, the values of liberal democracy, those same values that have been nurtured under nationalism, have to be sacrificed, as the history of the rise of the Third Reich in Germany has so vividly demonstrated.

Over the past 200 years or so, nationalism has not only served as a powerful secular religion, binding individuals and communities together, but because it has served this function it has also become an intrinsic part of our identity. While this may be especially so in the West, modeled on the ancient Greek city state, it has also been a powerful force in Eastern countries that have shifted from imperial rule to different forms of totalitarianism that remain circumscribed and defined by national boundaries. Increasing globalization and increasing economic development have brought in their wake vast increases in economic inequality. The American Dream that held the promise of both moral and material amelioration blossomed dramatically after World War II, only to reach a tipping point with the financial crash of 2008. The American Dream, at least in terms of its materialistic manifestation, was becoming a nightmare as its by-product, economic inequality, was becoming the new threat.

The scourge of inequality

In 2014, Thomas Piketty's groundbreaking treatise, *Capital in the Twenty-First Century*, was published and quickly rose to no. 1 on Amazon's best seller list. Its success was attributed to the fact that it constructs a well-documented frontal challenge to the inequality debate in economics and politics. Prior to this, leading politicians on both sides of the Atlantic have extolled free trade policies and tax benefits for corporations and inheritance, both of which generate inequality. In 2000, the CEO of Louis Vuitton boasted: "Businesses, especially international ones, have ever greater resources, and in Europe they have acquired the ability to compete with states … Politicians' real impact on the economic life of a country is more and more limited. Fortunately."

According to Robert Wade, a leading UK economist, most economists either don't think about inequality or believe in the self-adjusting market system—a view that has fundamentally supported political policies for decades. Poverty and wealth tend to be viewed as part of the natural order.

Obama, during his presidency, declared inequality "to be the defining challenge of our time." Pope Francis has also echoed this. Both have been accused by the wealthy of persecuting the rich. As predicted by Obama, rage against the rich (and the elites) has taken hold since 2008 and has prepared the ground for populism to take root. The rage was not unfounded. Wade points out, "In the period 2009–2012, 93% of the increase in the US national income accrued to the top 1%—and this in a stable democracy rather than a kleptocracy such as Equatorial Guinea" (2014, p, 1076).

In a report published in 2014, IMF researchers challenged the idea of a self-adjusting market system. They found that "Countries with a higher inequality tend to experience lower and more volatile growth; countries with lower inequality tend to experience higher and less volatile growth … in short, inequality is a drag on growth and fosters financial instability." Wolfgang Münchau of the *Financial Times* reported (2014), "The most likely trajectory is a long period of slow growth, low inflation, and a constant threat of insolvency and political insurrection."

Carol Graham, a US economist who studies inequality, has demonstrated that it is not simply the poor in the US who are being affected by economic changes, it is also the middle classes. She describes a "black box of no hope" that now characterizes much of middle class experience in the US. Graham (2017) makes the point that inequality is tolerable as long as people are optimistic about their opportunities to be upwardly mobile. When these opportunities disappear, inequality can no longer be accepted.

On the other end of the scale, among the rich and stemming from the financial crisis of 2008, there is increasing resistance to government regulation. In the US and UK, libertarian views that support the idea of a self-regulating market system and individual sovereignty are gaining strength and encouraging the disassembling of government institutions.

The threat of the Other

Although immigration figures in many European countries and in the US have fallen over the past few years since increased restrictions have been put in place, the prospect of future immigration, whether it is by economic or climate change refugees, looms large. Immigrants are perceived either as leeches, bleeding limited local resources or, on the other hand, as representing a new wave of upwardly mobile foreigners that are being given opportunities and help that are not available to the indigenous population. If immigrants do well, they evoke envy, if they remain dependent and poor, they evoke resentment. Either way they represent a threat.

Immigrants are also seen to threaten local identities and culture. Timothy Garton Ash (2017), writing about Germany, ironically points out,

> There is a striking inverse correlation between the number of immigrants (or people of migrant origin) in an area and the populist vote: East Germany has the fewest immigrants and the most AfD voters. As one participant in a demonstration organized by the far right, xenophobic movement Pegida (the initials stand for Patriotic Europeans Against the Islamization of the West) told a reporter: "In Saxony today there are hardly any immigrants, but there is a danger of the Islamization of Germany in fifty or a hundred years." An urgent matter, then.

Ash cites that

> 95 percent of AfD voters said that they were worried that "we are experiencing a loss of German culture and language," 94 percent that "our life in Germany will change too much," and 92 percent that "the influence of Islam in Germany will become too strong." Feeding this politics of cultural despair—to recall a famous phrase of the historian Fritz Stern—is a milieu of writers, media, and books whose arguments and vocabulary connect back to themes of an earlier German right-wing culture in the first half of the twentieth century. This is a new German right with distinct echoes of the old.

Ash (2017) also emphasizes that the AfD "is not a party of the economically 'left behind'. This strong presence of the educated upper middle class distinguishes populism from many other populisms." This phenomenon is not only evident in Germany but can also be seen across Europe and within the UK.

Immigrants not only threaten to dilute and contaminate indigenous cultures but, fleeing from disasters in their own countries, they are harbingers of the global dangers that defy borders. The increase in climate refugees is a case in point as it is often linked with problems of economic inequality. The political scientist, Ronald Inglehart, describes a "tipping point" in democratic societies in which social and economic inequality reaches an intolerable level and creates a backlash that paves the way for authoritarian governance (2018). Although climate change is not usually named as part of this process, it is an important factor. It is the poor who can't afford rising costs in food, oil, and housing. It is the poor who are vulnerable to becoming climate refugees. It is the poor who can't escape the path of the hurricane and, if they manage to, can't rebuild their demolished houses. It is also the poor and for that matter the middle class who will turn to populist leaders who acknowledge their need for a better life. As climate change affects us more and more, large-group anxiety is bound to intensify and, from our experience so far, this is likely to provoke greater authoritarianism. We can, for example, anticipate an increase in migration due to dwindling habitable land mass. Climate refugees are often portrayed as displaced immigrants in spite of the fact that within large countries such as the United States the most vulnerable populations live within the country. If we are not quick in developing alternative methods of food production, due to climate change and isolationist trade policies, we can also expect much greater competition for food and rising starvation. If we consider these conditions together, they constitute many of the factors that have led in the past to war and genocide—as a means of maintaining group identity in the threat of extinction.

Security in autocracy

As we saw in the case of Harry, when an individual is stripped of his belonging to a group and his function within that group, he loses an essential part of his identity. In this state of vanishing identity, the individual becomes highly susceptible to powerful authority figures who offer membership, security, and the eradication of conflict. When basic trust is broken, blind trust in a "totalitarian object" takes over (see Volkan, 2004). On a larger scale, the shift toward autocratic leaders indicates increasing levels of conflict and insecurity within national boundaries.

Despite polls that show the Z generation as largely supporting liberal elites, among millennials in Western countries there is greater support for autocratic leadership. The American journalist Sasha Polakow-Suransky writes:

> Those who believe millennials are immune to authoritarian ideas are mistaken. Using data from the World Values Survey, the political scientists Roberto Foa and Yascha Mounk have painted a worrying picture. As the French election demonstrated, belief in core tenets of liberal democracy is in decline, especially among those born after 1980. Their findings challenge the idea that after achieving a certain level of prosperity and political liberty, countries that have become democratic do not turn back.
>
> In America, 72 percent of respondents born before World War II deemed it absolutely essential to live in a democracy; only 30 percent of millennials agreed. The figures were similar in Holland. The number of Americans favoring a strong leader unrestrained by elections or parliaments has increased from 24 to 32 percent since 1995. More alarmingly, the number of Americans who believe that military rule would be good or very good has risen from 6 to 17 percent over the same period. The young and wealthy were most hostile to democratic norms, with fully 35 percent of young people with a high income regarding army rule as a good thing. (Polakow-Suransky, 2017)

It is not surprising that it is the young and wealthy who are reported as "the most hostile to democratic norms" as they are the ones under attack and who have the most to lose.

Political anomie

In psychoanalytic terms, we can understand the retreat of different countries into narcissistic isolationism as a regression into an illusory omnipotent past. The strong-man, narcissistic leader who is above the law belies the fragility of his position. Behind the carapace of postured strength, we find what Inglehart (2018) aptly refers to as the "existential insecurity" that has beset nations around the world, and will only increase with the challenges of climate change. Ideology and political ideals are scrapped in the scuffle for survival. When there is so much anxiety and uncertainty about the future and when facts are not reassuring it becomes hard to think clearly about the dangers ahead. The vacuum of ideological meaning is evident in the lack of political vision among many leaders who are preoccupied with staying in power and keeping their countries afloat. Suddenly, it seems that the idea of progress and what that means for individuals has turned sour. In an interview with the French writer Roger Errera in 1978, Hannah Arendt percipiently warned, "The law of progress holds that everything now must be better than what was there before. Don't you see if you want something better, and better, and better, you lose the good. The good is no longer even being measured." In our anxiety to survive within our own countries, are we becoming inured to the destruction that is being wrought in the name of nationalism?

Globalization has been central to the widespread belief in melioristic capitalism, that people's material standard of living will get better and better with the promise that poverty along with many associated social problems can be eradicated. Rather than wealth being shared in this utopian vision, it has increasingly come into the hands of large corporations and an elite few with the gap between rich and poor ever widening. The drive toward economic prosperity, starting in the 1990s, has spread like an infection—under Deng's premiership in China huge billboards saying, "Get Rich!" were erected over the highways; Putin has also made it clear the two aims for Russia are wealth and power; and other leaders, notably Trump, have followed suit. The "good" has become immediately aligned with power and stripped of ideological value, measured by wealth alone.

In her analysis of the new totalitarianism that has been inculcated by Putin in Russia, Masha Gessen refers to Yuri Levada's observation, based on research in Russia and China, that "Every totalitarian regime forms a type of human being on whom it relies for stability. The shaping of the New Man is the regime's explicit project, but its product is not so much a vessel for the regime's ideology as it is a person best equipped to survive in a given society" (2017, p. 59). In fact, ideology may get in the way of survival as it creates political inflexibility and dissent. Levada argued that the totalitarian system produced a certain kind of person, without self-agency and subject only to the rules of survival, and that this non-individuality led the way for authoritarian government. While Levada's theory has been widely criticized by social scientists (Sharafutdinova, 2019), he underlines the importance of the ideological vacuum that occurred with the implosion of the USSR at the end of the Cold War. The necessity to survive within the collective, especially toward the end of the Cold War when Russia's economy was suffering, morphed into the aim of materialist progress under Putin's capitalist autocracy. As Svetlana Alexievich (2013) so powerfully illustrates in her interviews with a cross-section of the Russian population during the early 2000s, the political ideals of the past, under Lenin, Stalin, Gorbachev, and Khrushchev, regardless of their differences, had died, leaving a painful vacuum in their wake. In such a vacuum, political identity is not informed by a set of beliefs and values so much as loyalty to a powerful autocracy. A whole generation of Russian youth, now in their twenties, has grown up with Putin as its only leader. Eduard Ponarin, professor of sociology at Russia's Higher School of Economics, describes this generation as, "Happy, apolitical and nationalist, to generalise ... and that is why politics is nothing to worry about, for most ..." (Foy, 2020). Politics is nothing to worry about when elections are predetermined and there is essentially no political choice, leaving nationalism as the only framework for belonging. Without an ideology that carries with it an image of the ideal citizen or member of the group, there is little to aspire to and little to bring people together in a common purpose—except anxiety for the future. Despite Ponarin's positive spin, Putin's failed promise of economic growth and state corruption are giving rise to protests led by Russian youths promoting citizens' rights. Without the foundation of political ideals, it is not surprising that these protests lack any sense of a cohesive worldview. This lack is not only apparent in Russia but it is apparent too in protests across the world from India to Turkey to the US. For example, in Hong Kong, protestors want what they have been promised under the Basic Law, but there is little vision of what is sought when this agreement expires and Hong Kong is fully absorbed into mainland China.

In the West, the ideals of democratic liberalism have been similarly eroded due to economic inequality along with corruption and mistrust in authority and institutions of government. We can understand the development of populist groups as an attempt to fill the ideological void, to restore former nationalist ego ideals and to reestablish group identity. However, populist beliefs as they are manifest today portray a vision of the past, not the future. They are retrogressive by their very nature; while they may provide a sense of security through familiarity, they cannot facilitate imaginative discourse and thinking in terms of creating a new future. The historian Timothy Snyder uses the phrase "the politics of eternity" to describe "the seduction by a mythicized past [that] prevents us from thinking about possible futures" (2017, p. 123). We use this mythicized past to obliterate the pain of loss. This was the conflict Harry experienced when his world fell apart. It was only when he was able to acknowledge that he could not replicate what he had lost that he was able to imagine a different life.

Adapt or die

The greatest threat to our identity is when the beliefs we have lived by have been overturned and we are left with no markers to point the way forward. When groups experience fundamental changes in their everyday life and expectations of the future, such as through modernization, displacement, or political upheaval, their response to these changes is vital to their identity and to their survival.

The most tragic response to massive change is that of suicide, whether of the group itself or of its members. This is the suicide brought on by humiliation and defeat in the face of an overwhelming force that has destroyed one's way of life and one's most important beliefs. At the end of the Reich, following Hitler's own suicide on April 30, 1945, a suicide epidemic swept across all of Germany. As the war was nearing its end and German losses were indisputable and severe, the prospect of suicide rose within the collective consciousness. The Reverend Gerhard Jacobi, perhaps aware of the anger and despair of his parishioners, preached in early March from his lectern at the Kaiser Wilhelm Memorial Church in Berlin on the evil of suicide. In an interview with a journalist at the time, the vicar said, "I have regular visits from parishioners who confide in me that they have procured ampoules of cyanide. They see no way out" (Huber, 2019, p. 77). The journalist had also noted that the congregation expressed "no surprise" at their vicar's warnings. He then spoke to a fellow journalist, loyal to the Nazis, who exclaimed, "I can't carry on … Everything I believed in is turning out to be madness and crime" (ibid.). Suicide featured "in newspapers, on state radio, and even in the Nazi leadership's rhetoric: 'Goebbels has changed his tune: he is talking of suicide as a last resort.' In a radio broadcast dripping with pathos, Goebbels had invoked the example of Frederick II, who had believed only in death or victory. Goebbels offered up the Prussian king as a martyr because he had once, at a time of military crisis, toyed with the idea of taking poison. Rarely had the propaganda machine appealed so heavy-handedly to the self-sacrificing spirit of the German people" (ibid., p. 79).

By early March, just as the Reverend Jacobi had feared, the suicide epidemic had begun, costing thousands of lives. While fear of brutal reprisals from the invading Russian soldiers was rife, fueled by German propaganda, it did not explain the extent and nature of the suicides that occurred. Many felt intense loyalty to Hitler and the Nazi regime, exacerbated by the scores of lives lost fighting to defend the Reich and the daily sacrifices made by those who survived. There was also shock that the beliefs that they had lived and died for had been destroyed along with their vision of the future. Others were shocked when they discovered the dark reality of the Nazi war crimes and the sudden disillusionment of their ideals. Repudiation and outright denial were also common. There was also the murderous rage of being defeated, a rage that was turned inwards in the act of suicide. Without their leader, German identity was suddenly left vulnerable. At this point of crisis, mass suicide, as in the case of religious groups under threat, can restore a group's identity and illusion of omnipotence. Volkan writes, "Identity enhancing massive suicides occur in religious groups when the members develop a shared conscious or unconscious fantasy that through death they join a divine power. Members of such a group physically die when they kill themselves, but, paradoxically (and illogically), just before their death they contaminate their group identity with omnipotence and believe that an omnipotent group identity will survive" (2004, p. 69). Even those who had not been Nazi supporters may have been susceptible to what was a form of mass hysteria. Robert Jay Lifton's study of the Japanese cult of Aum Shinrikyo (1999) provides a striking parallel to Nazi culture.

Lifton refers to "totalistic communities" as characterized by an emphasis on purity, ideological totalism, continual self-confession, spiritual truths, and the "dispensing of existence" in which those who are not pure do not have the right to live. Ultimately, the self-annihilation of the cult ensured its immortality.

For others still, the excitement and hope in building a new and better life had made them feel important for the first time in their lives. The Austrian novelist, Peter Handke, in *A Sorrow beyond Dreams*, describes the post-war depression of the narrator's mother, leading to suicide. Handke writes, "Personal life, if it had ever developed a character of its own, was depersonalized except for dream tatters swallowed up by the rites of religion, custom, and good manners; little remained of the human individual, and indeed, the word 'individual' was known only in pejorative combinations" (2019, p. 40). The humiliation of defeat, of poverty, and of the loss of what it meant to be an individual could also lead to despair. The narrator sees the changes in his mother's face, "gradually, in its daily effort to keep up appearances, her face lost its soul" (ibid., p. 48).

Sudden changes in our lives present huge losses that are painful and difficult to overcome, especially when they affect the world we live in and depend upon. The struggle to manage and adapt to these changes may in certain circumstances either be impossibly loaded or actually counter to the culture's belief system. The forced transition to modern life among undeveloped tribes, such as the Inuit in Arctic Canada, is a case in point. In his research on suicide among the Inuit, Michael Kral interviewed scores of young Inuit men who had attempted suicide and found that about 70 percent of suicide attempts occurred after romantic break-ups. This raised the question as to why Inuit young men seemed so much more likely to attempt suicide in this situation compared to other groups. Kral came up with an important finding reported by an Inuit government official. She explained, "The theory I have is that [Inuit] who commit suicide are doing it to protect the community … When we lived in small groups, we had a contract for survival. You lived for the collective, not for yourself. We're in this together. Children are conditioned to be calm. If someone explodes, that person is a threat to everyone. Then (the one who explodes) thinks, 'Everyone will be better off without me. I'm a problem because I can't handle my emotions.' It's hard to get that out of your head, because we're conditioned not be a burden to others" (Epstein, 2019, p. 18). Coming from a culture in which the harsh physical conditions required emotional strength and rationality for survival, any slip from this could endanger the group. The traditional ego ideal of the group that had ensured survival within their own native environment was, ironically, the greatest obstacle in preventing its members from adapting to the changes in their new way of life. By continuing to adhere to their old ideals, the Inuit have remained trapped in a past that can no longer provide them with a sense of self-agency.

Our traditional ego ideals guide us in our social behavior and are instrumental in inspiring how we see ourselves in the future. But what happens when these ideals are no longer helpful or even in some cases viable? A nineteenth-century story of two native American tribes and how each dealt with modernization elucidates the role of the ego ideal and whether it can perform a destructive or creative function in group survival.

By the end of the nineteenth century, the Crow Indians in Montana were facing extinction, like many other Indian tribes (Lear, 2006). As a young boy, the Crow Indian chief, Plenty Coups, had a dream foretelling the disappearance of the buffalo and the extinction of the Crow way of life. Not only did the Crow depend on the buffalo for their material survival but their identity, or their ego ideal, centered on being strong and brave hunters. Facing despair about the future, some years later Plenty Coups had another dream. In this dream, a little bird called the chickadee told Plenty Coups that the tribe needed to be like the chickadee to survive. For the Crow, the chickadee was a bird known for its ability to adapt to different conditions within its environment; it listened carefully and learned to adapt from what it heard. With this new vision, the tribe was able to shift from its traditional ideal of hunting and fighting to adopt a new ideal of listening and learning—a shift that enabled the Crow to maintain their identity as a group while adapting to the new world introduced by the white man. As a result, unlike many other Indian tribes, the Crow have been able to keep the majority of their land.

In contrast to the Crow Indians, the Sioux Indians became extinct. Their leader, Sitting Bull, insisted that continuing to fight and to fight even harder was the only way to win. His failure to accept their changing reality and to relinquish the tribe's ideal of themselves as warriors proved disastrous. What is vividly portrayed in the stories of these two tribes is the psychological devastation wrought within a group when their ideals cease to be realizable and "they cannot find ideals worthy of internalizing and making their own" (Lear, 2006, p. 140). In facing up to reality and recognizing forces beyond the Crows' control, Plenty Coups enabled his tribe to accept loss and to create a new ideal that could be internalized and sustain the tribe's identity in a new form. Sitting Bull tried to short-circuit reality by reinforcing his tribe's ideal as fighters with a disastrous result. The parallel here with modern day populist responses to the massive social changes that are already affecting us is only too clear. The lure of the past ultimately beckons us toward self-destruction.

Bravery and facing the new

Returning to Odysseus, we can see that despite his pleasurable sojourns on various islands with seductive goddesses and nymphs, he never abandoned his aim to reach Troy and then to return home. Odysseus's journey is a metaphor of life's struggles and how these shape our sense of ourselves and, ultimately, give meaning to our death. Driven off course by the fates and by his own failings, Odysseus overcomes each new challenge, resisting the temptation of the oblivion of immortality and resisting the temptation to cut his journey short and return to the human safety and warmth of Penelope's arms. Nicolson describes Odysseus as

> no victim. He suffers but he does not buckle. His virtue is his elasticity, his rubber vigour. If he is pushed, he bends, but he bends back, and that half-giving strength was to me a beautiful model of a man. He was all navigation, subtlety, invention, dodging the rocks, story-telling, cheating and survival. He can be resolute, fierce and destructive when need be, and clever, funny and loving when need be. There is no need to choose between these qualities; Odysseus makes them all available. (2014, p. 3)

Just as Odysseus may have been "a beautiful model of a man" to the ancient Greeks, he remains so today. The quality that is not mentioned, and conspicuous in its absence, is bravery. Odysseus's elasticity, his "rubber vigor," enables him to adapt and survive and yet, as Nicolson points out, he is "no victim." Odysseus is a heroic figure because he makes his own choices, often in defiance of the gods, according to what he knows he has to do. Although he is waylaid by sybaritic pleasures, he continues to be responsible for others, for his crew and for his countrymen, and he continues to face danger and uncertainty by binding himself to the mast of his principles. This is the binding required by bravery to face the changes of the future, both the losses and the new.

In a famous debate on the definition of courage, led by Socrates, one of the Athenian generals, Nicias, proposes that "courage is the knowledge of the grounds of fear and hope" (Plato, 380 BC). Socrates picks apart the meaning of knowledge, concluding that this is a virtue that encompasses courage and therefore cannot stand as a definition of courage per se. What Socrates fails to grasp is the meaning of Nicias's revealing juxtaposition between fear and hope. Nicias is making the point that courage is necessarily comprised of both fear and hope, the mortal fear that characterizes every act of bravery but also the hope that guides every act of bravery. Fear tempers the action that can be taken—there is always an assessment of risk in bravery—but without hope of a good, that is, life-preserving outcome, there is no point in acting bravely. Our hope in facing the future rests within our capacity to be true to ourselves and to the ideals that will light our way through the darkness ahead.

References

Alexievich, S. (2013). *Second-Hand Time*. London: Fitzcarraldo Editions.
Arendt, H. (1978, October 26). Hannah Arendt: From an interview. *The New York Review of Books*.
Ash, G. T. (2017, December 7). It's the Kultur, stupid. *The New York Review of Books*.
Dasgupta, R. (2018, April 5). The demise of the nation state. *The Guardian*.
Epstein, H. (2019, October 10). The highest suicide rate in the world. *The New York Review of Books*.

Foy, H. (2020, January 9). Generation Putin: How young Russians view the only leader they've ever known. *The Financial Times Magazine Life & Arts*.

Gessen, M. (2017). *The Future Is History: How Totalitarianism Reclaimed Russia*. London: Granta.

Graham, C. (2017). *Happiness for All? Unequal Hopes and Lives in Pursuit of the American Dream*. Princeton, NJ: Princeton University Press.

Handke, P. (2019). *A Sorrow beyond Dreams*. London: Pushkin.

Huber, F. (2019). *Promise Me You'll Shoot Yourself: The Downfall of Ordinary Germans in 1945*. London: Allen Lane.

Inglehart, R. (2018). *Cultural Evolution: People's Motivations Are Changing and Reshaping the World*. Cambridge: Cambridge University Press.

Lear, J. (2006). *Radical Hope: Ethics in the Face of Cultural Devastation*. Cambridge, MA: Harvard University Press.

Lifton, R. J. (1999). *Destroying the World to Save It*. New York: Holt.

Muller, J. W. (2018, November 26). What cold war liberalism can teach us today. *The New York Review of Books Daily*.

Münchau, W. (2014, June 16). Europe faces the horrors of its own house of debt. *Financial Times*.

Nicolson, A. (2014). *The Mighty Dead*. London: William Collins.

Piketty, T. (2014). *Capital in the Twenty-First Century*. Cambridge, MA: Harvard University Press.

Plato (380 BC). *Laches, or Courage*. B. Jowett (Trans.). Boston, MA: Actonian, 2010.

Polakow-Suransky, S. (2017, October 16). Is democracy in Europe doomed? *The New York Review of Books Daily*.

Sharafutdinova, G. (2019, April 29). R.I.P. "Soviet Man": Scrapping homo sovieticus in the spirit of Yuri Levada. In: *Woodrow Wilson The Russia File* [podcast].

Snyder, T. (2017). *On Tyranny: Twenty Lessons from the Twentieth Century*. London: The Bodley Head.

Volkan, V. D. (2004). *Blind Trust: Large Groups and Their Leaders in Times of Crisis and Terror*. Charlottesville, VA: Pitchstone.

Wade, R. (2014). The Piketty phenomenon. *International Affairs, 90*(5): 1076.

Wolf, M. (2018, December 18). The Faustian bargain of nationalism. *Financial Times*.

CHAPTER 6

Two facets of the pandemic: stigmatization and the psychopolitics of heroization

Deniz Ülke Arıboğan

> *Every group feels strong once it has found a scapegoat.*
> —Mignon McLaughlin

Introduction: the most challenging crisis in human history

The inhabitants of the global village were celebrating, almost with a holiday atmosphere, the end of the twentieth century, which went down in history as a period of total destruction, full of crises, conflicts, and two global wars. In the Millennium Declaration adopted at the United Nations Summit, the global values of the new era were listed as follows: freedom, equality, solidarity, tolerance, respect for nature, and shared responsibilities (United Nations General Assembly, 2000).

It was hoped that the new system of values would build the architecture of a new era on a more peaceful, more liberal, more unlimited, and more democratic model. Topics such as preventing hunger and poverty, increasing the schooling rate, realizing gender equality, reducing child mortality rates, and fighting against epidemics were among the main objectives of the summit. Instead of the obsolete history ending with the fall of the Berlin Wall in 1989, it was expected that the new millennium would start off with a clean slate and completely different political relations would be built. However, this expectation did not occur. The chain of terrorist attacks carried out on US soil on September 11, 2001 triggered the first major political crisis in the global world. The security concerns and the imagining of a global enemy, embodied in Al-Qaeda and radical Islamic terror, caused a serious shift at economic, political, and social levels. Economic resources began to be diverted to military spending; the securitization process on the social plane caused the suspension of fundamental rights and freedoms and the rise of the anti-democracy waves even in the liberal world. The concentration of power in the political sphere started to shift from civil society to central authorities.

The second major global crisis came with the economic collapse that broke out in 2008. The global economic earthquake triggered by the mortgage crisis that started in the US led to trillions of dollars in financial losses; it caused unemployment to reach abnormal levels and turned the economic growth performance of many countries negative. During the economic crisis, which had a particularly negative impact on global finance and investment companies, tens of thousands of companies went bankrupt. The state, on the other hand, as an economic actor, had the opportunity to return as a savior to the market which it had had to withdraw from significantly under the liberal conditions of the last decades.

The third global crisis of the twenty-first century erupted through a pandemic known as Covid-19. The viral disease, which was officially diagnosed in Wuhan, China in December 2019, spread all over the world in just a few weeks. It is already possible to say that this pandemic, which *"will forever alter the world order"* (Kissinger, 2020) will not only have significant effects on our perception of health and healthcare systems, but also in many other areas from the economy to social life, and from the individual-state relationship to the international environment. The potential impact of this crisis to affect very fundamentally the multilateral global balance developed since the Second World War, the world economy, and politics is highlighted by many social scientists.

Amitav Acharya (2020) summarizes this transformation as follows: "Above all, the pandemic will undercut support for the globalization process, which has been weakened by the rising nationalism and the policies of President Trump." With the spread of the virus all over the world due to human mobility, closing national borders against foreigners and the concept of "national sovereignty" becoming prominent again means the end of the dream of an unbounded world. In this sense, it is possible to say that the global pandemic will not actually change the trends that existed before the crisis. On the one hand, it may lead to the gradual death of neoliberalism. On the other hand, it may pave the way for populist autocrats to become more authoritarian (Rodrik, 2020).

Thomas Friedman (2020), claiming that the pandemic will be a new milestone for humanity—B.C. (before corona) and A.C. (after corona)—also argues that the reason the side effects of the pandemic are so great is that the world we live in is not only interconnected, but also "interdependent" and even "fused." However, Friedman's discourse of "the Earth is flat," which has become the motto of liberalism, does not mean, in the context of the virus, the removal of barriers raised by national borders, easier trade relations between states, convergence of cultures, and consolidation of the global economy. On the contrary, this concept now provides an explanation for a global level of activism encompassing closure of national borders, stagnation of the economy, and centralization of authority. The "flat Earth," which was supposed to be borderless and barrier free, paves the way for the virus to spread easily and turn into a pandemic. From the consideration of viruses, territorial boundaries are imaginary, just like the Equator line, and boundary walls that can be raised for people or commodities do not constitute any obstacles for these viruses. Instead, the pandemic, which managed to spread to almost every point around the world in just a few months, has also proved how actual the "global village" discourse is.

Pandemic, "infollution" (information pollution), and propaganda

Times of global crises, just like war settings, are periods when too much false and misleading information is produced, politicization is on the rise, and public opinion is consciously constructed by political actors. Many of the information platforms led by pseudo and false experts, deliberate deceivers, intelligence services, and partisan intellectuals create an information pollution that leads to negative psychological consequences in the social context. In the triangle of misinformation, disinformation, and malinformation (Wardle & Derakhshan, 2017), our severely damaged minds cause our fears and traumas to be politicized. However, it is impossible not to notice the vital consequences of political instrumentalization of the information that shapes a global crisis environment such as a pandemic. The fact that the pandemic has the potential to affect the attitudes and behaviors of large masses in economic, sociological, psychological, and political terms leads to the restructuring, censorship, and reproduction of all kinds of data regarding the pandemic by political or economic actors.

The concept of "infodemic," which was used for the first time by the World Health Organization (WHO) in its report, "Immunizing the Public against Misinformation" (2020), addresses the false knowledge and the fabricated information process that spread as the Covid-19 disease turned into a pandemic and points out the drawbacks caused by this process in controlling the effects of the pandemic. The circulation of fake, false, misleading, and even dangerous information not only increases the physical damage of the pandemic, but also paves the way for the development of individual and collective traumas. In the joint statement declared by the United Nations and WHO in September 2020, it was stated that, for the first time in history, a pandemic was experienced in an environment where social media and digital technologies had been in use, and the dangers of misinformation circulating in the same media were mentioned (Joint statement by WHO, UN, UNICEF, UNDP, UNESCO, UNAIDS, ITU, UN Global Pulse, and IFRC, 2020).

Directing and shaping data on epidemics by political authorities is not a new trend. As in wars, the first victims of epidemics are also facts, and this has been going on unchanged for centuries. Rather than preventing the epidemic, political actors have spent their time ensuring the dissemination of information according to their wishes, creating scapegoats and conveying the social response outward. This has naturally led to an increase in losses and the continuation of the fight against the epidemic on the wrong front. Psychological warfare has become one of the most important fronts since the beginning of the pandemic. In addition to the Spanish Flu label of a century ago, attempts to create scapegoats that point to the origins of the virus by using names based on ethnicity or nationality have always come to the fore in a short span of time. Names such as "The Spanish Lady," "French Flu," "Naples Soldier," "The Purple Death," "War Plague," "Kirghiz Disease," "Bolshevik Disease," "White Man's Disease," "German Plague," etc., all stem from the search to point out who the culprit is. Eventually, this tragedy is a story of failure that takes its place in history as a symbol of the pandemic's mismanagement for the sake of military interests (Davis, 2018, p. 14). The 1918 epidemic struck as a global tsunami wave and caused the deaths of 50 to 100 million people, corresponding to about 5 percent of the world's population, which is five to ten times more than the total losses in the world war. During war, people were often told that those who spread this unknown disease were the enemies they were fighting (Cotter, 2020; Davis, 2018, p. 18).

The Covid-19 pandemic, which emerged nearly 100 years after the Spanish Flu, is no different from its predecessors in terms of information pollution. From the very first moment, allegations such as withholding information, producing biased or incorrect information, and manipulating data were constantly expressed. These allegations reached the point of mutual accusations between countries, and became the most important issue in intranational debates between the governments and the oppositions. The information produced regarding perhaps the biggest global crisis of the twenty-first century has also paved the way for the production of conspiracy theories adopted by large masses in the "age of doubt" that we are thrown into (Galbraith, 1977). Theories such as the virus being a biological warfare tool, the crisis being produced by medicine and vaccine manufacturing companies (Big Pharma), Bill Gates being the person who produced the virus because he had mentioned the possibility of a global pandemic in a former speech, everything being caused by 5G technology, etc., accumulated a high currency among the masses in the communication platforms. "Deadly diseases, especially when there is no cure to hand and aetiology is obscure, spawn sinister connotation" (Porter, 1992, p. 179). A reflection of this state of obscurity and despair has been the creation of mysterious scapegoats that are partially abstract and hidden behind shadows, not implicitly defined but easily marked.

For example, during the 2020 presidential elections in the USA, President Donald Trump's whole strategy was built on the assertion that the pandemic was a crisis that had been magnified, if not created, for the purpose of preventing his being reelected. In this kind of crisis environment, where the future becomes uncertain and existential threats become evident, the focal point for the need to seek asylum may differ. Both for individuals and large groups, the search for asylum sometimes turns into a search for a leader of a group (whether it be a leader of a tribe, a sect, or a political party); sometimes that search is for a safe haven in science, sometimes in God, and sometimes in the state. Moreover, at a crisis point where the risk is at maximum level, holding on to the known past rather than accepting an uncertain future and following the traces of social traumas buried in collective memories is often the preferred route. For this reason, in the days of crisis, the report card of the culprit who caused us to fall into the pit and the hero who helped us out of the pit is shaped by the polished images engraved in our memories. The way we trace the culprits and those in charge as well as our savior heroes will mostly be shaped within the framework of our past practices and collective memory.

Global psychopolitics of the pandemic: political behavior against threat perception

Psychological factors are extremely important in understanding and managing social problems that arise in connection with the pandemic, such as blame, condemnation, marginalization, and hostility among societies. Anxiety about losing their health, loved ones, job, property, family, or security, and stress disorders resulting from this anxiety can affect people's entire lives (Taylor, 2019, pp. xv–xvi). The psychological reaction people develop from the moment they lose their security undoubtedly affects not only their social life but also their political decisions. According to Berezin, "Emotions operate as protective physiological cues that warn us individually or collectively that something is in flux" (2002, p. 47).

The Covid-19 struggle, which is defined by President Macron of France as "a war against an elusive and invisible enemy" (Didili, 2020), has an inconsistent and fluid effect that will reshape not only the healthcare system but also the attitudes and policies in the social, cultural, economic, and foreign policy fields. We tend to think of visible threats, such as weapons, bombs, and terrorism as extremely dangerous, yet invisible things—such as parasites, bacteria, and viruses—are known to create far more lethal consequences (Davis, 2018, p. 11). Moreover, in addition to these deadly physical health problems, psychological traumas that occur as a side effect of pandemics can cause as much havoc as the former in terms of social consequences. The impact of intense negative emotions, such as fear, anxiety, isolation, loneliness, and loss of trust, on our individual and collective social behavior, found its political expression in the consolidation of central political authority in some countries (e.g., New Zealand, Germany, and China) and has also led to a change in government holding office in some countries (e.g., the US).

According to research, events that threaten the system often lead to a conservative change in social and political behaviour (Jost, 2020). It is concluded by similar research that, compared to liberals, conservative people are more inclined to simplify problems and violate social distance rules (Rothgerber et al., 2020). This tendency makes it easier for conservative political entities to emerge from crises around the world with more effective and popular support. When people perceive a threat, the perception can become even stronger than objective reality. For centuries, politicians have preferred to highlight perceptual threats in order to tighten their groups and reinforce their supporters (Gelfand, 2018, p. 72).

The most powerful element that feeds conservative politics is when strong and radical winds of change are blowing and large masses perceive themselves in an uncertain and unpredictable environment. The inherent character of change is that it also triggers the tendency to "conserve and stabilize" as its own antithesis. Considering that today's world has undergone a great transformation, has surpassed the post-industrial civilization and moved to a new phase, sometimes described as industry 4.0, it is not surprising that conservative dynamics gain strength. In today's world, the monopoly of power which was traditionally in the hands of a few actors is broken. There is no consensus among current actors, and countries can no longer achieve what the US achieved in being the only superpower in 1945 (Haass, 2020).

The first difference between the administrations perceived as successful and unsuccessful in combating the pandemic is that, while the successful ones focused on the essence of the struggle—that is, to stop the pandemic—the unsuccessful ones focused on finding someone or something to blame for the ongoing disaster. Within this framework, it is possible to say that those who are successful develop practical and introverted strategies, and those who fail develop rhetorical and extroverted strategies. Second, it should be noted that there is a difference between those who try to cope with the crisis and those who instrumentalize it. Particularly, during the crisis, small countries with a narrow sphere of influence made an effort to minimize damage and save themselves from the effects of the pandemic. In the pursuit of gaining political leverage from the crisis, large countries with global claims heroized and sublimated themselves, or underestimated and blamed their rivals. Third, some countries have based their strategies on managing the negative effects of the crisis and the disaster, while others have focused on opportunities to occupy an advantageous position within the new economic and political architecture that may emerge after the disaster.

In the context of instrumentalizing or managing the crisis, we can see that many psychopolitical instruments have been deployed in order to sustain the resilience, productivity, and unity of populations. Since it is known by state authorities that, like all pandemics, this one will come to an end sooner or later, the main issue for many states is: from where and from what position to participate in the global competition when Covid-19 ends. As with any crisis, some global powers will rise and some decline. In such a prolonged crisis, the psychological resilience of the populace is as important as the economic, sociological, and political resilience. For this reason, it is an expected development that state authorities will produce a scapegoat, that is, in a sense, a negative focus of attraction onto which they can transfer the accumulated tension of the public; in other words, to create "the other" to be used during the crisis. It is a necessity of the human self-preservation instinct (DeAngelis, 2001).

On the other hand, because the same crisis requires a positive focus of attraction, so that people might take shelter under its wings, it is a politically meaningful action for political authorities to heroize themselves and glorify both their regime and national identity. Although heroism is a psychologically complex phenomenon, one definition argues that "modern heroes not only demonstrate the capacity for persistence in the face of failure but that they do so with a view to the protection and wellbeing of future generations" (Gumb, 2017, p. 211). For this reason, it is not surprising that the heroic stories of political actors are based not only on saving the moment but also on the future and leadership. It is possible to say that the country, company, or leader that came out of the crisis as a savior or hero will assume a permanent legendary identity, at least in the medium term.

Stigmatization: the policy of labeling the Other

Stigmatizing and blaming the other party are the most important psychopolitical tools used in today's competitive world. Stigmatization, in the most general sense, can be conceptualized as an attempt to show a negative bias that marks a person or a group, to humiliate and disparage him/her/it, or to discredit the other party by using negative evaluations and stereotypes (Major & O'Brien, 2005; Sayar, 2002). Stigma is a sign that justifies the bearer of that mark to be treated less humanely than those without the mark (Major & O'Brien, 2005). From the marked individual's point of view, it is not possible to display his/her true identity without getting rid of that imposed mark. The historical dynamics of politics always require such an approach. Especially in the new era we live in, where every individual and society is connected to each other through global information networks, and all potential crises are managed under the spotlights of the media in a way to satisfy the audience. The easiest way to appease the public in this medium is to create a scapegoat. In this way, incrimination/accusation becomes a product that is bought and sold just like other commodities and waits for its buyer in the market (Campbell, 2011, p. 18).

The act of scapegoating and stigmatizing is essentially a practice of getting out of crisis situations by unjustly playing the blame game. The target can be a person, ethnic or religious groups, business sectors, government departments, industry sectors, and sometimes an entire country. From a psychodynamic point of view, this process is fulfilled via projection or displacement as an implementation of unjust aggression, hostility, and disappointment on a person or group. In this respect, it can be described as a defense mechanism (Ee, 2017). Society's view of pandemics has not changed much historically. Since a disease appears suddenly and is something previously unknown to the communities affected, it is considered a normal act to put the blame on others. This is perpetuating a historical attitude which has led to the development of hatred, discrimination, and violence against those who are marginalized.

According to Niall Johnson, the main image of the disease in such epidemics is its "foreignness." Thus, the approach of "What is wrong or unnatural cannot be of us, but must be of the 'other'" is natural. One of the most obvious expressions of such externalizing of blame is when a geographical name becomes attached to a disease. The name suggests both disease origin and blame (Johnson, 2006, pp. 152–153). Precisely for this reason, the French called syphilis, which became an epidemic in Europe in the fifteenth century, "Neapolitan disease" or "Spanish disease." However, the disease was the "French evil" for the Germans. Russians called it the "Polish disease," the Polish and the Persians called it the "Turkish disease," the Turkish called it the "Christian disease," the Tahitians named it the "British disease," for the Japanese it was the "Chinese pox," and some other nations referred it the "Persian fire" (Frith, 2012) Those who were blamed for the cholera that spread in the USA in the nineteenth century were the Irish who had just started immigrating to the continent; it was named the "Irish disease." Usual suspects, the Jews, were scapegoated for bringing tuberculosis to the USA in the early twentieth century and held responsible for the epidemic known as "Jewish disease" or "tailor's disease" (mostly because it was the profession of Jews) (Mihm, 2020).

The phenomenon of hate that emerges at the social level during pandemic periods is an ordinary situation. According to Carlo Ginzburg, the extraordinary traumas caused by major illnesses intensify the efforts to seek a scapegoat as targets for any fear, hatred, and tension (1990, p. 124). "Why did this happen to us?" The desire to answer the question is very strong, and when the disease strikes and people begin to suffer, unfortunately it is inevitable for a scapegoat to be designated (McNeil, 2009). For this reason, it is not unexpected that Covid-19, the first major pandemic to affect the world on a global scale after a period of about 100 years, will have a similar side effect.

Considering the historical context up until today, defining Covid-19 as "Chinese virus" or "Wuhan virus" is a clear stigmatization and paves the way for a hidden or open discrimination against the Chinese and even all East Asians at the global level. The US was one of the countries with the most unsuccessful management of the pandemic and the Trump administration's "holding the other responsible" policy, which is a concrete example of the effort to deflect the wave of criticism emerging from the inside, did not have difficulty in finding supporters around the world. Especially in the first months of the pandemic, it was observed that the discrimination against people of Chinese origin and almost all East Asian people due to their physical resemblance increased significantly. In the US, around 650 virus-based discrimination and assault acts against Asian Americans were reported in the first week alone (Kandil, 2020). Such actions did not only take place in the US, but even in countries with high sensitivity to human rights such as England, Italy, Canada, and France.

Considering the relations between the US and Chinese governments in recent years and the political and cultural perception of modern China, it can be said that the concept of "Chinese virus" is effective in both concrete (life safety) and abstract (political and cultural conflicts) ways (Xu & Liu, 2020). The outcome of the "disease-spreading China" campaign led by Trump against the Chinese can be clearly seen in a PEW survey, which revealed that the negative opinions about China grew exponentially after the pandemic in countries neighboring China, such as Australia (81 percent) and Japan (86 percent) (Silver et al., 2020).

Although stigma, as a socially constructed psychological sign, is based on a concrete or symbolic perception of threat in the initial stage, it then becomes a part of the society that creates and ignores such attitudes, and ensures its continuity by sharing information about it frequently. Such stigmatization and exclusion, on the one hand, pushed Chinese and East Asian communities into the position of perpetual foreigners (for a study on the permanent foreign status of the East Asians, see Kim et al., 2011); on the other hand, it will turn into a motivating factor to enhance intra-group bonds by strengthening the group identity. For example, the Asian minority—a model minority in the US and defined as a part of the American dream as a well-educated, hardworking community that cares about its families (Chow, 2017)—being at the receiving end of this kind of stigma after Covid-19 causes these groups to become introverted and distrustful of the outside world.

The idea that determining the culprit of the pandemic will whitewash every other actor from guilt and responsibility has begun to be shared by other states. The growing negative approach toward China turned into a highly active global propaganda. In many countries, governments have chosen to suppress their desperation in fighting an undetermined foe they cannot deal with by directing the public toward a concrete enemy target. According to Richard Horton (2020), editor-in-chief of the well-known medical journal *The Lancet*, this approach—blaming China as responsible for everything—is nothing but an effort "to rewrite the history of Covid-19 and to marginalize the failings of Western nations." However, the speech of US President Trump to the UN General Assembly on September 22, 2020, should not be underestimated (The White House, 2020). As a matter of fact, many countries under the leadership of the US claimed that the Chinese government was late in acknowledging the virus and misinformed global public opinion, as they also expressed their demands for compensation against China. According to the report of the British foreign policy and national security think tank, the Henri Jackson Society, the sum of claims for compensations by only G-7 countries may reach approximately $6.5 trillion (Carey, 2020). US Secretary of State Pompeo's following remarks, "Every place I go, every foreign minister that I talk to, they recognize what China has done to the world. They will pay the price" (Macias, 2020), signal that a compensation lobby will be established under the leadership of the US.

The reaction of China to this stigmatization policy develops in multi-pronged ways. First, by emphasizing that they are not a criminal but a victim, they try to draw attention to the negative consequences of stigmatization since the beginning of history; to them, these discriminatory attitudes constitute a crime. Second, they claim that the fact that Wuhan was the place where the virus was first discovered does not indicate that the origin for the virus was Wuhan; indeed they claim that the virus came from elsewhere to their own country. Allegations that the virus had previously been seen in Italy (Hui et al., 2020; Vagnoni, 2020), and that US soldiers who came for military games carried the virus to China (Pickrell, 2020), are some of the tactics used to create clouds of doubt about the source of the virus. Another perception management method implemented by China is to present itself as the "restorative" country that first created the genome map of the virus and immediately shared it with the world, thus attempting to play a heroic role (Poitras, 2020). One of the most important tactics used by China within this framework is the "politics of generosity." The Chinese government, which has sent equipment such as masks, medical gowns, and ventilation devices abroad since the first days of the pandemic, has also implemented billions of dollars in economic aid packages. The claim of being the first country to overcome the pandemic and taking on the role of the hero with a success story was the ultimate tactic, and although this raised a lot of doubt about its authenticity, it was declared that life in the country had returned to normal. In this way, the Chinese government has mobilized all the means at its disposal and tried to purge the accusations against itself, at least in the eyes of the global community, through public diplomacy by directing the psychopolitical attacks against it from the Western world into another medium.

It is not surprising that the global effects of the pandemic have moved from the spheres of health care and the economy to the stage of politics. A trauma that can affect social psychologies so profoundly is expected to have political consequences not only at the national level but also at the international level. Directing and shaping the mass psychologies, thus instrumentalizing the pandemic, is a rational choice for dominant powers struggling with global competition because the pandemic is an enormous and very real crisis, one that can fundamentally affect global relations and even deconstruct the global system. On the global political ground, which has become suitable for the emergence of new alliances, new power centers, and new hostilities, a very fragile system of relations has been formed for the US, China, Russia, the EU and others. For this reason, state authorities try to make their positions more advantageous and pursue the systematically weakening of their global rivals by using various psychopolitical tools. Thus, while "Blame was, after all, turning into a calling card of all transnational epidemics" (Farmer, 2011, p. 191), it is also shaped as the main determinant element affecting political alliance systems, economic relations, legal attacks, and image/reputation management that will be formed especially with the end of the pandemic. Therefore, regardless of the definition of concept, all approaches that develop in the form of stigmatization, blame, labeling, or creating scapegoats are essentially political and do not serve the truth but the power relations between the dominant actors.

Psychological consequences of heroization

The efforts of the state authorities to prove how "successful" they are to the world's public opinion on the occasion of the pandemic, and their search for a reputation through this, is one of the positive disinformation initiatives that can be seen during the crisis. As in every pandemic or crisis scenario, the common expectation is that a hero will come and save all humanity. The purpose of the race for states, far beyond protecting their own citizens from this epidemic, is to reach the rank of heroism in the eyes of the global public. Competition over which state, which system, or which worldview is superior in dealing with the common enemy or crisis has also prioritized the need for new communication strategies for states. Some countries have tried to be the first to announce that they defeated the virus by declaring their victory with the end of the first wave; others highlight that women leaders are more successful in combating the pandemic, and others yet have sought to show that authoritarian systems can fight better than libertarian governments in times of crises. The question of "Who will be a hero?" triggers competition at different levels between political systems, between genders, between states, and between pharmaceutical companies (Big Pharma). From the point of view of political authorities, the race to prove the effectiveness of their state policies and political regime as well as their leadership to the world's public opinion is a perennial attitude. In this struggle, which has been going on since antiquity, the most important characteristic of the twentieth century was the introduction of the concept of "prestige policy" into the international relations literature, and the planning of the tactics applied to gain image and reputation for the global audience. Especially during the Cold War period, the "conquest of space" had been accepted as the most important determinant element of which system was more powerful. Sputnik's launch into space in 1957 was an important turning point in the increasing competition between NATO and the Warsaw Pact, and this tiny beach-ball-sized and silver-colored satellite shook the world balances. During the Sputnik crisis, the White House, CIA, and American Air Force worked confidentially with reliable defense companies on their own satellite to be sent into space. Few people know that the name of the satellite was CORONA (Dickinson, 2007).

Despite the prominence of the USSR in the space race with the launch of Sputnik into space, American astronaut Neil Armstrong, who took "a small step" for himself but "one giant leap for mankind" onto the moon on July 20, 1969, declared the US to be victorious. This step, which gave President John Kennedy a great psychological superiority as the first conqueror of space (Zimbardo, 2005), paved the way for the inter-block competition to focus on space and the moon from the late 1960s. Interestingly, maybe as an indicator of the continuity of history, the name given to the vaccine by Russia, which was developed as the first vaccine against coronavirus in the world, is "Sputnik V." Pushing the limits of space for the first time, Russia, this time pushing the limits of medicine, has sought to show the world its leadership in this field in which it has lagged behind for a long time (Corera, 2020). This symbolic branding is an interesting example of the use of a medical product for political prestige. The superpowers' use of the vaccine as a means of demonstrating their scientific abilities and proving that their political systems are superior can be regarded as an expansion of public diplomacy.

The "prestige policy," which classical theorists attach importance to in international relations, has gained much more importance especially in the twenty-first century world we live in, which is defined as post-truth. Political governments invest in the creation of information that will create impact and reputation at both national and international levels, with an approach that widens the difference between what happens and what is seen day by day. "Prestige policy," emphasizing visibility and reputation rather than content and efficiency, is a strategy that creates "cognitive dissonance" as described in social psychology. Instead of making an honest and self-critical assessment of the capabilities of states, it creates situations that require the transformation of facts into preexisting and firmly held beliefs (Sonntag, 2008, p. 78). Approaches such as "We were the first to find the vaccine," "We defeated the virus first," "We received the least damage," or "We helped the victims the most in the world" are in essence, post-truth approaches that engage in political propaganda rather than declaration of reality. But these approaches should not be perceived as acts of arrogance applied without strategy and unconsciously. One of the most important means of competition that states use in the international arena as soft powers (the term "soft power" was first used by Joseph Nye in 1990 and was defined as the new face of power; see Nye, 1990) is public diplomacy, used in the management of image and reputation. The perception of "the hero who ends the pandemic" can provide a great psychological advantage to that state's authority.

The declaration of being in "first place" in the race to heroism was made by Russian President Putin on August 11, 2020 (*BBC News*, 2020). Although the statement created a temporary excitement in world public opinion, it could not have optimum effect due to the reliability of the tests and the knowledge that the vaccine race had been used as a propaganda tool. Moreover, Putin's statement that his "daughter had been vaccinated," after stating that the vaccine had passed all checks and been approved, can be described as a perception maneuver aimed at establishing trust and eliminating doubts that might arise in the public response. Another heroic initiative undertaken by Russia was shaped in the context of showing how ready, willing, and equipped it was to help abroad. Despite being the country that suffered the most from the crisis, when Italy could not receive support from the European Union or the US, Russia sent a serious amount of aid to the region. Inspired by a James Bond movie, a quote "From Russia with Love" was written on the medical aid boxes.

Another example of a state seeking to be at the forefront of heroism is China, which consolidated its position as a great power in the global political arena of the early 2000s. China, while being declared as the main country responsible for the pandemic due to its perception as the source of the virus and being late in informing the world, is trying to position itself as the author of a heroic story. President Xi Jinping, at a ceremony where he gave medals of honor to the heroes in combatting the pandemic at the time when the whole world was just beginning to fall under the influence of the second wave (September 8, 2020), stated that 1.4 billion Chinese had passed an extraordinary test, and they were the first major state to defeat the virus and return to normal.

From one point of view, China has defeated the virus not because it has an authoritarian structure, but because of science and strong public healthcare policies. China has prioritized healthcare issues since the SARS (2002–03) epidemic and has managed to increase its capabilities in emergency health measures (Uretsky, 2020). In addition, not only the political system it implemented, but also the structure of the Chinese culture provided a great opportunity for the rulers (administrators) to successfully overcome the crises. As stated by Gregory Poland, president of the Mayo Clinic Vaccine Research Group, there is an attitude in Chinese culture that has internalized attaching more importance to the well-being of the majority. They do not have hyper-individualism, which causes resistance to the measures taken against coronavirus, as in the US culture. Likewise, in addition to the importance given to "science" in China's success, there are no anti-vaccine and anti-scientific movements to interrupt the struggle (Burki, 2020).

The fact that China clearly demonstrates its pursuit of leadership in the fight against the pandemic is an important threat to the US, which has taken the leadership of the world since the fall of the Berlin Wall in 1989. According to some, the fact that the Chinese developed the effective vaccine before anyone else created a shock wave similar to the one when the USSR sent cosmonaut Yuri Gagarin into space in 1961 (Sarkar, 2020). Moreover, the idea of producing the Chinese vaccine as a global public property is of great importance for China. In contrast to the egocentric US, which declared that it will not participate in the United Nations Joint Vaccine program, COVAX (Tooze, 2020), China's generous approach, which declares that the vaccine to be produced will be a public property, is an attitude that will be engraved on the collective memories of people suffering under severe trauma. In this way, the issue of vaccination has become one of the most powerful tools of the global propaganda war going on during the pandemic (Graham-Harrison & Phillips, 2020).

One of the negative examples showing that the level of scientific progress and economic development does not mean much alone and that cultural factors and social healthcare policies are as crucial is the European Union. Throughout the pandemic, countries preferred to close their borders instead of lending assistance to each other and embarked on a self-rescue quest. The fact that the EU could not agree on a common package of measures and campaign strategy, even on such an important issue, has damaged the idea of the "United States of Europe" built for decades. From the very beginning, some countries have opted for complete closure of borders, some have introduced hybrid systems, and some have tried to adopt herd immunity. Although the difference in strategy between countries seems to be an internal matter, since it has taken place in a geographic area with intensive integration, each strategy has turned into a disruptive factor that causes the collapse of the other. The isolated and selfish attitude of the countries and the ineffectiveness of the idea of the European Union in a time of crisis caused serious reactions among the member states. In a study by the European Commission covering nine countries that make up two-thirds of the population of the European Union, it was determined that only around 25 percent of Europeans think that the European Union shows sufficient interest in the issue. In Italy, one of the countries most affected by the pandemic, only 4 percent stated that they were satisfied with the support of the European Union, while 25 percent stated that the greatest support came from China (Butler, 2020). Subjected to intense criticism, the only method the European Union could find was to declare a financial support package worth 15 billion euros for its members (European Commission, 2020). In such a crisis, where subject matters such as the Common Market, monetary union, and the principles of the Schengen Treaty were completely eliminated and even the African and Asian countries (in much more difficult situations) showed better performance, the fragility of the idea of the Union also became more evident (Bongardt & Torres, 2020).

The result of all three crises in the first two decades of the twenty-first century is that the European Union is not resistant and prepared for global crises. In the crisis environment, the world's largest economy has been paralyzed, the world's most liberal societies have been panic-stricken, and the idea of "only for me" has become more prominent rather than an "all for one" policy. As in the statement of the president of the European Commission, Ursula von der Leyen, "When Europe really needed to prove that this is not only a fair weather Union, too many refused to share their umbrella" (Herszenhorn & Weathon, 2020).

The fact that the US—which influenced the twentieth century as the world's greatest political power and displayed leadership capacity at a level that would cause the last seventy-five years to be remembered as an "American Century" (White, 1992)—could not achieve a place among these heroic stories during the crisis period is one of the most interesting aspects of this pandemic. It was not possible for the US, as one of the countries that suffered the most from the pandemic, to direct its concentration to countries overseas and the global propaganda war due to the internal political turmoil and election atmosphere. When the Trump administration determined the strategy of only finding the culprit of the pandemic and using it as an election tactic, it settled into the position of a "victim" rather than a hero. In a setting where China and Russia seek to help and support countries abroad within the framework of the "generosity policy," even if it stems from their political interests, and the European Union tries to provide economic support packages to its members along with messages of unity, the Trump administration made the US perhaps the biggest loser in this global crisis, voluntarily renouncing its leadership status related to global health diplomacy. In contrast, the Biden–Harris administration announced that they will work towards restoring America's role in leading the world through global crises, advancing global health security and the Global Health Security Agenda, by rebuilding health security alliances, strengthening global pandemic supply chains, providing humanitarian relief, and building resilience for future epidemics and pandemics (The White House, 2021). Biden's late, but powerful entrance to the global health diplomacy arena might be considered as a signal that the US will push back against Russian and Chinese efforts to enhance their so-called soft diplomatic power by distributing vaccines to strategically important regions and prioritizing the global perspective after consolidating their power at the domestic scale (Wainer & Wingrove, 2021).

Conclusion

It can already be seen that the twenty-first century is conceived to have some developments different from the modern and postmodern era we have witnessed. In this period when the dominant powers in the world are preparing for a new distribution of power, it is necessary to focus on the psychopolitical grounds in determining the global power compositions as well as looking at how much the pandemic has harmed humanity. The pandemic is not just a health crisis; it is also a major earthquake that can trigger many structural changes in economic, sociological, cultural, and technological aspects, and may bring the reconstruction of political architecture into question. The political structure built by the ending of the Cold War has started to be shaken by a series of earthquakes, first with global terrorism, then with the global economic crisis, and finally with the pandemic. On which pillars the new political reconstruction will be built is a meaningful subject of discussion. According to some, a new world order will be formed under the leadership of China, and according to others, an economic and political fluctuation that will trigger China's collapse will begin. Likewise, the end of US leadership and the beginning of a renewed US leadership is also possible. Perhaps we are about to witness the emergence of a non-polar political structure, in which we cannot refer to a singular leadership.

From another perspective, the main issue is globalization, and this pandemic will either end globalization or start a new era of global cooperation. It is possible that the psychological environment caused by the pandemic will strengthen nationalities and nationalism and undermine the global economy; it is also likely that a tendency for global governance, solidarity, and integration that will enable the world to react against global crises collectively will become more evident. To make it more precise, no matter how it is perceived from different perspectives, the common ground on which almost everyone agrees is that nothing will ever be the same again. Therefore, it is not difficult to predict that the competition between the dominant powers over the reconstruction process of the new global structure—including how public perceptions will be shaped, what the global audience will believe and not believe, and what will be accepted as good and right or wrong and bad—will escalate.

Global actors, while dancing on the psychopolitical stage of the pandemic using all information and communication channels, will also try to construct the perception map of the post-epidemic landscape. Since the beginning of history, people have tended to identify the ones responsible for the evil that happened to them and to worship and to swear allegiance to the power that saved them from these evils. Scapegoats and heroes produced today are constructed on the traces of narratives and traumas that overflow from our collective memories. As Julius Caesar said, "Men willingly believe what they wish." The main thing is to convince them of what they want through a good story.

References

Acharya, A. (2020, April 18). How coronavirus may reshape the world order. *The National Interest*. https://nationalinterest.org/feature/how-coronavirus-may-reshape-world-order-145972 (last accessed August 13, 2022).

BBC News (2020, August 11). Coronavirus: Putin says vaccine has been approved for use. https://bbc.com/news/world-europe-53735718 (last accessed August 13, 2022).

Berezin, M. (2002). Secure states: Towards a political sociology of emotion. *Sociological Review, 50*(2): 33–52. https://doi.org/10.1111/j.1467-954X.2002.tb03590.x.

Bongardt, A., & Torres, F. (2020). Lessons from the coronavirus crisis for European integration. *Intereconomics, 3*: 130–131.

Burki, T. (2020). China's successful control of COVID-19. *The Lancet Infectious Diseases, 20*(11): 1240–1241. https://doi.org/10.1016/S1473-3099(20)30800-8 (last accessed August 13, 2022).

Butler, K. (2020, June 24). Coronavirus: Europeans say EU was "irrelevant" during pandemic. *The Guardian*. http://theguardian.com/world/2020/jun/23/europeans-believe-in-more-cohesion-despite-eus-covid-19-failings (last accessed August 13, 2022).

Campbell, C. (2011). *Scapegoat: A History of Blaming Other People*. London: Duckworth.

Carey, A. (2020, April 6). Report demands China pay $6.5 trillion in compensation. *NewsComAu*. https://news.com.au/finance/economy/world-economy/coronavirus-report-demands-china-pay-65-trillion-in-compensation/news-story/74710257a0881e8fc9f07603fed87ab6#.k14m0 (last accessed August 13, 2022).

Chow, K. (2017, April 19). "Model Minority" myth again used as a racial wedge between Asians and Blacks. *National Public Radio*. https://npr.org/sections/codeswitch/2017/04/19/524571669/model-minority-myth-again-used-as-a-racial-wedge-between-asians-and-blacks (last accessed August 13, 2022).

Corera, G. (2020, August 23). Coronavirus vaccine: Short cuts and allegations of dirty tricks in race to be first. *BBC News*. https://bbc.com/news/world-53864069 (last accessed August 13, 2022).

Cotter, C. (2020, April 23). From the "Spanish Flu" to Covid-19: Lessons from the 1918 pandemic and First World War. *Humanitarian Law & Policy Blog*. https://blogs.icrc.org/law-and-policy/2020/04/23/spanish-flu-covid-19-1918-pandemic-first-world-war (last accessed August 13, 2022).

Davis, K. C. (2018). *More Deadly Than War: The Hidden History of the Spanish Flu and the First World War*. New York: Henry Holt.

DeAngelis, T. (2001). Understanding and preventing hate crimes. *American Psychological Association*, *32*(10). https://apa.org/monitor/nov01/hatecrimes (last accessed August 13, 2022).

Dickinson, P. (2007, November 6). Sputnik's impact on America. *PBS Nova*. https://pbs.org/wgbh/nova/article/sputnik-impact-on-america (last accessed August 13, 2022).

Didili, Z. (2020, March 17). Macron says France is "at war" with coronavirus. *New Europe*. https://neweurope.eu/article/macron-says-france-is-at-war-with-coronavirus (last accessed August 13, 2022).

Ee, S. (2017, November 15). "Scapegoating"—What it is and how to understand it. *Psychology Practice*. https://thepsychpractice.com/plog/2017/11/15/scapegoating-what-it-is-and-how-to-understand-it (last accessed August 13, 2022).

European Commission (2020, April 8). Coronavirus: EU global response to fight the pandemic. https://ec.europa.eu/commission/presscorner/detail/en/ip_20_604 (last accessed August 13, 2022).

Farmer, P. (2011). *Haiti after the Earthquake*. New York: PublicAffairs.

Friedman, T. L. (2020, March 17). Our new historical divide: B.C. and A.C.—The world before corona and the world after. *The New York Times*. https://nytimes.com/2020/03/17/opinion/coronavirus-trends.html (last accessed August 13, 2022).

Frith, J. (2012). Syphilis: Its early history and treatment until penicillin and the debate on its origins. *Journal of Military and Veteran's Health*, *20*(4). https://jmvh.org/article/syphilis-its-early-history-and-treatment-until-penicillin-and-the-debate-on-its-origins (last accessed August 13, 2022).

Galbraith, J. K. (1977). *The Age of Uncertainty*. Boston, MA: Houghton Mifflin Harcourt.

Gelfand, M. J. (2018). *Rule Makers, Rule Breakers: How Culture Wires Our Minds*. New York: Simon & Schuster.

Ginzburg, C. (1990). Deciphering the Sabbath. In: B. Ankarloo & G. Henningsen (Eds.), *Early Modern European Witchcraft: Centres and Peripheries* (pp. 121–138). Oxford: Clarendon.

Graham-Harrison, E., & Phillips, T. (2020, November 29). China hopes "vaccine diplomacy" will restore its image and boost its influence. *The Guardian*. http://theguardian.com/world/2020/nov/29/china-hopes-vaccine-diplomacy-will-restore-its-image-and-boost-its-influence (last accessed August 13, 2022).

Gumb, L. (2017). Beyond trauma fiction: Constructing the recovery narrative and the ordinary hero. [PhD thesis, Murdoch University.] https://researchrepository.murdoch.edu.au/view/author/Gumb, Lynn.html (last accessed August 13, 2022).

Haass, R. (2020, December 29). The pandemic will accelerate history rather than reshape it. *Foreign Affairs.* https://foreignaffairs.com/articles/united-states/2020-04-07/pandemic-will-accelerate-history-rather-reshape-it (last accessed August 13, 2022).

Herszenhorn, D., & Weathon, S. (2020, April 7). How Europe failed the coronavirus test. *Politico.* https://politico.eu/article/coronavirus-europe-failed-the-test.

Horton, R. (2020, August 5). Anti-China feeling masks West's own COVID-19 failures. *The Lancet.* In: *Xinhua Net.* http://xinhuanet.com/english/2020-08/05/c_139267737.htm (last accessed August 13, 2022).

Hui, Z., Yusha, Z., & Juecheng, Z. (2020, December 10). Italy potentially had Covid-19 outbreak "Earlier than Wuhan", study shows. *Global Times.* https://globaltimes.cn/content/1209646.shtml (last accessed August 13, 2022).

Johnson, N. (2006). *Britain and the 1918–19 Influenza Pandemic: A Dark Epilogue.* London: Routledge.

Joint statement by WHO, UN, UNICEF, UNDP, UNESCO, UNAIDS, ITU, UN Global Pulse, and IFRC (2020, September 23). Managing the COVID-19 infodemic: promoting healthy behaviours and mitigating the harm from misinformation and disinformation. https://who.int/news/item/23-09-2020-managing-the-covid-19-infodemic-promoting-healthy-behaviours-and-mitigating-the-harm-from-misinformation-and-disinformation (last accessed August 13, 2022).

Jost, J. T. (2020, June 3). Will the pandemic change political attitudes? *Character & Context, SPSP.* https://spsp.org/news-center/blog/jost-pandemic-changing-political-attitudes (last accessed August 13, 2022).

Kandil, C. Y. (2020, March 26). Asian Americans report over 650 racist acts over last week, new data says. *NBC News.* https://nbcnews.com/news/asian-america/asian-americans-report-nearly-500-racist-acts-over-last-week-n1169821 (last accessed August 13, 2022).

Kim, S. Y., Wang, Y., Deng, S., Alvarez, R., & Li, J. (2011). Accent, perpetual foreigner stereotype, and perceived discrimination as indirect links between English proficiency and depressive symptoms in Chinese

American adolescents. *Developmental Psychology*, *47*(1): 289–301. https://doi.org/10.1037/a0020712.

Kissinger, H. A. (2020, April 3). The coronavirus pandemic will forever alter the world order. *Wall Street Journal*. https://wsj.com/articles/the-coronavirus-pandemic-will-forever-alter-the-world-order-11585953005 (last accessed August 13, 2022).

Macias, A. (2020, July 15). The world will make China "pay a price" over coronavirus outbreak, Mike Pompeo says. *CNBC*. https://cnbc.com/2020/07/15/the-world-will-make-china-pay-a-price-over-coronavirus-outbreak-mike-pompeo-says.html (last accessed August 13, 2022).

Major, B., & O'Brien, L. T. (2005). The social psychology of stigma. *Annual Review of Psychology*, *56*(1): 393–421. https://doi.org/10.1146/annurev.psych.56.091103.070137.

McNeil, D. G., Jr. (2009, August 31). Finding a scapegoat when epidemics strike. *The New York Times*. https://nytimes.com/2009/09/01/health/01plague.html (last accessed August 13, 2022).

Mihm, S. (2020, February 20). The ugly history of blaming ethnic groups for disease outbreaks. *The Japan Times*. https://japantimes.co.jp/news/2020/02/20/world/social-issues-world/history-outbreak-disease (last accessed August 13, 2022).

Nye, J. S. (1990). Soft power. *Foreign Policy*, *80*: 153–171. https://doi.org/10.2307/1148580.

Pickrell, R. (2020, March 12). Chinese official says US Army may have "brought the epidemic to Wuhan." *Military.com*. https://military.com/daily-news/2020/03/12/chinese-official-says-us-army-may-have-brought-epidemic-wuhan.html (last accessed August 13, 2022).

Poitras, C. (2020, January 23). Rapid data sharing and genomics vital to China virus response. *Yale School of Medicine*. https://medicine.yale.edu/news-article/22389.

Porter, R. (1992). The case of consumption. In: J. Bourriau (Ed.), *Understanding Catastrophe* (pp. 179–203). Cambridge: Cambridge University Press.

Rodrik, D. (2020, April 6). Will COVID-19 remake the world? *Project Syndicate*. https://project-syndicate.org/commentary/will-covid19-remake-the-world-by-dani-rodrik-2020-04 (last accessed August 13, 2022).

Rothgerber, H., Wilson, T., Whaley, D., Rosenfeld, D. L., Humphrey, M., Moore, A., & Bihl, A. (2020). Politicizing the COVID-19 pandemic: Ideological differences in adherence to social distancing. *PsyArXiv.* https://doi.org/10.31234/osf.io/k23cv.

Sarkar, S. (2020, May 8). Operation warp speed: The race to save US prestige and find COVID-19 vaccine. *Hindustan Times.* https://hindustantimes.com/world-news/trump-s-going-all-in-on-a-vaccine-he-may-still-get-beaten-by-china/story-xU6PKa9DG0QDYF8G9ZLB1N.html (last accessed August 13, 2022).

Sayar, K. (2002). Her Toplumun Stigması Farklıdır. *Popüler Psikiyatri Dergisi,* 9: 18–23.

Silver, L., Devlin, K., & Huang, C. (2020, October 6). Unfavorable views of China reach historic highs in many countries. *Pew Research Center's Global Attitudes Project.* https://pewresearch.org/global/2020/10/06/unfavorable-views-of-china-reach-historic-highs-in-many-countries (last accessed August 13, 2022).

Sonntag, A. (2008). The burdensome heritage of prestige politics. In: M. Maclean & J. Szarka (Eds.), *France on the World Stage: Nation State Strategies in the Global Era* (pp. 77–90). Basingstoke, UK: Palgrave Macmillan UK. https://doi.org/10.1057/9780230582934.

Taylor, S. (2019). The psychology of pandemics: Preparing for the next global outbreak of infectious disease. *Cambridge Scholars Publishing.* https://elibro.net/ereader/elibrodemo/124138 (last accessed August 13, 2022).

Tooze, A. (2020, September 19). The world is winning—and losing—the vaccine race. *Foreign Policy.* https://foreignpolicy.com/2020/09/19/the-world-is-losing-the-vaccine-race (last accessed August 13, 2022).

U.N. General Assembly (2000). United Nations Millennium Declaration, no. A/RES/55/2.

Uretsky, E. (2020, November 23). China beat the coronavirus with science and strong public health measures, not just with authoritarianism. *The Conversation.* http://theconversation.com/china-beat-the-coronavirus-with-science-and-strong-public-health-measures-not-just-with-authoritarianism-150126 (last accessed August 13, 2022).

Vagnoni, G. (2020, November 16). Coronavirus came to Italy almost 6 months before the first official case, new study shows. *World Economic Forum.* https://weforum.org/agenda/2020/11/coronavirus-italy-covid-19-pandemic-europe-date-antibodies-study (last accessed August 13, 2022).

Wainer, D., & Wingrove, J. (2021, May 5). Biden gets US into vaccine diplomacy race as stockpiles rise. *Bloomberg.* https://bloomberg.com/news/

articles/2021-05-05/biden-gets-u-s-into-vaccine-diplomacy-race-as-stockpiles-rise (last accessed August 13, 2022).

Wardle, C., & Derakhshan, H. (2017). Information disorder: Toward an interdisciplinary framework for research and policy making (DGI(2017)09). *Council of Europe.* https://edoc.coe.int/en/media/7495-information-disorder-toward-an-interdisciplinary-framework-for-research-and-policy-making.html (last accessed August 13, 2022).

White, D. W. (1992). The "American Century" in world history. *Journal of World History,* 3(1): 105–127.

White House, The (2020, September 22). Remarks by President Trump to the 75th Session of the United Nations General Assembly. https://whitehouse.gov/briefings-statements/remarks-president-trump-75th-session-united-nations-general-assembly (last accessed August 13, 2022).

White House, The (2021, January 21). National strategy for the Covid-19 response and pandemic preparedness. https://www.whitehouse.gov/wp-content/uploads/2021/01/National-Strategy-for-the-COVID-19-Response-and-Pandemic-Preparedness.pdf (last accessed August 13, 2022).

World Health Organization (2020, August 25). Immunizing the public against misinformation. https://who.int/news-room/feature-stories/detail/immunizing-the-public-against-misinformation (last accessed August 13, 2022).

Xu, C., & Liu, Y. (2020). Social cost with no political gain: The "Chinese virus" effect. *PsyArXiv.* https://doi.org/10.31234/osf.io/j4t2r.

Zimbardo, P. G. (2005, October 5). *Liberation Psychology in a Time of Terror.* The Dagmar and Václav Havel Foundation VIZ 97 Award for 2005, Prague.

Part II

Application

CHAPTER 7

American identity

Edward R. Shapiro

Is there such a thing as a national identity and a national mission that addresses the needs and history of its citizens and connects to the needs of the global society? The tumultuous politics of the last two decades, the forming and dissolution of international collectives, and the recent pull towards nationalism has brought that question to the fore in the United States (Shapiro, 2003, 2020).

Let me go back a bit. During the American presidential election of 2000 between George W. Bush and Al Gore, Americans witnessed a remarkable internal political polarization and an unprecedented politicization of the judiciary to solve the political impasse. In addition, there appeared to be systematic interference with voting in ethnic and lower income areas. The split vote was extraordinarily precise, dividing the country in half. The political map presented on newscasts illustrated this political division by delineating in red the Republican center of the country and, in blue, the Democratic coastlines. This chapter traces one speculative formulation of this precise political division in terms of the dynamic use of ethnicity in America and its relation to the evolution of American identity.

In this red and blue political map of 2000, I saw an illumination of a split national identity where our outer boundaries (at the ethnically diverse edges of our country) were liberally opening for contact with the outside world, while our internal life remained conservatively stable. It reflected to me a picture of national, political, and internal tension, with the center of our country holding a set of traditional Republican values about the importance of the individual and our outer boundaries illuminating the Democratic value of a differentiated community. It seemed to me as though the pressures of outside influences were leading us at our boundaries to renegotiate our identity, putting pressure on our internal sense of stability and familiarity.

Identity

Erik Erikson defined identity as developing congruence between a person's internal view of the self and the views of that self, coming from others (Erikson, 1956; Shapiro & Fromm, 2000). Identity formation is a developmental step in adolescence, negotiated through relationships with others as the adolescent's body changes and the child begins to individuate from the family, undertaking a more mature role in a larger community of adults. Impediments to taking up an adult role can include reluctance to give up certainty (Shapiro, 1982), intolerance of ambivalence and complexity, hatred of difference, projection of limitations, and other developmentally induced rigidities. A successful negotiation of identity requires a painful modification of the adolescent's narcissism. Beginning to recognize oneself in the less than idealized reactions of others marks a significant step toward maturity and strengthens the capacity for flexibly grasping the realities of the larger world with their complexity and limitations.

Erikson's formulation about identity formation can be applied to the identity of a nation, which is negotiated and renegotiated both between its citizens and across its borders. A mature identity would incorporate an increasing congruence between internal and external views and include mature openness to complexity, increasing tolerance of differences, and acceptance of limitations. Such a maturing identity would result in a modification of national narcissism and strengthen the capacity for flexibly grasping the realities of the global community.

AMERICAN IDENTITY   121

America, as a nation, emerged from its home in England over two centuries ago. American identity has developed over time and is in the process of continued development.

A review of the 1996 and 2000 presidential elections and the terrorist attacks of September 11, 2001 suggested the presence of a national struggle within the citizenry about grasping an American identity in transformation. Changes in the world were pushing Americans to give up a narcissistic position of moral superiority and move beyond subgroup identifications to find themselves as Americans in an increasingly global society and claim a role in the larger world. The subsequent elections of Barack Obama and Donald Trump suggested that these issues were far from resolved.

Studying the individual voter

Prior to the national election of 1996, I participated in a large study of selected unaffiliated voters for the Center for National Policy in Washington (Center for National Policy, 1996; Shapiro, 2000). Unaffiliated voters are those without clear party identifications. Their political significance lies in the recognition that their votes inevitably determine the election. As a group, unaffiliated voters illuminate issues that affect both parties and thus allow access to significant national trends. Psychologically, they are the leading edge of our identity-in-formation.

In addition to our extensive group interviews, I personally talked with randomly selected individual voters across the country. These voters, from all ethnic groups, were feeling a loss of shared values in this country and talked passionately of the loss of a sense of community, a breakdown of rules, and a view of America as "rudderless," without clear goals, direction, or a sense of vision. In a post-Cold War world where information technology, twenty-four-hour media coverage, economic globalization, and the presence of powerful multinational corporations are blurring national boundaries, people could not effectively discover a larger context that allowed them to link their experiences and values to those of other Americans in passionate, meaningful commitments. Beyond the familiar structures of their own family and church, and their untested but strongly experienced membership in ethnic subgroups, they could discern no larger framework. Their grasp of the larger social scene was obscured by social turbulence, economic insecurity, gender and racial tensions, political disenfranchisement, and disaffection. They spoke of a "loss of authority" in the country and resultant anxiety and uncertainty about the future. There was a widespread feeling that "life was not as it should be" in terms of their personal and family circumstances, their community life, the direction of the country, and "American life" in general. Many talked about feeling disconnected from wider social and political contexts, as if they were "all alone," "voiceless" or just "numbers" in a "political game" in which they simply did not count.

The voters had great difficulty articulating what America "stands for" today, although they were quite able to describe what it used to stand for. Voters could not identify core American values and beliefs. They were unsure of how to identify themselves in relation to others in a global community, and whether they could think of themselves as "American" or only in terms of their ethnic, racial, or religious group.

In the absence of an external enemy against which a shared national boundary could be discerned, ethnicity emerged as a binding framework that individuals could join. Though ethnic identifications frequently emerge in subgroups of white Americans, I am using the term here to refer to those who whites characteristically think of as "people of color," ranging from Native Americans to African Americans, Latinos, Hispanics, Asians, and the more recent immigrants from the Near East, the Moslems. For our voters, their ethnic identifications brought them together with others, linked them in a shared history that often included social trauma, and provided a framework for shared beliefs and values. For some, ethnic identifications offered a way of managing social projections.

For example, Frank was a thirty-eight-year-old black single waiter. He was interested in "diversifying his skill set." He knew there was no job security in waiting tables and he had no hopes for a management position. Frank said, "If a black man represents the restaurant, the customers get scared. Talent is not seen. You are seen as black first." Frank was adamant about social issues but didn't feel that there was any other source of power other than a general oppression. "Parents are working; the streets are raising the kids. Teachers are not paid enough to teach, so they don't care what kind of values they teach."

Frank's internal world, like that of many people I interviewed, is organized around his ethnic identifications. He does not experience himself as an individual American struggling with diverse opportunities and complex constraints. Instead, he locates his experience within the imagined context of other African Americans who, he believes, passionately and deeply share his picture of the ethnically oriented social world around them. He was quick to lump whites into an imagined privileged oppressor group against which he can organize his aggression and develop his adaptation; his only recourse, as he saw it, was an ethnic identification.

In addition to this repetitive ethnic focus, our voters associated their uncertain American identity with a perception of a declining work ethic. They felt the loss of a sense of a united society and of many conditions previously taken for granted (affordable education, safe schools, job security, community life, a manageable picture of crime and violence, recognizable national goals). Voters were deeply disaffected with politics and politicians, who they felt were manipulative, dishonest, and driven by self-interest. They felt the judicial system was inefficient and overly litigious, with a jury system increasingly racially polarized and unsympathetic to ethnic Americans. Despite their shared anxiety, cynicism, alienation, and loss of faith in the system, voters were aware of their need to renegotiate their connections with others and with changing work environments to respond adequately to turbulence and change. They needed help to do this.

It seemed to me that these voters needed an interpretation, potentially offered by their leaders, which would both affirm and help them bear their painful experience by placing what they had repressed or dissociated in a larger context. The search for this larger context that allows both sides the possibility of hearing how the other is "right" is the primary challenge to the possibility of bridging their differences as citizens (Shapiro, 2021).

Government leaders have the information and perspective to articulate the sources and social significance of rapid change, allowing voters to grasp their differentiated roles in an evolving free society. Such an integrating interpretation, plus resources to connect with others, might allow voters to escape their experience as isolated individuals and find new ways to join others to participate meaningfully in their world.

My interviews found they needed a synthesis of what they felt was the "partially" correct Republican picture (the need to mobilize individual competence) in combination with the Democratic view (strength in diversity and community and resources for those in need). They grasped that individualism without community leads to deadening isolation and that welfare programs can lead to an overdependence on outside help. They needed help in figuring out how people could work together to learn from their differences and discover a larger frame of reference.

To engage the spectrum of voters, political leaders needed to recognize individual competence while affirming the importance of neighbors, neighborhood, and community. We felt in this study that leaders needed to articulate the dangers of isolation, acknowledge resource limitations (including their own), and define a mission that capitalized on American strength in diversity, a central value this country represents to the larger world. Leaders might have demonstrated how painful differences could be both affirmed and transcended in the service of an American identity. This would allow citizens to move beyond identifications with others in their subgroups toward an identity that both affirmed their individuality and allowed them to join a larger common purpose. The political polarization was interfering with hearing how the other might be "right." Though the larger purpose required definition, what emerged in our study was the binding power of ethnicity and America's historical commitment to incorporating, recognizing, bridging, and transcending differences. This, it seemed, might be a recognizable American mission that citizens could have found a way to join.

The white majority and the election of 2000

These political trends in 1996 and the voters' wish for a synthesis contributed to the movement of both parties toward the middle. Despite significant differences in political philosophy, the election of 2000 showed little differences in the substance of the message from the two parties. While the issues—education, retirement security, how to use economic prosperity—captured the country's attention, there was no significant effort to mobilize the competence of the electorate toward a larger vision, or to link our internal national struggles to those of the outside world.

Just below the surface of these political discussions, the population was undergoing a significant change. Immigration, increasing ethnic identifications, and the emergence of major cultural voting blocks was changing the definition of "American." At the millennium ethnic subgroups, once considered minorities, were becoming a larger part of the population, and have since become the majority in many cities and states. This change coincides with a similar shift away from the majority of American families being a heterosexual couple with their own biological children. The politics of diversity was moving into a new era.

When the results of the election of 2000 were finally made clear, it was obvious that an overwhelming number of minorities had been conveniently forgotten. In American society, whites have always held power and used it to increase the economic gap with non-whites. The white majority has managed a sense of unity through projection of difference. The unconscious message is, "We whites are all the same; you minorities are different." These dynamics, characteristic of unconscious group functioning, provided external support for ethnic bonding in racial and ethnic subgroups. As my interview with Frank illustrated, the shared (and understandable) feeling was, "If we ethnics are not in power, at least we are unified."

In a country where disengaged and unintegrated citizens do not take up the complex work of democracy, the law increasingly regulates social and human issues. In 2000, the electoral process itself was handed over to the courts, de-linked from the democratic process and the Constitution. Perhaps in an unconscious recognition of the incipient loss of their majority, the white establishment seized power in a way that politicized the legal system and disenfranchised ethnic voters.

The events of September 11, 2001

For a period after the 2000 election, it seemed as if the antipathy to the election process would contribute to a mediocre presidency and a dispirited American public. Despite post-election rhetoric about bringing people together across the political spectrum, there was evidence of familiar American conservative trends in the government's abandoning the ABM treaty for a National Missile Defense, withdrawing from collaborative international efforts around global warming, and providing tax relief for wealthy individuals. All three policies represented a retreat from joining a differentiated and integrated community and the substitution of an isolated, intensely defended individuality.

The terrorist attacks of September 11 transformed everything. Suddenly, the unconscious anxiety that ethnics would take our country over from within (manifest most clearly at our Republican center) was transformed into a shared conscious anxiety that ethnics would destroy us from without. From the perspective of the internal national split, the attack could be understood dynamically as a return of a dissociated mental representation of historical racism, causing massive psychic disruption and reorganization. The right wing saw with shock their denied hatred of difference returning as an ethnic attack; the left saw their own disconnection from fundamental values returning as a rageful picture of America's godless liberalism. The shock of recognition indicated that this defensively split construction of our national identity had not worked; it demanded an internal shift to acknowledge a more complex reality. Facing this transformation was our conservative Republican president and a management team experienced in war.

If America was struggling with a developmental internal split with fundamental values held internally and differences projected to our outer boundaries, the terrorist attack evoked a crisis. Americans—as articulated by our president—were stunned that outside ethnic groups hated us. We faced a manifest identity crisis between our narcissistic self-idealization (President Bush called Americans "a good and kind people"), and a vicious external retaliation for our foreign policies that had contributed to the marginalization of ethnic subgroups.

Unlike the war in Vietnam, where the issues were complex and ambiguous and the dynamics suggested some form of American bullying, the war on terrorism gave us clearly delineated "bad guys," who were ethnically identifiable. The recognition that "they are trying to kill us" mobilizes powerful defenses, and with a clearly recognized "all bad" external enemy, internal differences in this country momentarily disappeared in a moving surge of patriotism. But the developmental tension between experiencing all difference as outside versus discovering a sense of "otherness" within remained.

"Are we all Americans, or just some of us?" This unresolved question was visible in the contrast between the moving obliteration of ethnic differences in the escape from the Towers and the episodic vicious murder, beatings, and harassment of Moslems and Sikhs across the country. Both responses are recognizable as historically American and evidence of an unresolved struggle about American identity and values.

The Republican government's response to the attack was sophisticated, multilateral, and determined. The election promises of genuine delegation and decisiveness seemed fulfilled, as were the potentials for bipartisanship. And the media moved us quickly into a massive educational forum about terrorism and a review of the motivations for such intense hatred of America. Citizens were beginning to learn about America's dynamic role in the world, the group projections into us, the intense stereotyping that we have invited by our policies. Though America has contributed to international humanitarian aid, our nation has regularly supported oppressive regimes that act against our national values. These policies have provided the basis for projective processes from abroad, supported by our wealth, power, and relative isolation. Newscasts, managed and filtered by the white power elites (Lewis, 2001), have maintained our isolation by focusing on local issues and paying scant attention to the larger world.

Terrified by our sudden vulnerability and facing an unprovoked attack, our response has necessarily been to use our vast military might to attempt to destroy those disaffiliated ethnic groups that we experience as Other. As one general put it, "We must destroy the conditions that lead to terrorism." While we have the power to be successful militarily, only our coalition building can support the deeper integration and renegotiation of identity that we need. Without the coalition, we run the risk of deepening America's regressive narcissistic position of invulnerability that contributes to isolation, withdrawal, and mutual projection. This solution—enacted later in Donald Trump's "America First" position—entrenches the country in a familiarly rigid defensive posturing in which "otherness" remains projected out, its illusion of internal goodness and certainty is maintained, and the integration of our internal differences is once more postponed.

America's sudden vulnerability, however, might also have been an opportunity to recognize the vulnerability of others and the need for Americans to help "ameliorate" rather than "destroy" the very conditions the nation had participated in developing. Recognizing internal ethnic tensions, Americans might have been more able to recognize their relatedness to the world's anger. This, sadly, did not happen.

We know about these dynamics. In my role as a therapist, for example, I have heard from some of my patients about their identification with the terrorists. I listen to their relentless hatred, envy, and wishes for retaliation and revenge against those with resources who withhold them to take care of themselves. When I worked with their families (Shapiro & Carr, 1991), I could see how this kind of polarization, rage, and marginalization could shift in treatment through identification with the Other to an increasing recognition of guilt, concern, and connectedness. This shift from rage and paranoia to identification and grief is hard to come by in the absence of containment and interpretation.

Erik Erikson (1954) describes "integrity" as a commitment to the most mature meaning available, requiring the discovery of larger social tasks to which the individual can become committed (Shapiro & Fromm, 2000). After the attack in 2001, Americans had the opportunity to recognize their internal polarization and participate in living out their values. Bush's retaliatory presidency did little to engage this opportunity.

Obama and Trump

The election of Barack Obama in 2008 mobilized an idealized fantasy of an America that could judge its citizens as Martin Luther King dreamed, "… not by the color of their skin but by the content of their character." Obama represented in his person the ultimate globalized ideal of integrating differences (black father, white mother, foreign upbringing). In the healing view that swept the country, many Americans discovered an identity that connected to their ideals and beliefs about the integration of difference—and America (transiently) deepened its ability to represent that identity to the world.

But underneath this phenomenon, the politics of isolation and the hatred of difference, so familiar in America's history, were intensifying. The frightening financial meltdown in 2008 had underscored the power of the coastal elites and illuminated Americans' perception of the corrupt (and, ultimately unpunished) exploitation of America's middle class. Despite Obama's competent management of the crisis, he increasingly came to represent to many from middle America both "otherness" and bi-coastal elitism. His support for marriage equality, respect for the gender spectrum, and willingness to stand up for liberal values became linked to the development of politically correct "trigger warnings" in colleges that protected the sensitivities of minorities and the traumatized and was perceived by conservatives as a limitation of their freedom of speech. The experience of middle America's voters in my 1996 interviews of feeling "left out, voiceless or just numbers in a political game in which they simply did not count," grew and politicians ignored it. Affirmative action, protection of "otherness," even the Black Lives Matter movement had contributed to the underlying fantasy in the center of the country that, as whites were moving into the minority, their opportunities were disappearing.

In response, came Donald Trump. The black writer Ta-Nehisi Coates (2017) called Donald Trump "the first white president," noting in *Atlantic Magazine*, "Trump arrived in the wake of [what he and his base considered] ... an entire nigger presidency with nigger healthcare, nigger climate accords, and nigger justice reform, all of which could be targeted for destruction or redemption, thus reifying the idea of being white." The Trump backlash was a familiar oscillation around America's identity challenge of integrating differences. Trump represented in his person the narcissistic isolation and repudiation of difference that has dogged America's history from its inception. His candidacy and his presidency mobilized ethnic hatred and racist behavior and was symbolized by the image of a wall that would exclude the Other. Like our waiter Frank, Trump could relate only to his narrow "base" considering others as "stupid," "rapists," and "enemies of the people." He could not take up membership, mature citizenship, join the larger society, and lead from that role. With his presidency, Americans were now looking at the worst representation of themselves and seeing clearly how difficult America's mission of integrating differences continues to be.

Individuals in authority roles have a large impact on people in organizations and society. To what extent does the personality of the leader have a major determining effect on the nature of the organization—or the state—and to what extent does the nature of the group, its tasks, structures, and relations with other groups influence the choice of its leaders? These questions have broad implications. If the group exists as an entity defined in relation to its task, then like the individual it is faced with the need to define itself in its context, that is, in relation to other groups. How and why now did America pick this particular leader? What is America saying to the rest of the world? What is the challenge now facing a disintegrating society?

Discussion

The dynamics of ethnicity have long been a major focus of irrational psychological and political behavior. Members of ethnic subgroups become symbols that hold emotional meaning; all diversity can serve as foci for projection (Barber, 1995). Black people in America, Aborigines in Australia, homosexuals, women in the workplace, the disabled—all these minorities and whatever differences can be discovered—mobilize passionate political polarization (Singer, 1999). The easy unconscious use of differences as receptacles where feelings of inadequacy, vulnerability, threat, and damage can be located outside of the self, leads to social disintegration that becomes manifest in the fragmentation of families, the breakdown of nations, the rise of tribalism, fundamentalism, and factionalism throughout society.

This polarity marks the understanding of irrational behavior in individuals, groups, and nations. American identity was first crafted in opposition to experienced tyranny. The openness, spaciousness, and freedom in our nation supported a powerful sense of American individualism. As it developed, the country recognized the significance of community, of interdependence, in accomplishing national goals. Is America's current collective use and misuse of ethnic boundaries a larger group manifestation of American individualism? Is the way its citizens so easily define themselves as individuals or in narrowly defined subgroups a collective defense against a difficulty in discerning a larger identity as Americans? Does America need an external enemy to discover the ways that freedom and interdependence are inseparable? Or is it possible for Americans to finally discover a collective identity in which they learn from their differences, integrate their unique history and values, and face—without flinching—others' complex reactions to them?

There may be congruence between the way the white power elite currently see this nation and the way it is seen from the outside. The collective picture of America as a nation run by affluent, powerful white men, while manifestly accurate, is also a defensive compromise formation, requiring a repression of its multiethnic complexity. Like any defensive structure, this view helps American citizens manage the anxiety derived from a full engagement with the nation's history and its internal diversity. Such a defensive American identity will inevitably continue to sap its citizens of the creative energy they might discover with a more complex integration of their differentiated strengths and capacities.

As Frank, says, "If a black man represents the restaurant, the customers get scared." As long as this is true in America, the nation will not be able convincingly to sell its mission of integration, interdependence, and democracy to the world's customers. Though it is manifestly simpler to form identities along ethnic lines, Americans have psychological and political work to do to identify themselves with the nation's range of multiethnic citizens. And, if citizens discover that they cannot identify with some of those who are different, they might, in the service of the national mission, be able to approach those differences as opportunities for learning from diversity rather than to hate these others as "not us." At the moment, this outcome still seems out of reach.

America, as a developing experiment in bringing together different ethnicities, histories, and capacities, can have a significant international role in reducing the projective distinctions between the "good guys" and the "bad guys." This might reduce the dangers of political disintegration as ethnic conflicts challenge the integrity of existing multicultural nation states (Ferguson, 2001). In assuming its own mature responsibilities for contributing to the marginalization of subgroups both within and without, this country can offer a realistic hope for transcending differences in the service of a larger integrative mission. The hope for a more complex vision of a global community may depend on the integration of America's identity and its willingness to recognize that the so-called "good guys" have to take their share of responsibility for their creation of disorder and rage in an evolving world.

References

Barber, B. (1995). *Jihad vs. McWorld*. New York: Ballantine.

Center for National Policy (1996). *Diagnosing Voter Discontent*. Washington, DC: Center for National Policy.

Coates, T. (2017, October). The first white President. *Atlantic Magazine*.

Erikson, E. H. (1954). The dream specimen of psychoanalysis. *Journal of the American Psychoanalytic Association, 2*(1): 5–56.

Erikson, E. H. (1956). The problem of ego identity. *Journal of the American Psychoanalytic Association, 4*: 54.

Ferguson, N. (2001, December 2). 2011. *New York Times Magazine*.

Lewis, J. (2001). *Constructing Public Opinion*. New York: Columbia University Press.

Shapiro, E. R. (1982). On curiosity: Intrapsychic and interpersonal boundary formation in family life. *International Journal of Family Psychiatry, 3*: 69–89.

Shapiro, E. R. (2000). American voters: Optimistic and disenchanted. *American Psychoanalyst, 34*: 14.

Shapiro, E. R. (2003). The maturation of American identity: A study of the elections of 1993 and 2000 and the war against terrorism. *Organisational and Social Dynamics, 3*: 121–133.

Shapiro, E. R. (2020). *Finding a Place to Stand: Developing Self-Reflective Institutions, Leaders and Citizens*. Bicester, UK: Phoenix.

Shapiro, E. R. (2021) "Why do I have to do this?": Institutions, integrity, and citizenship. *Organisational and Social Dynamics, 21*: 197–211

Shapiro, E. R., & Carr, A. W. (1991). *Lost in Familiar Places: Creating New Connections Between the Individual and Society*. New Haven, CT: Yale University Press.

Shapiro, E. R., & Fromm, M. G. (2000). Erik Erikson's clinical theory. In: B. J. Sadock & H. I. Kaplan (Eds.), *Comprehensive Textbook of Psychiatry*. New York: Lippincott Williams & Wilkins.

Singer, T. (Ed.) (1999). *The Vision Thing*. London: Routledge.

CHAPTER 8

Moral-psychological aspects of ethno-political conflicts in Russia and other post-Soviet countries

Alexander V. Obolonsky

T his chapter was written before the invasion of Russian troops into Ukraine. Now, in May 2022, I must add a few more sentences and say that this event became the hardest and most terrible shock, both for me and a lot of people around me; that I am completely against these inhuman actions of the Russian government; and that I consider it a huge political, moral, and psychological mistake with many long-term negative consequences. For me personally, the invasion has become, possibly, the most tragic blow and disappointment to all I believed, valued, and attempted to do in my professional scholarship and my life in general. Moreover, during my long lifetime, I have tried to do everything I could, both as an academic and as a citizen, to preclude the movement of events in this kind of terrible direction. Tragically, I failed in this, like many other similarly minded people in my country.

I am afraid that currently I am not in the appropriate moral and psychological condition for detached academic analysis of all of this. On the other hand, I think that the following text corresponds rather closely with this problematic, and, hopefully, might serve both for better understanding *of the psychological basis for these terrible, inhuman events and for a prognostication of their future development, to the extent that is possible at all.*

* * *

Perceiving "interesting times" as inconvenient and even dangerous for the daily life of ordinary people dates back to Confucius. This idea has been reproduced in various times and versions regarding various periods of history, including the twentieth century. I, personally, do not fully share it. It was indeed true for the periods of transition in which Russia and post-Communist societies of Eastern Europe found themselves at the turn of the century, and where, mentally, they still largely are, even now. I propose to discuss in this context the moral-psychological aspects of interethnic conflicts and collisions within particular times and places.

Russia is the main country under examination, though not the only one; there are elements of comparative analysis. I also decided not to divide the moral and psychological factors, which are so closely intertwined in this context. Methodologically, I will rely, primarily, on the psychoanalytical ideas and approaches developed for several years by members of the International Dialogue Initiative. The mission of the IDI is to understand the psychological grounds for the barriers in the way of peaceful resolution of interethnic and intercultural conflicts, and, thus, facilitate their overcoming. For the IDI, large-group identity is a critical area of study; the effort is toward a psychological analysis of the emotional aspects of historical and other conflicts between large groups, which have formed over time according to ethnic, religious, or other stable characteristics.

I am not sure whether to consider the psychoanalytical approach as comprehensive for the study of human motivations and behavior but I find it very useful in analyzing and understanding ethno-political conflicts in times of transition.

A phenomenon of post-traumatic society

We, in present-day Russia, are living in a past, and still experienced, trauma of our national consciousness and psychology. Lack of understanding of this on the part of many does not change the situation; rather it makes it worse and prevents finding adaptive solutions. We are, by no means, unique in our condition. All societies who went through a war or collapse of a political regime experience a similar situation. This is true to various extents, not only in Russia, but in all the post-Communist countries of Eastern Europe going through a transition period. However, our situation is more complex and challenging, not only due to the long duration of the Soviet regime and the number of its victims, but also because its consequences have not been overcome, even on the subjective, psychological level. We, as a society, are far from being healed, that is, from a cure by way of forming an adequate memory of the past and a respectful attitude toward it in our collective national consciousness.

The present state of ambiguity was aptly described by historian and cultural scientist Alexander Etkind (2016). Here are a few quotes from his book. "If the executioners have not been convicted, the victims' damages have not been compensated for, the criminal institutions have not been banned, and monuments to victims have not been erected, the memory of the disaster acquires peculiar forms" (p. 66). "In the USSR, those same people and institutions that organized mass violence exposed it later ... It's a unique situation—the criminal regime had to expose itself" (pp. 56–57). Hence, there is a crucial difference between Russia's situation and that of post-Nazi Germany, as well as of post-Soviet countries of Europe and the Baltic states, a difference which is critical for the analysis and understanding of the resentment over Russia's collective experience in the 1990s, leading to significant steps back from the reforms of that period (Obolonsky, 2018, pp. 47–57). That difference has to do with the effects of trauma on both the society and the state. We face, therefore, a cumulative effect of *both a post-traumatic society and a post-traumatic state*, including, in particular, the problem of lustration. Russia is the only country among the successors of the Soviet regime in Eastern Europe that has not conducted even minimal cleansing of the state apparatus from the officials of the preceding political system.

The problem of lustration (vetting in official UN terminology) has, beyond its political and legal aspects, serious psychological specifics and nuances. It seems to produce dual long-term effects, both positive and negative. On the one hand, lustration is a sort of delayed and quite moderate retribution for the previous "sins" of those bureaucratic servants who directly "served evil," so to speak, but with consequent forgiveness toward them. In the original Latin meaning of the word, lustration means repentance with pardon to follow. So, this process should support in people's minds a certain trust in the final triumph of moral justice—a kind of moral satisfaction—and give them some hope of avoiding similar injustices in the future. Applied to authoritarian and totalitarian regimes, lustration addresses, first of all, the law enforcement system that conducted the political repressions on behalf of the state. Therefore, the very fact of lustration—and of public accountability—after that state's demise has a potentially healing effect.

But, on the other hand, lustration frustrates and traumatizes those rank-and-file public servants who didn't consider themselves part of the state's offenses. They begin to feel discriminated against and betrayed, because, according to their vision of the past, they simply fulfilled orders from their bosses, followed the rules and laws of the previous regime, the standards of that time, and supposedly acted just "as everybody must do in my place." I think, however, that this is a convenient but wrong and even dishonest position, because it presumes an absence of personal responsibility for one's own actions and for finding ways to deal with the challenges that arise in one's way of life. In general, I believe that Russia's refusal to conduct even minimal lustration in the post-Soviet state brought many more negative than positive consequences, which the current situation and political dynamics unfortunately seem to confirm.

In contemporary psychoanalytical theory, for healing to occur in a post-trauma society, the collective consciousness should fully acknowledge the fact of the trauma, grieve for its victims and losses, and go through a genuine mourning process. Awareness of the scale and horror of the collective crimes against humanity committed on behalf of the state by its obedient servants should become deeply rooted in societal consciousness. Otherwise, the traumatic stress will not be overcome, and even worse, this may, among other things, legitimize psychologically the acceptance of violence against various Others. The negative image of those "bad guys," of Others who are supposedly responsible for all our griefs, is either shaped by long-held views and myths of the masses, or those Others are directly "appointed" as such by the authorities along ethnic or other criteria, in order to create enmity and present the current leadership as saviors (Ochberg, 1988; Volkan, 1988, p. 201).

The Federal Republic of Germany may well be the most successful case of adequate understanding of this danger and constant effort to prevent its possible recurrence (Baum, 2015), although even there, the understanding and all the efforts do not always preclude outbursts of intergroup enmity and aggressive rejection of Others. Even more so, some analysts view the German case as not quite successful (Eppleh, 2020), though it certainly is in comparison to others. Although post-Soviet Russia has also done something along these lines, regrettably, it is much less and in a far more formal fashion. We never had genuine de-Stalinization. Moreover, the political practice of Stalinism involved persecutions, not only on class or ideology-driven grounds, but also along ethnic lines. Even worse, one can see today the explicit reincarnation of the Stalinist ideological and political paradigm with its inevitable attributes of violence and cruelty, albeit to a more modest degree. It is now a matter of policy to cultivate nostalgia for Stalinist and, more broadly, Soviet times.

Consumerism propagated on a massive scale also hampers the development of the feeling of collective guilt and any thoughts in this direction. One should admit that for the first time in a century and thanks to the market reforms, albeit implemented not in the best way possible, Russia's consumer market has been saturated with goods. And the generations of Russians who grew up amid the total shortage of goods and who can now for the first time enjoy consumer store-bought abundance, proved to be ready to sacrifice political and liberal values for the so-called "consumer Paradise," although this sacrifice did not appear inevitable during perestroika and the first post-Soviet years. Another post-Soviet "carrot" was that after three quarters of a century of insularity, people could now travel freely around the world.

What we may have seen here is the inertia of the process of cultural change lagging behind the change in material conditions of life, at least by one generation. The intergenerational lag during transition to the so-called post-materialistic society is described in detail in Ronald Inglehart's (2018) work, *Cultural Evolution: People's Motivations Are Changing and Reshaping the World*, which became a classic overnight. The view of IDI's Frank Ochberg and Ed Shapiro on "the three-generational" cycle of the overcoming of trauma is in close agreement, in psychological terms, with Inglehart's conception. This serves to partially explain, in my opinion, the shocking phenomenon of nostalgia for Stalinism among some young and middle-aged Russians. Psychologically, this may reflect an imaginary, self-deceiving compensation for the disappointment in one's present life conditions and a lack of positive prospects for the future.

The mythologizing and idealization of the past sometimes becomes a "blind eye syndrome" toward the multiple evils and crimes of the Stalinist regime. It is based on three things: first, the younger group's poor knowledge about the reality of how hard life was then, with all its horrors; second, the intentional imposition of official propaganda, on TV, etc., showing a distorted and embellished version of the Soviet period of history; third, the same kind of symbolic gestures coming from political leadership. The most important point in this context is the approval, in official statements, documents, and even federal laws, of a simplified, narrowly one-sided, and exaggeratedly heroic version of the Great Patriotic War, represented as the single possible interpretation for events of that time and prohibiting other visions and concepts.

True, there is also an encouraging phenomenon of a dramatic growth in the share of youth among active participants in street protests and other nonconformist actions, in response to the government "screw-tightening" policy. That policy, in my view, has gone beyond both legal (let alone constitutional) and simply rational limits, even from a purely survival perspective of the regime itself. One method for the government's return, morally and politically, to a Stalinesque logic has been to enhance and expand the policy of criminalizing its political opponents, both at the legislative level (the notorious "anti-extremist" laws, and the laws on "foreign agents" and "undesirable organizations") and at the law-enforcement level. Unpunished, unpunishable, and often cruel police violence against peaceful citizens—participants in explicitly nonviolent protests and even casual bystanders—with further quasi-legal "legitimation" of conspicuously unlawful actions of the police and the so-called RosGuard, through blatantly unlawful courts' biased decisions—has become the norm. Massive civic protests in Moscow in the summer of 2019, in response to denial of access of undesirable candidates to municipal elections, and even more massive protests across the whole country in the winter of 2021, triggered by the obviously unlawful incarceration of Alexei Navalny and subsequent repressions against protesters, are striking examples of this.

At the interethnic level, trauma that has not been overcome is an ever-existent nutrient solution for feelings of enmity and intolerance toward Others who have a different group ethos and cultural traditions. The extreme case, regrettably quite frequent during military conflicts, is to dehumanize enemies. In other words, one creates the image of the enemies as having a set of exclusively negative features, making them not quite human, which morally legitimizes any cruelties toward them and creates a moral-psychological basis for politically oriented manipulation of "our kind," through fear-mongering about the dangers to our accustomed national identity, allegedly coming from the Others. If the enmity has interethnicity or something similar as its basis, the cruelty and atrocities against the Others may go beyond imaginable limits or any rational paradigm of human behavior.

Conflicts that erupted on the ruins of the disintegrated Yugoslavia, especially in Bosnia, abound in terrifying cases of mass cruelty, including sheer barbarity. Outside of the European region, recent decades have seen the most horrible mass atrocities in African countries. One will recall waves of genocide in Nigeria, genocide against the Tutsis in Rwanda in the early 1990s, followed by the Tutsis' revenge, similar in scale, following a military coup a year later. In the context of this paper, one should note the dehumanization of those exterminated; thus, in the lexicon of the Hutus, the Tutsis they were killing were called "cockroaches."

Such "insectization," though, is just one method of dehumanizing enemies being killed. There are other ways, seemingly less offensive: ethnic jests and jokes, for instance, in which the image of the Others has little to do with reality. Such caricatures exaggerate, as a rule, some features of a particular ethnic group, disregarding others and inventing the rest. Besides, these chosen Others are turned into a sort of a target for projecting one's own deficiencies and vices, that is, the negative features of one's "own kind." And those Others, consisting of nothing but vices and deficiencies, monsters or blunderers, are made to look so bad that no one feels sorry for them, while getting rid of them seems even useful. The ways of "elimination" can vary subject to circumstances—from all kinds of percentage quotas, professional disqualifications, and multiple other discriminating restrictions to creation of territorial ghettos and even direct physical extermination.

It is difficult to apply the concept of dehumanization to the extreme, diabolic cruelty displayed toward Others who are not part of an interstate conflict, but are on different sides of civil wars, where neighbors and even relatives—people who have lived next door for decades, who were friends, who shared common interests, including married couples—become implacable enemies.

It is clear that disagreements and conflicts between parties in conflict normally should not transform people at an interpersonal level into irreconcilable political enemies. Having analyzed the scale, forms, and, more importantly, the motives of violence in civil wars, using the cases of Russia, Greece, Bosnia, and Chechnya, a US political scientist, Stasis Kalibas (2019) concluded that ethnic and ideological differences are a camouflage for self-serving and/or security motives. Perhaps too the seemingly trivial hunt for privileges, a higher status, and various material benefits are also important factors. In fiction, one finds this "justifying" turnabout of the mind in early Soviet literature, for example in Mikhail Sholokhov's *And Quiet Flows the Don* and Alexander Fadeyev's *The Rout*, and later in bard Vladimir Vysotsky's song: "I'm tired of being a gangster and bandit … I'd better join the anti-Semites …"

Such things also happen, in gentler forms, in times of peace, not in the form of physical violence, but, primarily, in the form of negative mental attitudes and moral constructs; for instance, in connection with mass migrations and even temporary movements of Other ethnic groups to other countries in search of jobs. In everyday life, one can observe this in the negative attitude toward labor migrants coming to Central Russia from Central Asia. Unfortunately, such attitudes are sometimes stoked by the actions of the authorities, discriminating against the migrants. The phenomenon itself emerges not only at the level of consciousness, albeit loaded with myths and prejudice, but in the unconscious as well (see, for example, Covington, 2017).

One manifestation of post-traumatic societal thinking is the post-totalitarian mind syndrome. The Russian mass consciousness, infected by the post-totalitarian virus, has proved to be far more severely injured than some would think, even quite recently. This revealed itself in such psychological phenomena as "Stockholm syndrome," "victimization," conspicuous super-conformist pro-government aggressive activism, a reduced or even switched-off empathy for government-designated "enemies," unpunished cruel actions against those "enemies," not excluding their physical elimination, for which Hanna Arendt's (2006) "banality of evil" appears to be quite a fitting description.

The post-totalitarian syndrome manifests itself differently at different levels. For some politicians and a certain part of the political environment, its features include political cynicism, an impudent style of political behavior, and a demonstrably aggressive rejection of the views and positions taken by the appointed Others who are stigmatized with such pejorative clichés as "the fifth column," "traitors of the nation," etc. At the level of the "man in the street," it appears rather in "little man" or "lonely man" syndromes, and a view of politics as, admittedly, an immanently dirty business, supposedly incompatible with morality, and dangerous into the bargain (see in detail Obolonsky, 2016, pp. 76–77).

Ethnic enmity through the lens of psychoanalysis

Psychoanalysts who are interested in large-group psychology hold the view, generally shared by scholars from many other research domains, that ethnicity as a sign of personal and group identity is rooted not in nature, but only in the minds of people. The alternative, "genetic" biological approach to defining nations was dominant up until middle of the last century. But Nazism had a sobering effect. For the wartime and subsequent generations of Europeans, such words as "national spirit," "the soil," "national idea," and "racial purity" came to be associated with camp watchtowers and gas chambers. Besides, serious ethnographic and anthropological research has shown that such perceived pillars of national community as language, history, and culture do not always work to assign national identity, and, in any case, are not suitable for formulating universal criteria to define nationality. There is only one indicator that proved to be universal: that is a person's self-attribution and sense of belonging to a specific nationality or ethnic group.

In a healthy society, this sense of belonging lifts a person, putting them in national "cothurni," and thereby providing an additional basis for their self-respect through a sense of sharing in the successes and achievements of fellow countrymen and fellow citizens. But, on the other hand, it makes the person more vulnerable in the case of a national crisis or a significant large group's failure. Then, the positive patriotic national feeling is easily turned into a misanthropic nationalism, hostile to others. The malignant "ladder of nationalism" has been described by many Russian writers, starting with late nineteenth-century Christian philosopher Vladimir Solovyov.

In the context of this problem, it appears important to note a frequent psychological feature of such situations—finding a "scapegoat," which means looking for the cause of one's troubles not in oneself, but in the intrigues of various foreigners, a neighbor, or "betrayals" within one's own country, that is, "internal enemies," "fifth column," etc. The Soviet regime applied this approach at full scale in a total and extremely brutal, inhuman way. In 1944–46, fourteen (!) ethnic national groups had been stigmatized as "nations of betrayals" and all members of them had been completely exiled from their places of permanent, many-generations-long habitation and deported to Siberia and Kazakhstan. Among victims of such operations, conducted by special military detachments within one to two days, were about ten nations of the Northern Caucasus and Crimea. Earlier, in 1941, during the first months of the War, the population of the Volga German Autonomous Soviet Socialist Republic in the middle Volga area—about a half million people, descendants of emigrants from German states living together as a group since the eighteenth century—followed the same path of total deportation to the East (see, for example, Solzhenitsyn, 1987).

Unfortunately, this kind of repression, directed against a whole nation, is not unique in the history of different states. Similar actions happened in various parts of the world. Remember, for example, the punitive removal of all Japanese from the West Coast of the USA in 1942 to special camps. Many other similar cases happened in many other countries. However, the Soviet case differs not only in its brutality, the horrible conditions of transporting exiles and their treatment in exile, but also for the time it occurred and the reason for the deportation. It took place not as a preventive step caused by fear of a "fifth column"—the existence of a true or imaginary "inside enemy" at the beginning of war; in the Soviet Union, exile took place at the very end of war (except for the deportation of Germans), when this kind of threat did not exist at all, even in the pathologically suspicious brain of Stalin. So, this massive deportation can only be considered to be a "revenge" of the state against nations or ethnic groups designated, for political reasons, as "bad," as potentially "betrayers." It served as a convenient opportunity to erase certain nations and national groups from the map of the Soviet empire.

This psychological context explains, at least partially, the outburst of aggressive brutal nationalism in post-socialist Yugoslavia and—fortunately in not so extremely brutal ways—in the massive ethno-national conflicts accompanying the dissolution of the USSR. These conflicts also brought many human tragedies—even the conflicts of the same period in Eastern European and Baltic countries—which, though they did not result in killings, in my view were of the same ethno-phobic nature in their basis. The collapse of the Soviet multinational empire opened a Pandora's box for numerous historical grievances and nationalistic phobias, both old and new, some of which were constructed for short-term, self-serving political purposes. Their exploitation served as a primary tool for politicos. Those who made and implemented the formal ethnic policy in the USSR over the course of seven decades used a wide range of methods—from a fairly flexible cultural policy and purposeful development of new national elites to near-genocidal repressions against whole nations, including mass deportations and forced assimilation.

One paradox of nationalism is that, with all the ostentatious conceit of its promoters, it appears to camouflage a deep-seated *inferiority complex*. This complex can be either aggressive or, on the contrary, defensive and apprehensive. The latter is characteristic of small nations who do not believe they have enough cultural, moral, and material resources to resist cultural oppression, assimilation, and political absorption by more powerful nations. However, paradoxically, it may also manifest itself in ethnic and cultural giants like the Russian nation, and is reflected, for example, in the ideological narrative of "the special path" (see, e.g., Travin, 2018), and in tendencies toward isolationism, "Westernophobia," and hostility toward the outside world. However, there is no impenetrable wall between the aggressive and defensive types of the complex. They are context-dependent and easily pass into each other. Both relate to the post-traumatic condition.

Trauma itself can be quite real and grave in terms of its consequences for a country and its people, with lingering pain (in Russia's case, from the Patriotic War). In other cases, it may be not very grave, psychologically, but it may have been purposely constructed from partly mythologized events, covered with the patina of time. In Serbia, this role was played by the defeat of the Serbian army in the battle with the Ottomans at Kosovo Polje, which took place over six centuries ago, and about which, before the acute phase of the Kosovo conflict at the end of the 1980s and early 1990s, ordinary Yugoslav citizens, I suspect, had not known much, and, to which, no doubt, they had given little thought in their daily life.

Yet, irrespective of reality, recent and old, partially imagined traumas become, under certain circumstances, a major factor in determining the psychological state of large ethic groups. Vamık Volkan (1988) importantly introduced the idea of a "chosen" collective trauma to describe this phenomenon. According to him, a chosen event, experienced by ancestors and recognized as a common tragedy, makes a large group of people (an ethnic group in this case) feel like a humiliated victim of the vicious actions of Others. The event, "fatal" for long-ago members of the group, becomes psychologized and mythologized, and appears to embed the image of the event into the very core of the group's self-identity. Once the real trauma transforms into "a chosen trauma," the actual historical facts as such stop playing any significant role of their own. What is now important is only their psychological construct, becoming, sometimes, a pillar of the sense of ethnic community. The concise Israeli "Never again" slogan, referring to the Holocaust, is sometimes cited as a case in point. The reader will easily find in real life quite a few empirical examples of this phenomenon.

This explains the psychological inability to mourn trauma in a positive way, and thereby, eventually "bury" it and in some way come to terms with what happened. Such unreadiness to adapt to a new situation, according to Volkan, also has practical negative implications. Having been excessively humiliated, or on the contrary, being implacable to the enemy who inflicted the trauma, the group turns out to be incapable of a compromise with this enemy. This plays out in politics, for instance, as outright rejection of the sheer possibility of any territorial concession to the former adversary. And the real value of the disputed territory is unimportant. It acquires a symbolic, almost sacred value for both parties to the conflict, passing from generation to generation. An example of such an impasse may be, in my opinion, the issue of the four small northern islands of the Kuril Ridge, which, for fifty years has created problems for both Russia and Japan, blocking solutions to far more important issues, but remaining for politicians on both sides a symbolic "red line" not to be crossed.

When Albert Einstein asked Sigmund Freud if there was any way to protect humankind from the threat of wars, the latter said it was useless to try to control people's aggressive drives, and that conflicts between them were rarely resolved without violence, adding, though, that the development of civilization is accompanied by certain changes in the human mind, which, in the future, may help partially repress aggressive instincts and even control, to some degree, destructive impulses. But in contemporary psychoanalysis, the original Freudian scheme is being critically debated and modernized. Current psychoanalytic thinking is generally more optimistic in assessing the possibility and prospects for dealing with negative impulses. The positive things this entails are the subject of the section below.

Psychological perspectives on easing the impact of ethno-traumas

Let us now discuss whether at least a partial adaptation to this kind of trauma is possible. On the one hand, people have a basic psychological need for an enemy as a stabilizer of a person's sense of identity. Yet there is also another side to this concept: an equally significant and basic need to have allies, and better still, friends. This was suggested in philosophical terms well before Freud. The outstanding Russian thinker and public figure of anarchist persuasion, Pyotr Kropotkin, developed the idea that alongside Darwin's law of the struggle for survival in the animal and human worlds (it's worth noting that Darwin himself did not deal with intra-species struggles; the "credit" for the latter goes to the subsequent development of Social Darwinism), there is also, as a counterbalance, the opposite law of cooperation and mutual aid.

Pyotr Kropotkin wrote a book entitled *Mutual Aid: A Factor of Evolution* (Kropotkin, 1902). Interestingly, this book was first written and published in English; it was never published in Russian until the fall of the USSR. The book examines the view that it is not struggle, but mutual aid that served as the engine of humankind's progress, including moral progress, and that further human evolution should follow this direction. This appealing and optimistic hypothesis appears to agree with the thesis of psychoanalytical theory about the need to have both enemies and friends. Volkan and IDI colleagues, based on this need, are trying to build unifying "bridges" in the collective consciousness of traumatized groups. Thus, the destructive is given a chance to turn into something positive. But for this to happen, one must change one's approach to the past, its events, tragedies, and victories.

Let me explain this, using, as an example, an exhibition dedicated to World War II entitled "Different Wars." Held in 2016–17 in several European cities and countries, including Moscow, its main concept was to show, using the cases of Russia, Poland, Lithuania, and Germany, how differently the events of WWII are portrayed in different countries. It was not about the distortion of or silence about the established facts, but about something totally different; it was about the social-psychological aspects of specific events from that time, which were picked up by the national collective consciousness and integrated in various ways, including, for example, their finding their way into school textbooks.

The French historian Marc Ferro, in his book, *Comment on raconte l'histoire aux enfants: À travers le monde entire* (published in English as *The Use and Abuse of History: Or How the Past Is Taught to Children*), describes several regional, national, and religious variants of history, concluding that "There is no more world history, because it was nothing but Europe's mirage, with Europe making it as it liked … it would mention other nations only in passing, to the extent their ways crossed Europe's ways" (Ferro, 1986, p. 305). His general conclusion is directly related to the topic in question: "Every society facing attempts to belittle its history, needs to create its own history, hidden from the eyes of the victors … Under the circumstances, it is a sign of either deceitfulness or tyranny to extract 'the world history' from one source or even one institution. Whereas liberty seeks to let different historical traditions co-exist and even compete with each other" (ibid., pp. 305–308). Different versions of history, according to Ferro—including alternative counter-histories living in the minds of the defeated, in works of art, especially in films, or sometimes, even in parallel oral histories told on behalf of the "small" people—are as real as religious beliefs or as the formal powers' actions and orders.

The above-mentioned exhibition emphasized not political, but human aspects of war, not "big," but "small" histories, focusing on the stories about the lives of concrete people. Each of the stories was an account of human traumas, including psychological traumas. This, according to psychologists, serves to shape the attitude towards the war as a shared trauma, helping it to be jointly experienced, and leading eventually to reconciliation, at least on the interpersonal level. In psychoanalysis, this is called adaptive mourning, and creates, at the minimum, one, but one significant, step toward overcoming trauma (Ochberg, 1998).

"Small history" can cure traumas inflicted by "big history"—the history of nations, states, political leaders, and certainly the history of wars, with heads of states, marshals, and generals as major heroes or villains. Taking the problem to a human, interpersonal level—the level of ordinary people who found themselves, because of war, in unusual and difficult circumstances—one could see how these circumstances can change their life attitude. The book *Forced Labor in the Third Reich* (2018) joins under one cover three different life stories of young, inexperienced, and rather poorly educated woman—Polish, Czech, and Czech Jew—who had been conscripted to compulsory work as *Ostarbeiterinnen* in labor camps of Nazi Germany. They are very relevant in this regard. Using illustrations and photos, the stories show how each girl managed to survive, despite hard and degrading forced labor conditions. The important point for us is that they did not simply survive; they also came to a deeper understanding of the meaning of human life, of the critical importance of direct people-to-people contacts, of the possibility for the individual to choose how to behave—despite the imposition of brutal restrictions—and of the moral responsibility of each human for others. Their potentially traumatic experiences changed their lives in the post-war years and influenced their behavior for the rest of their lives.

It is also important to recognize that, during personal encounters, veterans who were on opposite sides in past wars do not usually feel or express any hatred toward one another. Long ago a war veteran (who later became a famous film director and whom I happen to work with), Grigory Chukhray, told me that, during one post-war meeting between former Russian and German military officers, one of them exclaimed in horror: "Oh, boy! We might have killed each other!" Certainly, such moods of reconciliation, and an overcoming of past feelings of hostility, evolve not immediately and need both time and special circumstances. In this respect, there is a remarkable story, meant to be included in a movie, about the changes in behavior of two military pilots—one Finnish and one Soviet—who shot down each other's planes practically simultaneously, then managed to parachute to almost the same field in a wild and swampy forest near the line of fire between their troops. Despite their common desperate situation and the same need to survive in the face of hunger and cold, they continued their efforts to kill each other by shooting from revolvers.

Gradually, as the story goes, step by step, they abandoned their shooting and even began to cooperate, though cautiously and in a limited way. For example, they helped each other in a cooperative attempt to catch a fish in the small lake. There was a good end to this story. When they neared a village, at last, but did not know which side controlled the area, the feelings of mutual distrust and hostility revived in them again. Then they saw a teenager running and asked him warily the crucial question. The boy shouted in response: "The war is over!" Certainly, this story sounds like a tall tale, perhaps simplifying reality. But, on the other hand, it also seems like an almost metaphorical description of the existence of opposing motives in each person's soul and the tense competition between them. Sadly and perhaps symbolically, the film including this story was never made.

Another question to be noted is the issue of guilt and responsibility for actions committed. Here, too, the situation in post-Soviet countries is far from positive. People may have adapted to the new reality and challenges, but not fully. And Russia in this respect is not alone. Let me start, by way of illustration, with perhaps the most horrifying case of mass military crimes against humanity—the responsibility for the Holocaust. In the minds of the citizens of Russia, Ukraine, Poland, and Lithuania (the last of these to a lesser but significant degree), the Holocaust is a crime the responsibility for which solely belongs to Others, the diabolic enemies, whereas we, of course, were just victims, saviors, (at worst) indifferent bystanders, or even, allegedly, unaware of what was going on. As if there were no other modes of behavior among the population of the occupied countries. It's as though the very idea that substantial groups of "my" compatriots participated actively in these crimes by providing direct assistance to the Nazis in the imprisoning and extermination of Jews is unthinkable, despite the existence of reliable documentary proofs.

Yet quite a few sources tell us that the reality was, sadly, somewhat different. Indeed, without the active, and sometimes unsolicited, "assistance" of local collaborators, the Nazis would have been physically unable to carry out the genocide against Jews in occupied territories on the scale that was perpetrated. This appears to have been indirectly corroborated by post-war anti-Jewish actions—even pogroms—by the local population and by seemingly anti-Semitic policies pursued in some Eastern European countries, especially Poland and the Soviet Union, which understate the scale of the Holocaust and maintain silence about its main purpose of exterminating Jews as a people. One moral question merits attention here: Is it a moral duty for society to accept at least a share of the guilt and responsibility for what happened, even if at a minimal or symbolic degree? Such a position of denial of one's share of guilt is extremely significant and destructive in terms of its political and psychological implications. New generations, no doubt, cannot and should not be held accountable for events that took place long before they were born. However, we are responsible for our current positions with regard to history. And the Holocaust is just one but perhaps the greatest and most tragic example.

In macro-political terms, there are two obvious topics that merit mention: the Munich Agreement of British Prime Minister Chamberlain with Hitler and the Molotov–Ribbentrop Pact. The former has long been assessed as a tragic political mistake, for which several generations of British politicians have been apologizing in all kinds of ways. Thus, half a century after Munich, during Margaret Thatcher's visit to Czechoslovakia, in her speech to the country's Federal Assembly in Prague, she once again apologized for the actions of her distant predecessor, Neville Chamberlain: "We failed you in 1938, when a disastrous policy of appeasement allowed Hitler to extinguish your independence. Churchill was quick to repudiate the Munich Agreement, but we still remember it with shame" (Riks, 2019, p. 171).

As to the official Russian attitude to the Molotov–Ribbentrop Pact, it has undergone cardinal changes and continues to change within a broad range, depending on the political situation of the day—from its unqualified approval in Soviet times as, allegedly, a brilliant political maneuver, to its complete denunciation in perestroika and post-perestroika times, as an immoral and wrong political act, and then, back to its political rehabilitation in a neo-Soviet spirit in the present day. This is directly linked, in my view, to the question of our responsibility before history and for its interpretation. I believe that today's attitude to past mistakes and crimes, to the awareness of one's own collective guilt, is closely related to the concept of "different wars" and to essentially their different perception and interpretation in mass consciousness in different countries.

Incidentally, the once fashionable politicians' formal apologies for the actions of their predecessors, though they carry an important symbolic message at the level of "big politics," have no serious psychological effect. We can see it in the first half of the 1990s, during multi-ethnic roundtables in the reborn Baltic States. The participants on the Russian side would express their deep apologies, in various contexts and forms, for the Soviet occupation and other state crimes during Stalin's time. However, the other side would not accept those apologies, because they were not ready to forgive. The time might not have come yet for such steps; the traumas were probably too fresh. It is appropriate in this regard to invoke again Frank Ochberg's (1988) idea about the three-generational cycle of trauma mourning.

As to adaptive mourning, I think it can be an effective medicine in the attempt to change the image of "the scapegoat," "appointed" as responsible for the group's troubles and misfortunes. In Russia, in Eastern Europe, and elsewhere, this role has been and is still played by either a neighboring ethnic group or state, or by the Soviet regime, or by all Russian people because they supposedly represent the imperial politics of the national state and, therefore, share responsibility for its actions and consequences. At times, all three targets are used. One should recognize that, in some cases, the enemy image is not at all fiction. Each side cites reasons based on historical traumas and grievances. However, adaptive mourning means the acceptance of trauma as a tragic but completed event. Interestingly, it can even be achieved where the ruling regime is also the scapegoat. Its main assertion would be: "We are all victims of the same Moloch; but it is no longer around, and we, enriched with our hard-earned understanding of the nightmare of totalitarianism, and having liberated ourselves from it, are now creating a new society based on new principles." This position, objectively speaking, has an element of idealization and oversimplification of reality. Reality itself is more complex (see, e.g., Yurchak, 2019). And the ghosts of the past are still hovering above us, sometimes coming back in somewhat modernized, but in their essence, quite negative and offensive forms. The first quarter of 2021 in Russia saw, unfortunately, many dreadful manifestations of this on the part of the government.

Yet, to have hope for convalescence from the post-totalitarian syndrome, some moral and psychological readiness to accept a share of responsibility for past crimes of the totalitarian regime and its obedient servants seems necessary. It appears to be the only way to acquire a sense of a shared common trauma, which would bring together groups differing in other respects. The kind of symbolic common "funeral feast" or "brothers' *trizna*" for the USSR and similar regimes in Eastern European countries could have become an integrating and unifying factor for all. This, sadly, never happened. It also seems that alongside the mourning feast and mournfully going through the past national tragedies, a seemingly opposite thing could in some cases become a cure—laughter at and scornful ridicule of former political leaders and "rulers of minds." Satire directed toward Hitler, Stalin, authoritarian dictators of that time in countries of Eastern Europe, their associates and entourage, ironically shows their intellectual and moral squalor. There are many books and films of this kind about Hitlerism and Hitler. We Russians, unlike others, have progressed far less in overcoming Stalinism using these art tools. In fact, ridicule of this kind has been banned by a kind of censorship: One may recall the direct and unexplained ban of the release in Russia of the sardonic English comedy *The Death of Stalin*.

Another method of dealing with shared historical trauma is a transition from "chosen trauma" to "chosen glory." Every nation has not only something to mourn, but also something to be proud of; it has reasons not only for national mourning, but also for a feeling of pride over various successes, victories, and achievements. These may be military victories, advances in democratic development, sports victories, achievements in science and art, etc. When such achievements are made as a result of cooperation of two or several allied countries or their citizens, who came together to achieve a common goal, this can become a powerful integrating factor, contributing to mutual understanding, respect, and, eventually, the overcoming of enmity.

A classic situation of this kind is an alliance and joint victory in a war, especially, over the universally recognized evil of fascism. After the World War, the alliance, unfortunately, fell apart, which was followed by almost half a century of confrontation. The memory of the alliance would occasionally be revived in a limited fashion, for example in the spirit of meetings of Normandie-Niemen fighter squadron veterans. Today, though, there is not so much talk about the wartime alliance, but rather about one's own country's greatness as the main, if not the only, victor, diminishing the contribution of the other allies, and using, among other things, a fairly strange argument about the size of wartime human losses of our own citizens, compared with those of the others, as if this were the key yardstick to assess the contribution to the common victory.

Still, the approach to healing societal trauma through shared "chosen glories" is not utopian. One will recall, specifically, the Apollo-Soyuz space project that operated with success in a seemingly unsuitable period, during an acute phase of the Cold War. One can find many such cases of cooperation in various areas: scientific, cultural, economic, environmental, and others. And in each of the mentioned areas, it is not only general agreements at the level of governments or other large entities that matter, but also interpersonal contacts between the people involved. The latter seem crucial for eventual success. Earnest cooperation creates a special psychological atmosphere, and people genuinely immersed in it are unlikely to "shoot" at each other, even metaphorically speaking.

A positive role could be played, for example, by the Immortal Regiment march on Victory Day and other related events, held not only in Russia, but also, on a smaller scale, in Israel and in member countries of the anti-fascist coalition. As it was originally conceived, the march has a significant, if underutilized, positive, unifying psychological potential, though in real life, there have been some distortions, even later profanations, for political purposes of the day. Of course, there can always be manipulations, speculations, and provocations. It is hard to avoid them altogether. But they follow an entirely different logic. The proponents of Social Darwinist concepts and geopolitics are stressing and exaggerating, not without some gratification, the supposed inevitability of enmity and permanent intergroup and interpersonal struggle as, admittedly, an immanent attribute of human nature. In my view, the Social Darwinist view of humanity, specific to geopolitics, is an extremely dangerous kind of false consciousness—a view of the world as solely an arena of "intra-species" struggle of states and ideological doctrines, religious beliefs, etc. So, from this perspective, certain temporary tasks, intermediate goals, possible coalitions and methods may change, but not the essence: Peoples are immanent enemies, the world is a ring, states are wrestlers fighting in it, etc.

This geopolitical phantom cost humankind two global and a multitude of "small" wars, as well as wars with "inner enemies," inevitably accompanying the former. It has brought death, untold misfortune, and suffering to innumerable millions of people. I consider as far more constructive and encouraging Pyotr Kropotkin's above-mentioned view on human interaction as not only about fighting or struggle, but as a sphere of cooperation and mutual aid. The arguments on behalf of prevailing force and cruelty—the banality of evil—should be challenged at least, morally and psychologically, using an opposing set of arguments concerning the duality of human nature—the human capacity for creative goodness and even the "banality of heroism" (Zimbardo, 2013). These arguments underlie both the world's religions and its principal philosophical and ideological doctrines and are exemplified by many people's readiness to deliberately take risks and accept inevitable troubles and losses for the sake of keeping a sense of personal dignity, and/or out of solidarity with one's reference group. While I am by no means claiming to offer an in-depth treatment of this fundamental philosophical and moral problematic, I want to recall Vaclav Havel's (see, e.g., *Gosudarstvo. Obschestvo. Upravlenie*, 2013), the dissident slogan about "the power of the powerless," and the idea of the pragmatics of political idealism, which became the title and content of one important book of the 1990s (Kovalyov, 1999).

The range of problems dealt with in this chapter is by no means limited to the aspects discussed. There are many other aspects that matter for the practice of international and interethnic negotiations. One example is the so-called "narcissism of small differences," depicted by Volkan (2013) in one of his books, where people from ethnic groups that are close culturally, ethnically, and historically deny their commonality in a number of features, and are inclined to accentuate and even make a show of the existing small differences. Seemingly this is driven by a fear of losing their identity and "soul," and being assimilated by another nation that appears more advanced, "greater," and stronger, which, as a rule, is a geographic neighbor.

Related to this and of further psychological interest is the "accordion effect" (Volkan, 2013), frequently occurring during negotiations, where the parties alternately get closer, emphasizing the commonality of their interests, closeness of origin, mutual liking, etc., but in spite of that begin, at some point, to distance themselves from each other to the maximum, stressing sometimes in a tough manner their distinctions, contradictions, conflicting cultural traits, and other purportedly irreconcilable differences. This is sometimes underlined symbolically by the unwillingness even to sit at the same negotiation table or shake each other's hands. Again, becoming closer seems to threaten identity. There are, though, so many other aspects to the symbolic politics. And there is, of course, the inescapable problem of historical guilt and responsibility for the crimes of the past. This topic, which may be a key psychological issue, is beyond the scope of this chapter. And words alone will not resolve it.

References

Arendt, H. (2006). *Eichmann in Jerusalem: A Report on the Banality of Evil*. New York: Penguin.

Baum, G. (2015). *Spasti prava grazddan (To Save Civil Rights)*. Moscow: Fond Fridrikha Naumana (Friedrich Naumann Foundation).

Covington, C. (2017). *Everyday Evils: A Psychoanalytic View of Evil and Morality*. New York: Routledge.

Eppleh, N. (2020). *Neudobnoe Proshloe: pamyat' o gosudarstvennykh prestupleniyakh v Rossii I drugikh stranakh (Inconvenient Past: Memory of the State Crimes in Russia and Other Countries)*. Moscow: Novoe literaturnoe obovrenie.

Etkind, A. (2016). Krivoe gore. Pamyat' o nepogrebennykh (*Warped Mourning: Stories on the Undead in the Land of the Unburied*). Moscow: Novoe literaturnoe obozrenie (New Literary Observer).

Ferro, M. (1986). *Comment on raconte l'histoire aux enfants: À travers le monde entire*. Kak rasskazyvayut istoriyu detyam v raznykh stranakh mira (*The Use and Abuse of History: Or How the Past Is Taught to Children*). Moscow: 6 36.6 Publishers, 2014.

Gosudarstvo. Obshchestvo. Upravlenie. (*State, Society, Governance.*) (2013). Moscow: Al'pina Publishers.

Inglehart, R. (2018). Kul'turnaya evolutsiya (*Cultural Evolution: People's Motivations Are Changing and Reshaping the World*). Moscow: Mysl'.

Kalibas, S. (2019). Logika nasiliya v grazhdanskoy voyne (*The Logics of Violence in Civil War*). Moscow: Pyatyy Rim.

Kovalyov, S. A. (1999). *Pragmatics of Political Idealism*. Moscow: Institute of Human Rights.

Kropotkin, P. A. (1902). *Mutual Aid: A Factor of Evolution*. Moscow: Labyrinth, 2011.

Obolonsky, A. (2016). Politicheskiy tsynizm: konsept, praktika, al'ternativa (Political cynicism: Concept, practice, alternative). *Obshchesvennye nauki I sovremennost'*, 2: 76–77.

Obolonsky, A. (2018). Liberal'naya i byurokraticheskaya mental'nosti i rossiyskaya transformatsiya kontsa XX—nachala XXI veka (Liberal vs. bureaucratic mentalities and the Russian transformation at the end of late 20th and in early 21st century). *Obshchesvennye nauki i sovremennost*, 4: 47–57.

Ochberg, F. M. (1988). *Post-Traumatic Therapy and Victims of Violence*. New York: Brunner/Mazel.

Prinuditel'ny trud v tret'em reykhe (*Forced Labor in the 3rd Reich*) (2018). Moscow: Post Bellum. International Memorial.

Solzhenitsyn, A. (1987). Archipelago GULAG 2(6), Chapter 3 (pp. 385–404). Paris: YMCA Press.

Travin, D. (2018). *Osoby put' Rossii: ot Dostoevskogo do Konchalovskogo* (*The Special Path of Russia: From Dostoevsky to Konchalovsky*). St. Petersburg, Russia: Saint-Petersburgian European University.

Volkan, V. D. (1988). *The Need to Have Enemies and Allies: From Clinical Practice to International Relations*. Northvale, NJ: Jason Aronson.

Volkan, V. D. (2013). *Enemies on the Couch: A Psycho-Political Journey through War and Peace*. Durham, NC: Pitchstone.

Yurchak, A. (2019). *Eto bylo navsegda, poka ne konchilos* (*Everything Was Forever Until It Was No More: The Last Soviet Generation*). Novoe literaturnoe obozrenie (New Literary Observer).

Zimbardo, P. (2007). *Efect Lutsifera: pochemu khoroshie lyudi prevrashcha-yutsya v zlodeev* (*The Lucifer Effect: Understanding How Good People Turn Evil*). Moscow: ATF, 2013.

CHAPTER 9

The German "welcoming culture": some thoughts about its psychodynamics

Regine Scholz

Introduction

In the following chapter, the reader will find some thoughts concerning the psychic backgrounds and dynamics of the so-called and much discussed summer fairy tale of August/September 2015, when the German government decided not to close its borders to refugees who were stuck in the Balkans after Hungary closed its borders. Just as a reminder: In 2015, Germany took in about one million refugees. On August 31, Chancellor Merkel spoke the now world-famous words: "Wir schaffen das!" (We can do this!) The complete quote was: "Deutschland ist ein starkes Land. Das Motiv, mit dem wir an diese Dinge herangehen, muss sein: Wir haben so vieles geschafft—wir schaffen das!" ("Germany is a strong country. The motivation to approach these things must be: We already managed so many things—we can do this!") What happened since then became known as the "German welcoming culture": the unscheduled and unforeseeable wave of helpfulness by German people—volunteers as well as officials—to accommodate these huge numbers of people.

Picture 1: Arrival of refugees at Munich central station. Photo Sven Hoppe, copyright: picture alliance/dpa

The picture above was taken in the Munich main train station on September 9, 2015. Not only there, but all over the country, thousands of people wanted to help; they volunteered, went to the stations where the trains with refugees arrived, welcomed them, provided them with food, warm tea, and clothes, toys for the children, etc. That was the real summer fairy tale—completely unexpected inside as well as outside the country. Everybody knew it wouldn't last forever, but, for a moment though, people were united in that nearly euphoric atmosphere and in a warm feeling of fusion.

Of course, this surprising wave of readiness to help soon called for explanations. Interestingly enough, these came more from outside the country. One widely shared theory about this group phenomenon is to be found in Vamık Volkan's recent book *Immigrants and Refugees*, where in the preface he writes, referring to a situation he experienced in 2015 in Berlin, "… the Germans … especially the younger ones, wanted nothing to prevent them from taking care of the suffering of Others and reverse their Holocaust-related guilt feelings" (Volkan, 2017, p. xiv). Similar arguments were discussed in many European and overseas journals, for example, the *National Geographic France* (Kunzig, 2016), *20 Minutes* in Switzerland (Gabriel, 2015), *The Washington Post* (Stanley-Becker, 2017), and *The Guardian* (Freedland, 2015).

This argument contains a more or less subtle turn, one that suggests that the actions were not aimed at the refugees, but at the emotional well-being of the helpers. From that perspective, the refugees served the function of a remedy for the transgenerationally wounded soul of the helpers, whose own suffering was being treated. This turn in the argument could be seen as its speaker's effort to regain the moral authority—and to reestablish the old moral order—by implying that the helpers' altruism just covers up their selfish motivation.

Every argument has a content and implies at the same time a statement about the sender. Let us start with the content of this argument: It hurts and it is shaming—because in the moment of joy and satisfaction about doing something good and meaningful, the helper is called a hypocrite, an egoist who is hiding his own wounds and using the misery of the refugees to heal—or at least to mitigate—his own pain. For "his" read "her" too.

The problem is that there is some truth in that. The argument hints at a deep-rooted pain and shame. Volkan explicitly refers to the younger ones. For them, in addition to guilt and shame, a profound helplessness is also involved: the task of carrying something that you had no influence on or responsibility for (see Connolly's interview with Bernhard Schlink, in *The Guardian*, September 16, 2012). Being identified with and identifying oneself as German results in an emotional impasse: feeling guilty for something you didn't do, but, because you are connected to a family history, carrying the guilt and shame the (grand-)parents were so often denying.

This is the moment where the Other—other persons as members of the formerly attacked groups, like the opponents in war or the victims of the Holocaust and their offspring—become important. Their acceptance of current good deeds, verifying the message—"Look, I'm not bad (anymore)," and also "I'm not like them, who murdered, humiliated, or at the very least didn't help the persecuted and needy ones"—is urgently wanted or needed to calm down the helper's inner drama.

In addition, being encouraged to welcome the refugees by the most powerful person in the country, the then chancellor, Angela Merkel, allowed for this differentiation without having to lose connection. "We can do it" enabled people to break the emotional impasse and move forward without denial. This freeing element, in the context of the complex psychic background of the welcoming culture in August/September 2015, mainly contributed to the mesmerizing atmosphere of those days. Though, because all this happened in a disguised—mainly unconscious—manner, it always risked carrying a somehow false tone, which was attentively registered by some observers.

Identification with the refugees I

The argument that Holocaust- and WWII-related guilt feelings played a crucial role in the psychodynamics of the mass movement to help refugees in summer 2015 does not exclude the possibility of genuine altruism nor other possible psychic dispositions that might add to an explanation. Some other factors, covered by this first layer, should be taken into consideration too.

First there may have been a deep identification with the refugees, along more than one dimension: for instance, the experience of being bombed and generally living through the horrors of war; the suffering from traumatic flight with its accompanying violence; the shock of being displaced, the pain of not being welcomed, and much more.

Look, for example, at this picture of the long lines of people on their way through the Balkans in 2015:

Picture 2: Migrants walk to the border with Hungary after arriving by train at Botovo, Croatia. Photo: Laszlo Balogh, copyright: picture alliance/ Reuters

The next picture shows people after WWII on their way towards the West. According to the Bundeszentrale für Politische Bildung (2018), 12 million people (other sources mention 14 million) came, between 1945 and 1950, to the Western parts of Germany (including the former GDR), and an estimated 2 million did not survive the trek (Zeidler, 2012). They came from formerly German territories in the East (East Prussia, West Prussia, Pomerania, Silesia, etc.), fleeing from the approaching Russian army, but also from areas in the Baltic States, the Soviet Union, Hungary, Romania, Czechoslovakia, Slovenia, etc.—the whole German diaspora. Before these treks, there was, of course, the Holocaust and there was the war; there was Coventry and Rotterdam, Oradour and Lidice, Auschwitz and Treblinka. These incredible crimes committed by Germany before and during the war secured broad international support for the geopolitical decisions made at the Potsdam Conference in the summer of 1945 to expel ethnic Germans from these traditional areas where they lived.

Picture 3: Displacement. Photographer unknown, Repro Ahles (private)

In Germany, not much is spoken about war, bombing, flight, and expulsion. Building up a new living in the devastated country absorbed everybody's energies and helped to split off the mourning of the lost innocence and the grandiose aspirations connected to the "Führer." It hindered the emotional realization of the amount of guilt connected to the crimes committed by Germans (Mitscherlich & Mitscherlich, 1967), and it also blocked feelings related to the physical and emotional wounds of war, flight, and displacement. To bear in the mind and the heart just one of these mass crimes and horrors is already too much; more than that is simply unbearable. Consequently, and for various reasons, most of the traumatic material had to be split off.

Nonetheless, the pictures of the war in Syria brought back the memories of some of these horrors. This picture below was taken on March 22, 2015 in Kobane, Syria.

Picture 4: Syrian Kurds in Kobane. Photo Çağdaş Erdoğan, Depo, copyright: picture alliance/abaka

It might resemble for many elderly Germans the situation shown below, in a picture taken in 1952 (!) in West Berlin.

Picture 5: Boys on ruins. Photo Herbert Maschke, copyright: Cornelius Maschke

If you let yourself be touched by these photos, the idea might not be so far-fetched that many Germans—though the generation that lived through fascism, through the war, and post-war times is, for the most part, not alive anymore—from their own childhood experiences and by intergenerational transmission have a deep connection to these scenes of bombed cities, ruins, flights, and refugee treks. These memories must have been reactivated by pictures of recent events, leading more to identification and compassion than to fear of the Other.

Also transferred in these post-war families were the experiences of an unfriendly (to say the least) welcome of those from formerly German territories coming to the West. At that time, they were simply not considered to be Germans (belonging to us) but foreigners with different accents, habits, and sometimes religions. Moreover, they came into a destroyed and bitterly poor country—there was not much to share. Mostly, the original population remained hostile, displaying all the well-known stereotypes to be heard again nowadays: the newcomers are dirty, they stink, steal, and rape. Sometimes they also were accused of being Nazis. Of course, that often was true—though not more or less so than for the autochthonous population. To defame the newcomers as Nazis was an unfair attempt to whitewash one's own guilt by projection.

It is always said that the integration of these millions of people went without problems. That's not true (Kossert, 2008). What is true is that, in the end, it worked out. The cities were rebuilt; Germans of all origins eventually were considered as one nation and consider themselves now as such. To preserve peace and allow integration into the Western world, the whole complex of war, flight, and expulsion was more or less excluded from public discourse—only taken up and exploited by the far right. The world-famous German memory culture—born in decades of post-war disputes—originally imposed by the allied forces and then taken on inside the (divided) country by its inhabitants—refers mainly to German war crimes and the Holocaust (about this developmental process, see Frölich et al., 2012). My hypothesis is that the intertwined though mainly split off complex of Germany's own direct traumatization also showed up indirectly in the 2015 compassion for current refugees, which allowed some expression of the old pains while circumventing the intractable moral conflicts around war crimes and the Holocaust.

Identification with the refugees II

Another split that became visible on the issue of welcoming and integration is a clear gap between Western and Eastern parts of Germany, mirroring the division of Europe by the Iron Curtain and causing different developments in response to immigration. The West is usually friendlier than the East, though almost no foreigners live in the East (Bertelsmann Stiftung, 2017). One reason might be that the former West Germany has a longer tradition of taking in people from faraway countries and therefore had the possibility—though in an often-painful process—to adapt emotionally to these changes over a longer period of time. Reacting to a lack of workers, West Germany, beginning in the mid-1950s, made treaties with Italy, Spain, Portugal, the former Yugoslavia, and Turkey asking for "guest workers." Until 1973, 14 million had followed this call. While 11 million returned to their homelands, the others brought their families. For comparison: In 1989, only 93,000 foreigners lived in the territories of the GDR, mainly as contract workers, accommodated separately from the German population—thereby remaining in the role of the Other.

Picture 6: Italian "guest workers" at VW—1970. Photo Fritz Rust, copyright: picture alliance/Fritz Rust

The picture above shows the arrival of Italian workers in Wolfsburg.

There are more groups that settled in (mainly West) Germany: Refugees from East Germany (1949–61: 2.7 million, later 700,000 until 1989), resettlers from formerly German settlements in the nearer (Poland) and further away (Kazakhstan) eastern parts of the European and Asian continent (3.2 million since 1953), refugees of the Balkan war in the 1990s (440,000, some of whom returned), Jews from the former Soviet Union (1989–2009: 219,000), asylum seekers from different countries, such as from Hungary after 1956 (c. 16,000), Czechoslovakia after 1968 (c. 4,000), from Chile after 1973 (c. 2,500), from Vietnam after 1979 (38,000), in the 1980s from Iran, Poland, and Turkey, but also from

Sri Lanka, Pakistan, Ghana, and other countries (see Garschagen & Lindner, *Mediendienst Integration*, 2015).

Picture 7: A former immigrant, who came to Germany in the 1970s, answering questions from refugees at Munich main station. Photo and copyright: Karim El-Gawhary

Many of these people—and eventually their children and grandchildren—also volunteered to welcome refugees in 2015. The photo above from September 8, 2015 shows on the right a then seventy-three-year-old man from Egypt, at that time living for decades in Germany. Here he is answering questions from men who had just arrived from Syria.

In 2019, of the population living in Germany, 26 percent had what is called a "migration background," meaning either they themselves or at least one of their parents was not born in Germany; more than half of them had a German passport (*Mediendienst Integration*, Facts and Figures in English, 2019). Members of this group, when volunteering and helping the refugees, have a different agenda from those who have longer and therefore deeper family ties in Germany, which result in more dense psychic connections with German history. For groups who themselves have been immigrants, it is more about telling indirectly their own, somewhat different stories: They demonstrate their success—that they made it in Germany—thus reassuring themselves about the difficult road they traveled, and at the same time encouraging the newcomers by their example.

In addition, while volunteering, they also show the wider German public, "Look, this is how people in need have to be welcomed," thus communicating something about the hardships of their own way into this society and what they would have wished for. In that respect, they resemble those coming from the Eastern parts of Germany after the war, though they differ in their connection to German history. One might say that the "migration background" group has a lesser part in the "German neurosis" mentioned in the beginning of this chapter. Of course, it might also occur that there are people belonging to both groups: one parent originally from abroad, the other parent a descendent of someone who came after the war from the East.

A complementary perspective

Let us return to the issue of German guilt feelings being a (main) motivation for the "welcoming culture" in 2015. As discussed earlier, that is true—for large parts of the population—though on a conscious level, which can be accessed by conducting telephone surveys, revealing that guilt feelings are not the first layer that shows up. A 2018 study by MEMO (Multidimensionaler Erinnerungsmonitor) indicates that only 10 percent admit guilt feelings, though a great majority (84.3%) feel a high responsibility for preventing the return of National Socialism in the future. This appears to me to be, to some degree, the classical turnaround of the time sequence often observed in trauma contexts: Instead of confronting painful feelings connected to the unchangeable past, the problem is located in the future, where it can be fought.

In contrast to the low number of people reporting guilt feelings in this survey, clinical experience shows a different picture and gives us ample evidence of the transformation of real guilt denied by the perpetrator generation into guilt feelings in the unconscious life of their children and grandchildren (Bar-On, 1989; Gobodo-Madikizela, 2020; M. Hirsch, 1997; Jokl, 1997; Lohl & Moré, 2014). I can confirm these findings from my personal perspective—as one of the second generation from the perpetrator's side—and my clinical experience, especially as one of the organizers of the "Voices after Auschwitz" conferences where the offspring from both sides meet.

Now, in a second step, I want to return to the change in perspective mentioned earlier, from which we might explore what the argument about German guilt tells us about the conscious or unconscious motivation of those who use it. The question in this context might be dangerous and seen solely as a defense, and given the immense guilt connected to the war and the Holocaust, defense always is lingering. Nonetheless, that doesn't change the well-known fact that every communication not only has a content; it also gives some information about the speaker.

What is at first striking in the various interpretations of German guilt is the intensity associated with this psychological argument, an intensity not so often heard in political debates, even if it might be helpful. And of course, if you go for psychological explanations, this argument gets close to labeling somebody as being neurotic: she or he is ill, but perhaps can be cured. It does not easily allow for the possibility that there could be something actually rational in the behavior. Second, the argument could imply that the one who is diagnosing is not ill, but rather is healthy. This could further imply that their opinions and actions—which, in the political sphere, might include an argument against taking in refugees—are the correct ones and not subject to debate. As usual, this is a power play; who is allowed to define whom, even in psychological terms, becomes a political action for political purposes. Third, the German guilt argument is a confusing one, because for a long time, German guilt feelings were demanded, and sometimes exploited, by the larger world. In that era, who would have dared to say the Germans should leave their guilt feelings behind?

A major question could be: Which psychic function was it that the Germans and German mass crimes fulfilled for the Allied nations?

For years, and partly still today, these crimes were the reason to identify the Germans as the international "bad guy," and thereby the others as the good ones. Splitting creates order, and here it allows for a certain kind of defensive veiling of, for example, a nation's own collaboration with the Nazis or their own crimes of colonization and slavery. France had the Vichy government, Great Britain had Oswald Mosley and Lord Londonderry with their followers (Kellerhoff, 2017), the US had a flourishing Nazi scene recruited mainly from German immigrants after WWI (Diamond, 1974). Nonetheless, it was not until 1995 that the then president of France, Jacques Chirac, finally acknowledged French responsibility in the deportation of the French Jews in July 1942 (Chirac, 1995), which was confirmed by his successor Emmanuel Macron in July 2017 (*Le Monde*, 2017).

Connected to the question of French collaboration during German occupation and perhaps even more difficult to remember is the history of colonization. In France, it took until 1999 to name the war of independence in Algeria a war; previously it was referred to as "events of Algeria." Slowly in the 2000s, the admission of atrocities (including torture) in connection with this war surfaced (Kormann, 2021). Unsurprisingly, the topic stirred up a heated debate (Knipp, 2011). Eventually in 2020, the now President Macron placed an order to compile a report about the different ways these events are seen and how to reconcile the different societal groups (Stora, 2021).

For the UK and the US, one might say that—though some of their citizens were not immune to Nazi ideas and collaboration—the crimes of their nation connected to colonization and slavery predominate over their involvement with Nazism and were hidden behind their contribution to freeing Germany and the Nazi-occupied countries. Thus, their connections to Nazism during the 1930s and 1940s, the crimes of the British Empire, and the disgrace of slavery—none of these found much attention by the governments and people of these countries until recently.

Even in 2020 in a YouGov poll, more than 30 percent of Britons revealed their belief that colonies were better off as part of the British Empire, and the Empire was something to be proud of (Booth, 2020). Though things are changing, the change is rather slow: It took until 2012 for victims of colonialism to be given the right to claim compensation from the British government (Wessely, 2017). For this special case (and only for this, in an attempt to avoid making it a precedent) in 2013, there followed an official apology by the then foreign secretary William Hague.

While in 2017 the British were still waiting for a museum dedicated to the history (which often means crimes) of the British Empire (A. Hirsch, 2017), now there is, since 2018, a joint British and Kenyan initiative to explore British colonialism and its aftermath (Museum of British Colonialism). Racism from a different angle—how (black, Caribbean) immigrants from the former colonies were treated in the UK—surfaced, when the Windrush scandal occurred in 2018 (Petter, 2021). It stirred up and is part of a rather broad discussion, which unsurprisingly is heated and highly emotional. A symbolic expression of this long-suppressed pain and rage was enacted in the tearing down of the monument to the slave trader Edward Colston in Bristol in June 2020 (*BBC News*, June 7, 2020).

At the moment, as this text is written, the US is probably the country where we find the sharpest divisions over how and what to remember and who is to define the moral standards. The US is hesitantly confronting its violent history of genocidal attacks on the American Indians and its long and bloody history of slavery. Meanwhile, there is a National Museum of the American Indian (since 2004), and, since September 2016, the history of African Americans and their contribution to their country was recognized by dedicating to them their own museum (Kendrick, 2017). White Americans have to face (or prefer to deny) the fact that their beloved country is to a large extent built on crimes. That poses the painful question, articulated by a comment in the *Washington Post*, "How can you love a place while knowing the crimes that helped produce it?" (Gerson, 2021). Mr. Gerson's answer to his fellow citizens is: "By relentlessly confronting hypocrisy and remaining 'woke' to the transformational power of American ideals" (ibid.). Not everyone in the States follows this route as the killing of George Floyd in 2020 and the following uprisings, reactions, and counterreactions show. The struggles and discussions are ongoing—and probably will not be finished soon. The monstrosity of the Nazi/German crimes—incredible in amount and executed not in faraway countries but in the heart of Europe and the Western world—served for a long time to cover over these problems and frictions. It allowed people of the Allied nations to maintain the feeling that "We may have our shortcomings, but we are the good ones. Indeed, we suffered ourselves. We might not be perfect, but the others/the Germans are the ultimate evil." The possibility that Germans could also be nice, warmhearted, and friendly people did not exist in this picture (viz. the English and American movies/fiction until today; for a detailed analysis, see Scholz, 2004 and/or Bredella et al., 1994—and for fun, the gorgeous John Cleese in the classic scene of "Don't mention the war," *Fawlty Towers*, 2009). Given this construction, the pictures and TV news from Germany in summer 2015 must have been, to some degree, confusing, challenging the defensive split and thus threatening the ego-balance of people abroad. To declare these Germans to be ill—they are crazy, these Germans—also helps to reestablish the old order. And when the first terror attacks occurred in Germany, everyone could feel justified in this interpretation.

Summary

In a way, this whole chapter is about splitting, denial, projection, and the disavowal of inner and outer realities, both inside and outside one's country. It is not about the rational consideration of how best to deal with the challenges of mass migration. It is about some historical facts and largely unconscious reactions to these facts that shape personal and collective mentalities, the inner lives of millions of people when dealing with present situations in Europe—here focused on the summer of 2015 in Germany.

As main factors for the overwhelming willingness to help, in addition to the attempt to mitigate feelings of guilt and shame related to war crimes and the Holocaust, two long-neglected complexes were identified: The first is the long-lasting disavowal of war-related traumata in Germany. This slowly is changing due to an aging society. The children (see Bode, 2004) who lived through war and experienced heavy trauma during the times around 1944–45 and after the war are now elderly people; their defenses weaken and sometimes they come into therapy (Peters, 2018). The now slowly opening discourse about the psychic impact of this part of German history could help to disentangle some psychic knots in dealing with the challenges of the current international situation. There still is much work to do to bring together opposing, even antagonistic experiences: the memories of the Holocaust, of the persecution of all those who opposed the regime (though not enough in number to change its course), and of other war crimes, and, on the other hand, the memories of war, flight, displacement, and post-war hardships.

The second additional factor to be considered in the motivation for the summer of 2015 is the long-denied fact that Germany is an immigration country—until recently without a real immigration law. This situation was cautiously changing in 2020, when the so-called "Fachkräfteeinwanderungsgesetz" (immigration law for qualified persons) was introduced (www.bundesregierung.de). Mainly because of the demographic changes in the workforce, experts find this law still not sufficient. Currently the chairman of the federal employment agency Detlef Scheele underlined the necessity for 400,000 qualified immigrants per year (Hagelüken, 2021). That is in sharp contrast to the fact that the experiences of immigrants who came into the country over the last decades were mainly disregarded by the wider public—their contributions and their pains, their aspirations and their dreams, their successes, and their problems of belonging also constitute an important background of 2015.

Integrating these diverging experiences and the connected emotions into a larger narrative of "being German" is still a task that at best has just begun. One of the main difficulties in opening up these encapsulated wounds is a difficulty related to the various perpetrator-victim constellations of the subgroups involved; these painful conversations can lead to aggressive explosions, mutual blaming as well as to falling bitterly silent. Years after the war, a German woman with Jewish roots—asked by her daughter why she doesn't show a family album to her friends—answered: "I prefer not to talk about these things. I don't know how they would react. I also don't know if they were Nazis. Then they will only say 'We also went through hard times.' I never mention it. It's better like that" (Zeuch-Wiese, 2010, p. 259). Keeping silent is a legitimate and understandable act of self-protection (against disappointment, pain, rage, etc.)—though not helpful in the long run.

In the summer of 2015, these complexes found a somewhat displaced and disguised expression, largely on unconscious levels. Visible was enormous splitting as a central element in Germany, then and later.

The good ones helped the refugees, the bad ones warned—or worse (in 2015, 1,031 attacks on asylum shelters were counted, mostly committed by the far right) (Migazin, 2017). The ambivalences of the whole situation were put aside for the moment (and came back later), in the context of the people feeling an urgent need to help and a strong optimism that all problems could be and would be solved. This quasi-erotic fusion went along with the intense split between the good and the bad ones; there was not much space for sober contemplation of the situation or to look for longer lasting solutions. The next wave of high emotion came with the now infamous New Year's night in Cologne, when all the suppressed anxieties seemingly found their justification (for the facts, see Brenner & Ohlendorf, May 2, 2016) and were soon exploited by a well-organized right wing/neo-Nazi scene, which played on the old topos of the black man raping white women (Mysorekar, 2018; Pilgrim, 2000). Tracing these counter movements would entail another chapter, though; this one has limited itself to focusing on the welcoming culture.

Despite some sobering of the welcoming euphoria and having to deal with rather complicated realities, there is still much solidarity with the refugees. In the summer of 2017, research carried out by the Institut für Demoskopie Allensbach (the Allensbach Institute, which carries out public opinion polls) indicated that, from 2015–17, 55 percent of the population in Germany had been involved in volunteer work and 19 percent still were active. Meanwhile, much formerly volunteer work was taken over by official institutions—with good results in housing, language skills, and bringing people into jobs.

This ongoing support for refugees—even in spite of terror attacks—is not reflected much in TV and print media, which focus more on the problems and the radical opposition to the intake of refugees, thus mirroring more the split than the actual situation and attitudes toward migrants. An opinion poll on behalf of "More in Common" found not just two but five major groups of attitudes toward immigration and refugees: humanitarian skeptics 23 percent, liberal cosmopolitans 22 percent, economic pragmatists 20 percent, moderate opposers 18 percent, and radical opposers 17 percent. Humanitarian skeptics, for example, were in favor of offering shelter to people in need after fleeing from war and warlike situations, though they had some concerns about the possibilities for long-term integration; economic pragmatists welcomed refugees as a help to the aging German workforce while being very much aware of the complexities of the situation (More in Common, 2017). Further studies and analysis on these topics are highly desirable.

The tasks of integrating immigrants are enormous, as are the social and psychic energies needed to deal with these challenges. The world order that was established after WWII is changing, not only in Germany, and the topic of this chapter—the overwhelming willingness to help and its psychic backgrounds—is only a minor part of it. The future probably holds huge tasks that every community, nation, and person must face. Let us be prepared; there is no way back. Much courage will be needed, including the courage to look in the mirror and face the multifaceted, often contradictory realities—the good, the bad, and the ugly ones.

References

Bar-On, D. (1989). *Legacy of Silence: Encounters with Children of the Third Reich*. Cambridge, MA: Harvard University Press.

BBC News (2020, June 7). Slave trader statue torn down in Bristol anti-racism protest. https://bbc.com/news/av/uk-52954994 (last accessed October 15, 2022).

Bertelsmann Stiftung (2017). Willkommenskultur im "Stresstest." Einstellungen in der Bevölkerung 2017 und Entwicklungen und Trends seit 2011/2012. Ergebnisse einer repräsentativen Bevölkerungsumfrage (Welcome culture in the "stress test"—people's attitudes in 2017 as well as developments and trends since 2011/2012). Gütersloh, Germany.

Bode, S. (2004). *Die vergessene Generation—Die Kriegskinder brechen ihr Schweigen (The Forgotten Generation—The War Children Are Breaking Their Silence)*. Stuttgart, Germany: Klett-Cotta.

Booth, R. (2020, March 11). UK more nostalgic for empire than other ex-colonial powers. *The Guardian*. https://theguardian.com/world/2020/mar/11/uk-more-nostalgic-for-empire-than-other-ex-colonial-powers (last accessed October 15, 2022).

Bredella, L., Gast, W., & Quandt, S. (1994). Deutschlandbilder im amerikanischen Fernsehen (Images of Germany on American television). Tübingen, Germany: Gunter Narr.

Brenner, Y., & Ohlendorf, K. (2016, May 2). Time for the facts: What do we know about Cologne four months later? *The Correspondent*. https://thecorrespondent.com/4401/time-for-the-facts-what-do-we-know-about-cologne-four-months-later/740617958817-a498b7c3 (last accessed October 15, 2022).

Bundesregierung (2020, March 1). Mehr Fachkräfte für Deutschland (More qualified workers for Germany). https://bundesregierung.de/breg-de/aktuelles/fachkraeteeinwanderungsgesetz-1563122 (last accessed March 30, 2020).

Bundeszentrale für Politische Bildung (2005). Zwangswanderungen nach dem 2. Weltkrieg (Forced migration after WWII). http://bpb.de/gesellschaft/migration/dossier-migration-ALT/56359/nach-dem-2-weltkrieg (last accessed February 15, 2019).

Bundeszentrale für Politische Bildung (2018). Bevölkerung mit Migrationshintergrund in absoluten Zahlen, Anteile an der Gesamtbevölkerung in Prozent, vom 04.04.2018 (Population with migration background in absolute figures, as percentage of the overall population, from 04.04.2018). http://bpb.de/nachschlagen/zahlen-und-fakten/soziale-situation-in-deutschland/61646/migrationshintergrund-i (last accessed October 15, 2022).

Chirac, J. (1995, July 16). Discours prononcé lors des commémorations de la Rafle du Vél' d'Hiv' (Speech given during the commemorations of the Vél' d'Hiv' Roundup). https://fr.wikisource.org/wiki/Discours_prononc%C3%A9_lors_des_comm%C3%A9morations_de_la_Rafle_du_Vel%E2%80%99_d%E2%80%99Hiv%E2%80%99 (last accessed August 15, 2019).

Connolly, K. (2012, September 16). Bernhard Schlink: Being German is a huge burden. *The Guardian*.

Diamond, S. (1974). *The Nazi Movement in the United States, 1924–1941*. Ithaca, NY: Cornell University Press.

Fawlty Towers—BBC (2009). "Don't mention the war" scene in The Germans episode. https://youtube.com/watch?v=yfl6Lu3xQW0 (last accessed October 17, 2022).

Freedland, J. (2015, September 11). Mama Merkel has consigned the "ugly German" to history. *The Guardian*. http://theguardian.com/commentisfree/2015/sep/11/merkel-ugly-german-history (last accessed October 17, 2022).

Frölich, M., Jureit, U., & Schneider, C. (Eds.) (2012). *Das Unbehagen an der Erinnerung—Wandlungsprozesse im Gedenken an den Holocaust (The Discontents of Remembering—Changing Processes of Thoughts about the Holocaust)*. Frankfurt am Main, Germany: Brandes & Apsel.

Gabriel, O. (2015, September 7). Migrants: Pourquoi l'Allemagne accueille à bras ouverts les migrants (Why Germany welcomes migrants with open arms). *20 Minutes*. https://20minutes.fr/economie/1681419-20150907-migrants-pourquoi-allemagne-accueille-bras-ouverts-migrants (last accessed October 17, 2022).

Garschagen, T., & Lindner, J. (2015). Welche Migrationsbewegungen haben Deutschland geprägt? (What were the formative migration movements for Germany?) https://mediendienst-integration.de/artikel/fluechtlinge-asyl-migrationsbewegungen-geschichte-einwanderung-auswanderung-deu (last accessed July 5, 2019).

Gerson, M. (2021, May 27). When it comes to knowing U.S. history, we should all be "woke." *Washington Post*. https://washingtonpost.com/opinions/2021/05/27/american-history-we-should-all-be-woke (last accessed October 17, 2022).

Gobodo-Madikizela, P. (Ed.) (2020). *History, Trauma and Shame: Engaging the Past through Second Generation Dialogue (Cultural Dynamics of Social Representation)*. New York: Routledge.

Hagelüken, A. (2021, August 24). Wir brauchen 400,000 Zuwanderer pro Jahr (We need 400,000 immigrants per year). *Süddeutsche Zeitung*. https://sueddeutsche.de/wirtschaft/zuwanderung-arbeitsmarkt-coronakrise-afd-1.5390143?reduced=true (last accessed October 17, 2022).

Hirsch, A. (2017, November 22). Britain's colonial crimes deserve a lasting memorial. Here's why. *The Guardian*.

Hirsch, M. (1997). *Schuld und Schuldgefühl—Zur Psychoanalyse von Trauma und Introjekt (Guilt and Guilt Feelings—About the Psychoanalysis of Trauma and Introjection)*. Göttingen, Germany: Vandenhoeck & Ruprecht.

Institut für Demoskopie Allensbach (2018, February 7). Engagement in der Flüchtlingshilfe. Ergebnisbericht einer Untersuchung des Instituts für Demoskopie Allensbach im Auftrag des *Bundesministeriums für Familie, Senioren, Frauen und Jugend* (Commitment in helping refugees. Report of the results of research by the Allensbach Institute for Public Opinion Polling on behalf of the Federal Ministry for Families, the Elderly, Women and Youth). https://bmfsfj.de/bmfsfj/service/publikationen/engagement-in-der-fluechtlingshilfe/122012 (last accessed October 17, 2022).

Jokl, A. (1997). *Zwei Fälle zum Thema Bewältigung der Vergangenheit* (*Two Cases Concerning the Issue of Coming to Terms with the Past*). Frankfurt am Main, Germany: Jüdischer Verlag.

Kellerhoff, S. (2017, July 27). So viele Freunde hatte Hitler in Großbritannien (So many friends Hitler had in Great Britain). *Geschichte.* https://welt.de/geschichte/zweiter-weltkrieg/article144397997/So-viele-Freunde-hatte-Hitler-in-Grossbritannien.html?wtrid=socialmedia.email.sharebutton (last accessed October 17, 2022).

Kendrick, K. M. (2017). *Official Guide to the Smithsonian National Museum of African American History and Culture.* Washington, DC: Smithsonian.

Knipp, K. (2011, March 3). Französisch–algerische Altlasten (French–Algerian legacies). *De Qantara.* https://de.qantara.de/inhalt/interview-mit-benjamin-stora-franzoesisch-algerische-altlasten (last accessed October 17, 2022).

Kormann, J. (2021). Weshalb der blutige Krieg in AlgerienFrankreich bis heute prägt (Why the bloody war in Algeria is formative for France to this day). *Neue Zürcher Zeitung.* https://facebook.com/143694099006529/posts/5350261045016449/?sfnsn=scwspmo (last accessed October 17, 2022).

Kossert, A. (2008). *Kalte Heimat: Die Geschichte der deutschen Vertriebenen nach 1945* (*Cold Homeland: The History of the German Displaced Persons After 1945*). Munich, Germany: Siedler.

Kunzig, R. (2016, November 9). Comment l'Allemagne accueille-t-elle les réfugiés? *National Geografic France.* https://nationalgeographic.fr/histoire/2016/11/comment-lallemagne-accueille-t-elle-les-refugies (last accessed October 17, 2022).

Le Monde. (2017, July 16). Macron réaffirme la responsabilité de la France dans la rafle du Vél' d'Hiv (Macron reaffirms France's responsibility in the Vél' d'Hiv roundup). https://lemonde.fr/societe/article/2017/07/16/macron-reaffirme-la-responsabilite-de-la-france-dans-le-vel-d-hiv_5161159_3224.html (last accessed October 17, 2022).

Lohl, J., & Moré, A. (Eds.) (2014). *Unbewusste Erbschaften des Nationalsozialismus. Psychoanalytische, sozialpsychologische und historische Studien* (*Unknown Legacies of National Socialism: Psychoanalytical, Social-psychological and Historical Studies*). Giessen, Germany: Psychosozial.

Mediendienst Integration (2019). Facts and figures in English. https://mediendienst-integration.de/english/facts-figures.html (last accessed April 5, 2020).

MEMO Deutschland (2018). Trügerische Erinnerungen—Wie sich Deutschland an die Zeit des Nationalsozialismus erinnert. Institut für interdisziplinäre Konflikt- und Gewaltforschung der Universität Bielefeld und Stiftung "Erinnerung, Verantwortung und Zukunft" (Deceptive memories—How Germany remembers the time of National Socialism. Institute for interdisciplinary research, conflict and violence at the University of Bielefeld and the Foundation "remembrance, accountability and the future").

Migazin (2017, November 7). Immer noch täglich ein Anschlag auf Asylbewerberheim (Still everyday an attack on shelters for asylum seekers). https://www.migazin.de/2017/11/07/bka-statistik-immer-anschlag-asylbewerberheim/ (last accessed March 2, 2023).

Mitscherlich, A., & Mitscherlich, M. (1967). Die Unfähigkeit zu trauern (The inability to mourn). Munich, Germany: Piper.

More in Common (2017). Attitudes towards national identity, immigration, and refugees in Germany. https://www.moreincommon.com/media/r4dd05ba/more-in-common-germany-report-english.pdf (last accessed October 17, 2022).

Museum of British Colonialism. https://museumofbritishcolonialism.org (last accessed October 17, 2022).

Mysorekar, S. (2018). Rassismus in den Medien vs. diskriminierungsfreie Berichterstattung (Racism in the media vs. discrimination-free reporting). https://djv.de/fileadmin/user_upload/Mysorekar-Rassismus_in_den_Medien.p (last accessed April 5, 2020).

National Museum of the American Indian. https://americanindian.si.edu (last accessed October 17, 2022).

Peters, M. (2018). *Das Trauma von Flucht und Vertreibung—Psychotherapie älterer Menschen und der nachfolgenden Generationen (The Trauma of Flight and Displacement—Psychotherapy of Elderly People and Subsequent Generations)*. Stuttgart, Germany: Klett-Cotta.

Petter, O. (2021, June 22). Windrush scandal: Everything you need to know about the major political crisis. *Independent*. https://independent.co.uk/life-style/windrush-day-2021-scandal-history-b1870442.html.

Pilgrim, D. (2000). The brute caricature. *Ferris State University*. https://ferris.edu/jimcrow/brute (last accessed October 17, 2022).

Scholz, W. (2004). *Formen und Funktionen der narrativen Inszenierung nationaler Selbst- und Fremdbilder in zeitgenössischen englischen Romanen (Forms and Functions of Narratives Referring to National Self-images and Images of the Other in Contemporary English Works of Fiction)*. Munich, Germany: GRIN.

Stanley-Becker, I. (2017, July 26). In Germany, Merkel welcomed hundreds and thousands of refugees. Now many are suing the government. *Washington Post*. https://washingtonpost.com/world/europe/merkel-welcomed-hundreds-of-thousands-of-refugees-now-some-are-suing-her-government/2017/07/20/2d9e13aa-68a7-11e7-94ab-5b1f0ff459df_story.html?utm_term=.a1efbb722bda (last accessed October 17, 2022).

Stora, B. (2021). Les questions mémorielles portant sur la colonosation et la guerre d'Algérie (Memorial issues relating to colonization and the Algerian war). https://elysee.fr/admin/upload/default/0001/09/0586b6b0ef1c2fc2540589c6d56a1ae63a65d97c.pdf (last accessed December 5, 2021).

Volkan, V. D. (2017). *Immigrants and Refugees: Trauma, Perennial Mourning, Prejudice, and Border Psychology*. London: Routledge.

Wessely, A. (2017, October 6). The Mau Mau case—five years on. *Leigh Day*. https://leighday.co.uk/Blog/October-2017/Kenyan-colonial-abuses-apology-five-years-on (last accessed October 17, 2022).

Zeidler, M. (2012). Flucht und Vertreibung der Deutschen aus Ostpreußen, Westpreußen, Danzig, dem Warthegau und Hinterpommern (Flight and displacement of Germans from East Prussia, West Prussia, Danzig, the Warthegau and Outer Pomerania). In: A. Surminski (Ed.), *Flucht und Vertreibung, Europa zwischen 1939 und 1948 (Flight and Expulsion, Europe between 1939 and 1948)* (pp. 66–100). Hamburg, Germany: Ellert & Richter.

Zeuch-Wiese, I. (2010). Spuren suchen oder: Vom langsamen Erkennen (Looking for traces, or: About slowly recognizing). In: *Der halbe Stern: Verfolgungsgeschichte und Identitätsproblematik von Personen und Familien teiljüdischer Herkunft (The Half Star: History of Persecution and Identity Problems of Persons and Families with Partly Jewish Origins)* (pp. 247–260): Giessen, Germany: Haland & Wirth.

CHAPTER 10

Identities in flux in a globalized world

Abdülkadir Çevik

Introduction

Globalization, an agent of change that has been accompanied by great resistance, has been a highly discussed topic over the last three decades. The world we live in today is so connected that interactions between cultures, societies, and economies are far more accessible to individuals. News, trends, and social movements transcend boundaries and quickly travel from one end of the globe to the other. Millions are connected to each other in virtual communities, which then form subcultures. Experiences that previously may have affected only one specific group or society now affect others outside that group. For example, it is hard to imagine a world in which the refugee crisis only impacted the countries that have a direct influx. The current interconnectedness of the globalized world and the way that has created the networked individual have paved the way for global political trends, such as rising nationalism and resistance to change, both inevitable responses to the effects of globalization. In the twenty-first century, we are now witnessing a conservative and nationalist backlash as the psychological effects of globalization are felt more keenly.

Therefore, globalization for societies can simultaneously mean progress, resistance, and shared, regressive responses to change. Globalization is intertwined with the loss of the pre-globalized world and requires a shared mourning process for many large groups, including ethnic, national, religious, and ideological groups. In this regard, the psychological process of globalization is comparable to that of migration where loss, and therefore mourning, are essential for a healthy transition. In various ways, we are witnessing how globalization plays into phenomena such as nationalism and the refugee crisis, and this does not even take into account the effects of global problems like climate change and the pandemic.

Change is an inevitable element of life, but is often the cause of resistance. The transformations associated with globalization often represent a threat, both to individuals' and large groups' internal and external adaptations to their surroundings and lives. Although generally understood in positive terms—for example, the way that a globalized economy has lifted some groups out of poverty—such transformations also contain an element of loss. Clinical work demonstrates that loss and drastic changes are always accompanied by resistance, and that the transformations leading to change are often perceived as threats to existing individual and large group identities. This is true in spite of the fact that the individual or large group may acknowledge that such change makes economic or political sense. No meaningful change is accepted until the individual or the society has gone through an effective amount of the shared work of mourning (Freud, 1917e), which needs to run its course before aspects of globalization can be assimilated.

This chapter embarks from the understanding that migration and globalization have a dyadic, interconnected relationship. Mass migration is a direct result of globalization, especially because various borders have been further erased since the end of the Cold War. The interconnected world in the post-Cold War era also brought an unexpected trend of nationalism—similarly eminent during the interwar period—and this nationalistic wave goes hand in hand with feelings of loss and anxiety. With this backdrop, this chapter examines the psychodynamic processes involved in globalization by comparing individuals' and societies' responses to its infiltrating influences and by examining immigrants' adjustment to their new surroundings. It also looks at the dyadic relationship between host and guest in the context of globalization. I will first provide an overview of the psychodynamics of globalization, then discuss the psychology of migration, and finally conclude with remarks on how globalization, similar to migration, can be a double-edged sword: It has advantages for both the society and the individual, but is very difficult to integrate into one's individual or shared identity. This chapter sheds light on the intersection of globalization, migration, and nationalism by drawing from the case study of Turkey.

Globalization

Globalization has enabled the relatively equal economic participation of the developing nations, particularly in the global South, as more accessible means of communication have allowed people to have physical and social connections. However, with the increase in income inequality and international conflicts—to some degree driven by climate change—the first two decades of the twenty-first century saw a mass refugee crisis. The response to globalization from the developed North has sometimes been hostile, manifesting itself in former US President Trump's Mexican border wall project, the UK's Brexit under Boris Johnson, and the authoritarianism of Hungarian President Orbán.

These reactive changes took place as both an individual and group dynamic, and brought out the complexities and layered nature of globalization. On the surface, the prospects of globalization refer to a voluntary step toward the enrichment of an individual or a large group's life, including through developing a more international, worldly identity and a sense of being a global citizen embracing diversity and universality. But, at the level of anxiety, there are troubling associations to globalization in the West and in the East. For some in the West, globalization is directly linked to terrorism in the Islamic world and the latter's attack on "Western values," particularly after 9/11. This overlaps, in the minds of many in the West, with the idea that non-Western cultures do not belong in the West—witness the EU's resistance to Turkey's becoming a member—and that the world should operate in its own image (İlhan & Çevik, 2013).

On the other hand, many developing countries perceive globalization as an attempt by the West to invade their cultures. In both cases, globalization has triggered a ripple effect that has not been imagined by its liberal proponents. For example, Iran's religious revolution was made possible both because of the use of "Western" technology (e.g., the distribution of Khomeini's messages via recorded tapes) and because of a refusal to allow unwanted aspects of the "West" to infiltrate Iranian territory (e.g., fundamentalist Shi'ite Muslims in Khomeini's Iran perceived many other aspects of the Western influence as a threat to their brand of Islam and its traditions). Indeed, the current rise of nationalism—a conservative trend—is greatly amplified by new technology, such as Facebook and Twitter. Ironically, globalization as a form of liberalization provides the technology—and the motivation—for nationalistic, even racist, agendas.

Globalization leads to major psychological processes for both individuals and large groups. Large group identity is based on shared mental representations of ancestors' legends, realistic and fantasized history, and past heroes (Çevik, 1999; Volkan, 1997). Globalization inevitably introduces images of new and foreign legends, histories, and heroes. These images compete with the existing mental representations within large groups before a psychic continuum is created between them. This process of giving up, or at least modifying, existing representations and of accepting new ones may induce difficult emotions, like guilt and shame, which in turn, may lead to aggressive expressions, either against one's own society, now "invaded" by these difficult-to-integrate images of itself, or against those perceived as "invading" that society's positive self-image.

It is imperative to look at the root of large group responses to globalization. In his writing about large group psychology, Volkan illustrated that societies need both allies and enemies (1988). Concepts of "allies" and "enemies" primarily refer to the members of one group externalizing their difficult-to-integrate images of themselves and others to outside "suitable reservoirs"—mostly neighboring large groups. Emotionally toned concepts of "we" and "they" are built on the psychological meanings of such reservoirs. For example, in Finland, the sauna becomes a suitable reservoir that absorbs all Finnish children's "good" unintegrated self and object images. By using the same reservoir, Finnish children are linked to each other in an invisible way. In Cyprus, Turkish children use pigs as a suitable reservoir (Muslim Turks do not eat pork, and the Muslim culture considers pigs "foreign"). The children are connected by the externalization of their "bad" unintegrated images into the same reservoir; the pigs stand for the "foreign" Greeks who also live in Cyprus. These psychological processes are the result of identification with parents and important caretakers within the same society, whose unconscious attitudes play a formative role in separating "us" and "them." Utilizing the same reservoirs and identifying with others in the same culture paves the way for the later division of the adult world into "allies" and "enemies."

The imagined enemy of a society is suddenly and simultaneously real if there is an active or intractable conflict between groups. As anthropologist Howard Stein (1982) stated, enemies are both real and fantasied. As long as a society has foreign "enemies," the images, with their associated "bad" feelings and thoughts projected onto them, do not boomerang back and harm the society. One's own potential "badness" is safely projected and contained by others. Globalization threatens this psychological balance by bringing different groups into more and deeper contact with each other. It thereby challenges a group's ability to maintain "enemies" as well as "allies" in that simplistic but powerful psychological sense, and thus is a threat to large group identity. By way of globalization, boundaries loosen, creating an ongoing source of anxiety for large groups interacting with one another. The more visible the Other becomes, the more the differences between groups—on which each group has built a psychological mythology—evaporate and lead to the disconcerting question: Who are we now?

An example of large-group anxiety related to globalization is Turkey's relationship with the European Union (EU) and its aspiration of full membership in the early 2000s. In a way, Turkey's journey toward inclusion in the EU can be conceptualized as a process of globalization that triggered large-group processes in Turks and EU member states. The possibility of Turkey's EU membership induced anxiety in both Turkey and Europe, expressed by various political parties, leaders, media organizations, and some citizens.

One way that Turkish citizens initially expressed their anxiety was in reference to "kokoreç," a traditional Turkish food made of sheep tripe. A common belief among Turks in the early 2000s was that Europeans perceived kokoreç as something bad, inedible, and a food that might infect the eater with bacteria. The popular thinking among Turks who shared this belief was that if Turkey were to become part of the EU, Turks would be prohibited from preparing and eating kokoreç (*Deutsche Welle*, 2003). There seemed to be a shared psychological meaning attached to the preoccupation with kokoreç: as a "dirty" (aggressive) tool that could be digested safely by "tough" Turks, but was a "weapon" that would sicken people from the "Western" cultures. Thus, Turkey's joining the EU might rob the Turks of their "toughness" and make them "weak." With the stalemated relations between the EU and Turkey and in the context of rising nationalism, Turkey became more wary of the EU, even to the degree of spreading such conspiracy theories in order to appeal to its domestic constituents.

The countries that belong to the EU also experienced anxiety about having Turkey as a member. EU states share a sense of "togetherness" and of common identity, particularly in terms of religion, history, currency, and values. They fear the migration of Turkey's Muslim culture into the predominantly Christian EU; they fear the presence of something "foreign" in their midst. This sentiment was openly verbalized by the former French president, Valéry Giscard d'Estaing—also the head of the Convention on the Future of Europe—on November 8, 2002, when he told the French newspaper *Le Monde* that those who backed Ankara's candidacy to join the EU were "the adversaries of the European Union." He went on to say that Turkey's capital is not in Europe and that the admission of Turkey into the EU "would be the end of the European Union" (*The Guardian*, November 9, 2002).

In the second half of the 2010s, Europe witnessed a nationalist surge partially instigated by the influx of Syrian refugees. In turn, this process was projected onto relations with Turkey and the Turkish people. In fact, anti-Turkey sentiments have been integral to the rise of the far right in Europe. In this respect, immigration and the refugee crisis are directly linked to globalization: the Brexit campaign was fueled by the unfounded claim that Turkey was going to join the EU. It stoked fears of uncontrollable immigration and put Turkey into the role of the scapegoat (Kirişci & Ekim, 2016). Most recently, Belgium instituted a ban on halal and kosher meat (*BBC*, 2020), and France has banned the slaughter of halal poultry (*FR24 News English*, 2021). As nations approach each other to move toward the goals of peace and prosperity, the psychological anxieties about what in that process is taken in—whether that be people, foods, or ideas—speak to a society's deep need to protect the boundaries around large-group identity.

Psychology of migration

While there have been limited in-depth studies of globalization that apply a psychodynamic understanding to the problem, there is ample research on the psychology of both voluntary and forced migration (Akhtar, 1995, 1999; Çevik, 1999; Grinberg & Grinberg, 1989; Volkan, 1979, 1993). Forced migrations occur due to wars, warlike conditions, and racial or ideological persecutions. We know a great deal about how forced migration influences the outcome of an immigrant's adaptation or maladaptation to a new location. In general, voluntary migration allows an immigrant to make a better adjustment. The study of migration, forced or voluntary, must also include an examination of an immigrant's mourning process. The immigrant who is capable of effectively mourning can put his or her pre-migration self-images alongside his or her post-migration self-images, and over time can come to experience a continuum in his or her identity. Applying what we know about the psychodynamics of immigrants' adaptation to a new country, culture and patterns of thinking or behavior can tell us something about reactions to globalization as well, particularly how individuals and societies use what has "migrated" into their territory in adaptive or maladaptive ways.

An immigrant's struggle with identity issues is necessarily accompanied by a mourning process. Initially, an immigrant experiences a "cultural shock" (Ticho, 1971) because of the inevitable changes in his or her "average expectable environment" (Hartmann, 1939). For the immigrant, the new environment is an unpredictable one, especially if he or she has been forced to go into exile. Garza-Guerrero shows how a new immigrant who effectively completes a mourning process for what has been lost can form a new identity that is neither a total surrender to the new society, culture, and traditions, nor the sum of bicultural endowment (1974). Seeing a positive aspect in this kind of "good" adjustment, Julius argues that an immigrant can keep his or her previous and new identities on a continuum and belong "totally to both" (Julius, 1992). Akhtar (1995) suggests that the adaptation of the immigrant is like a third individuation phase, following the first one in childhood (Mahler, 1968) and the second one during the adolescent passage (Blos, 1979). Individuation means internally separating one's own identity from the images of those to whom one is emotionally very close (Çevik, 2019). This enables a greater internal freedom to decide which images of others to keep (through identifying with them) and which images to modify or discard.

Of course, there are many complications in the process of an immigrant's adaptation. Leon and Rebecca Grinberg (1989) examine in detail the immigrant's various defense mechanisms used to deal with what has been left behind and what has to be changed internally. Feelings of guilt about the change or the loss of part of the self may complicate an immigrant's mourning process and adaptation. If the guilt is "persecutory," the past and present are confused and "resentment, pain, despair, fear [and] self-reproach" may emerge (Grinberg & Grinberg, 1989). An immigrant with persecutory guilt may be more vulnerable to expressing violence either toward the self or others.

On the other hand, migration psychology is important for host communities as well. There is significant psychological work to be done by the host community for a peaceful transition; the host community must embrace and accept the migrant community as part of its own culture, which may mean letting go of some core elements of identity. During the 1990s, following the influx of Iraqi refugees fleeing Saddam Hussein's violence and the Gulf War, Turkey gained a significant Kurdish population. In the latter half of the 2010s, approximately four million Syrian refugees found shelter in Turkey. Particularly with the recent refugee influx from Syria, Turkey's own psychological and physical boundaries have been tested. In addition to living in state and internationally funded refugee camps, many refugees have taken up residence in border Turkish towns, which changes the ethno-linguistic makeup of those cities. Refugees have established local ghettos with stores decorated in Arabic font. While the Turkish government has welcomed the Syrian refugees, several incidents of violence and ethnic strife point to an anxiety about identity felt by the broader Turkish society as it hosts large groups with an Arab identity.

In between two cultures

Any immigrant needs to adapt to influences that infiltrate his or her internal world from the new cultural, societal, and political environment. On the other hand, a person (or society) subjected to globalization has to adjust to influences that infiltrate the internal world (or the societal, cultural, and political norms of the society) from the outside. In the latter situation, the individuals remain at the same location, but face changes or losses almost as though they were immigrants. The following story of Turkish immigrants arriving in Belgium from a central Anatolian village will help us to understand the similarity between the psychodynamics involved in immigration and globalization. This example involves a "society" rather than an individual and thus illustrates a societal response to changes in culture and other norms.

In 1987, I was invited to Belgium as a consultant to Turkish families who had begun to settle in the Schaerbeek district of Brussels in the early 1960s. Economic difficulties had forced them to migrate to Belgium. Initially, they had come to Brussels as guest workers; their spouses and children later joined them. The Turks living in Schaerbeek had come from Emirdağ, a small town in central Anatolia about 200 kilometers southwest of the Turkish capital, Ankara. Most of them had lived in the same district of Brussels since the early 1960s. I was asked to study this group because of the prevalence of depression and various psychosomatic symptoms, such as peptic ulcers, among them. What struck me was the fact that most of the people living in this district did not speak Dutch, French, or German—all official languages in Belgium—and because of this, they could not express their feelings in a language that most people around them could understand. They also could not effectively use Turkish to communicate these feelings, because they felt surrounded by a foreign culture that would not respond to their own language. Any expression in Turkish against this "invading" culture would be useless. Internalizing this, they could not use their own language to express their frustrations, even within their own enclaves. They expressed their troubled state of being—caught between their original central Anatolian culture and their new Belgian one—through depression and somatization, rather than through verbalization and direct discharge of emotions.

The people of Emirdağ are moderately religious and nationalistic, and the immigrants living in the Schaerbeek district of Brussels come from such a tradition. However, the Turkish families I visited in Brussels were more religious and nationalistic than those relatives and friends who had remained in Emirdağ. I concluded that although this Turkish group in Brussels had migrated voluntarily, they resisted the Belgian way of life and resisted including aspects of it in their daily lives. Instead, because their traditional identities were threatened, they exaggerated their traditional values, particularly their religious and nationalistic commitments. They also created a ghetto-like environment, thus putting a "border" around their community in order to protect themselves against the infiltration of Belgian culture and traditions. Indeed, they had little contact with native Belgians. The threat to their identity had induced frustration and aggression in them. Their aggression turned inward, resulting in depression, somatization, and increased dependency on drugs and alcohol, the latter symptoms differentiating them from their relatives in Emirdağ. In their minds, alcohol and drugs were a part of Belgium culture; they could only identify with the "bad" qualities of the host country, and only in maladaptive ways could they find a continuum between their past and present lives (Çevik, 1999).

In 2009, I conducted another study, this time in several prominent Belgian cities, such as Brussels, Ghent, Anvers, and Liege, that had significant Turkish migrant populations. I interviewed first, second, and third generation immigrants in these cities, and this research, twenty years after my initial study, showed very similar findings. Most families never went outside of their enclaves and did not know much about life outside their immigrant circles. They lived, shopped, and dined in the same areas, regardless of which generation immigrant they were. Integration into the mainstream Belgian culture was not encouraged as the fear of assimilation overshadowed acculturation. The idea of intermarriage was, to put it lightly, frowned upon. They stayed away from trying local foods and dining at local non-Turkish restaurants, mostly because of halal guidelines and anxiety about the unknown. Most of the interviewees had limited command of French, Dutch, and German, and some spoke exclusively Turkish. Today, the integration of Euro-Turks is still very difficult, in part because immigrants are more connected to Turkey than to their host countries. What could seem distant and far away is closer because of increased international connectedness. Therefore in this case, globalization is adding to the problem of immigrant acculturation.

The mid-2000s were marked by feelings of rejection, isolation, and rising anti-Islamic sentiments in Europe. Toward the latter half of the 2010s, nationalism became prominent both in Turkey and Europe, in a sense feeding off each other. In recent years, Turkish president Erdoğan has organized rallies in various European cities and consolidated his religious and nationalistic base in what many call "Erdoğanism." As a result, the Turkish migrants in Europe have become an extension of Turkey, and many identify Erdoğan as the defender of the oppressed. So, even though this Turkish community migrated to Belgium willingly, in pursuit of better lifestyles and economic independence, they in fact have resisted transformation. And while it is certainly providing opportunities, globalization also induces shared anxiety, experienced as a threat to shared identity. In response, nationalism, even among immigrants, is seen as a solution.

Conclusion

Globalization, like migration, creates a threat to individual and large group identity (Çevik & Ceyhun, 1995). Certainly, it can be conceptualized as an avenue of change that can lead to adaptive and peaceful togetherness. But under conditions where there is a perceived threat to large group identity and where political leaders inflame such a threat, it can also fuel violence and even terrorism. The psychology of globalization should be considered when organizations and governments make international attempts—political, commercial, legal, or otherwise—to create increasing amounts of direct and indirect contact and cooperation between cultures and societies.

References

Akhtar, S. (1995). A third individuation: Immigration, identity and the psychoanalytic process. *Journal of the American Psychoanalytic Association,* 43(4): 1051–1084.

Akhtar, S. (1999). *Immigration and Identity: Turmoil, Treatment, and Transformation*. Northvale, NJ: Jason Aronson.

BBC (2020, December 17). EU court backs ban on animal slaughter without stunning. https://bbc.com/news/world-europe-55344971 (last accessed July 12, 2021).

Blos, P. (1979). *The Adolescent Passage*. New York: International Universities Press.

Çevik, A. (1999). Avrupa'daki Göçmen Türklerde Kimlik Sorunlarının Reaktivasyonu ve Bunun Kimliğe Yansıması: Yas Kimlik Sorunları ve Somatizasyon (Reactivation of identity problems in immigrant Turks in Europe and its reflection on identity: Mourning identity problems and somatization). *Türkiye Klinikleri Psikiyatri Dergisi, 1*(1): 55–62.

Çevik, A. (2019). *Birey Olabilmek: Bireysel Bütünlükten Toplumsal Bütünlük ve Barışa Giden Yol. Politik Psikoloji Seminerleri (Being an Individual: From Individual Integrity to Social Integrity and the Path to Peace. Political Psychology Seminars)*. O. Herdi, R. S. İlhan, & A. Çevik (Eds.). Ankara, Turkey: Barış Kitap.

Çevik, A., & Ceyhun, B. (1995). *Psikopolitik Yönden Kimlik Gelişimi ve Etnik Terörizm. Politik Psikoloji Serisi Sayı, 1 (Psychopolitical Identity Development and Ethnic Terrorism. Political Psychology Series Issue 1)*. Ankara, Turkey: Medikomat Basın Yayın.

Deutsche Welle (2003, August 26). Turks troubled by possibility of tripe ban. https://dw.com/en/turks-troubled-by-possibility-of-tripe-ban/a-956200 (last accessed July 12, 2021).

FR24 News English (2021, March 21). Muslims in France outraged by decision to ban the slaughter of halal chickens. https://fr24news.com/a/2021/03/muslims-in-france-outraged-by-decision-to-ban-the-slaughter-of-halal-chickens.html (last accessed July 12, 2021).

Freud, S. (1917e). Mourning and melancholia. *S. E., 14*: 237–261. London: Hogarth.

Garza-Guerrero, A. C. (1974). Culture shock: Its mourning and vicissitudes of identity. *Journal of the American Psychoanalytic Association, 22*: 400–429.

Grinberg, L., & Grinberg, R. (1989). *Psychoanalytic Perspectives on Migration and Exile*. N. Festiner (Trans.). New Haven, CT: Yale University Press.

The Guardian (2002, November 9). Turkey must be kept out of the Union. https://theguardian.com/world/2002/nov/09/turkey.eu (last accessed August 10, 2022).

Hartmann, H. (1939). *Ego Psychology and the Problem of Adaptation.* D. Rapaport (Trans.). New York: International Universities Press, 1958.

İlhan, R. S., & Çevik, A. (2013). Önyargıların Psikolojisi: Psikodinamik Bir Gözden Geçirme (The psychology of prejudices: A psychodynamic review). *Nesne Psikoloji Dergisi, 1*(1): 50–64.

Julius, D. A. (1992). Biculturalism and international interdependence. *Mind and Human Interaction,* 3: 53–56.

Kirişçi, K., & Ekim, S. (2016, June 23). Brexit, the politics of fear, and Turkey the boogeyman. *Brookings Institute.* https://brookings.edu/blog/order-from-chaos/2016/06/23/brexit-the-politics-of-fear-and-turkey-the-boogeyman (last accessed October 8, 2022).

Mahler, M. S. (1968). *On Human Symbiosis and the Vicissitudes of Individuation.* New York: International Universities Press.

Stein, H. R. (1982). Adversary symbiosis and complementary group dissociation: An analysis of the U.S./U.S.S.R. conflict. *International Journal of Intercultural Relations,* 6: 55–83.

Ticho, G. (1971). Cultural aspects of transference and countertransference. *Bulletin of the Menninger Clinic,* 35: 313–334.

Volkan, V. D. (1979). *Cyprus—War and Adaptation: A Psychoanalytic History of Two Ethnic Groups in Conflict.* Charlottesville, VA: University Press of Virginia.

Volkan, V. D. (1988). *The Need to Have Enemies and Allies: From Clinical Practice to International Relationships.* Northvale, NJ: Jason Aronson.

Volkan, V. D. (1993). Immigrants and refugees: A psychodynamic perspective. *Mind and Human Interaction,* 4: 63–69.

Volkan, V. D. (1997). *Bloodlines: From Ethnic Pride to Ethnic Terrorism.* New York: Farrar, Straus & Giroux.

CHAPTER 11

Cultural exchanges between Turkey and Israel: set for reset

Senem B. Çevik

Introduction

Culture is an often neglected tool in managing conflicts between nations. It certainly is not the first thing that comes to mind about diplomacy but shared culture can be a powerful tool in strengthening existing relations and fostering cultural appreciation. Various aspects of culture have been used as vehicles to establish mutual understanding between communities. With its universal appeal, music can reverse biases and transform the unknown other into a familiar other. The universal nature of music serves as a cultural engagement platform that can demonstrate the commonalities between people and help build bridges between societies. To be sure, cultural engagement does not offer a solution to conflicts but with the increased agency role of non-state actors in international affairs, the potential of cultural engagement cannot be overlooked.

Relations between Turkey and Israel have always been very complex and dependent on outside factors, including regional political dynamics, regional alliances, and the Arab–Israeli conflict. Although trade has been on the rise consistently, diplomatic relations between the two countries have simultaneously been eroding due to disagreements between Israeli and Turkish administrations in the last two decades. Turkey and Israel appointed respective ambassadors in the fall of 2022. Nevertheless, citizens of Turkey and Israel have found ways to engage with one another through melodies that resonate with both cultures. Although many of these musical exchanges take place unofficially, based on the initiative of private citizens, or result from unintended efforts, political will from both sides of the aisle could more easily help transform public opinion. In addition to musical exchanges, the rising popularity of Israel-based Netflix series *Fauda* and *Shtetl* and Turkish television series creates positive steps toward cultural understanding between societies. Encouraging these exchanges may not directly lead to the resumption of diplomatic relations at the ambassadorial level, but it will sustain the inter-cultural connection and prepare the societies for when diplomatic relations improve.

Diplomacy *by* the people *of* the people

The art of negotiation, or diplomacy as we know it, is one of the most essential mechanisms of a nation's relations with its outside world. Traditional diplomatic practice involves career diplomats engaged in negotiations, mediations, and dialogue taking place behind closed doors. The public has very limited if any access to these conversations (Berridge, 2015). This kind of diplomacy, which is often called track-one diplomacy, is conducted away from the public gaze and therefore faces challenges related to its exclusionary communication style. Especially at times of conflict, it fails to offer sustainable grassroots solutions and omits the dynamics that depend on rapprochement between peoples. Traditional diplomacy attempts to manage the conflicts between nations without necessarily taking account of confidence-building measures at the grassroots level. Despite maintaining its fundamental function, diplomacy today has an additional application as a result both of advances in communication technologies and in the way that democratic culture empowers civil society.

The public has a broader agency role in twenty-first-century diplomacy through the ability to engage as active participants. United States career diplomat Joseph Montville recognized the importance of activities taking place outside of the realm of official, track-one diplomacy. Davidson and Montville (1981) argue that track-two diplomacy is "an unofficial, informal interaction between members of adversary groups or nations that aims to develop strategies, influence public opinion, and organize human and material resources in ways that might help resolve their conflict" (p. 155). Track-two diplomacy is a method that assists official (track-one) diplomacy and seeks to assess alternative scenarios that satisfy the basic security and needs of the parties in conflict by facilitating discussion at the grassroots level (Azar, 2002; Montville, 1991). These efforts can involve opinion leaders, academics, artists, and scientists as well as diplomats. To be sure, track-two diplomacy is not an alternative to track-one diplomacy. However, its success in informally bringing the public into the conversation provides added value to official diplomatic efforts between nations. By emotionally preparing societies to understand one another, track-two diplomacy serves as a vital tool in establishing the necessary psychological foundations for genuine rapprochement.

Track-two and multi-track diplomacy, now a prevalent form of diplomatic practice in international relations, emphasizes grassroots interaction between citizens of two or more nations. Citizens have a role as agents in multi-track diplomacy. With this perspective, Herbert Kelman and Ronald Fisher (2003) place emphasis on the role of non-state actors such as the public in building relationships between nations in conflict. Harold Saunders (2001) argues that the human dimension is central to peace-building processes and that citizens can transform conflicts by building relationships beyond the formal state structures. Citizens become active participants through continuous interaction, which is also called citizen diplomacy. As a result, foreign policy involves a more public dimension (G. H. Fisher, 1972). These grassroots interactions include relationship-building initiatives related to different forms of culture, including music and other arts (Jarman, 2009). Saunders (2005, 2014) describes these interactions as the public peace process, where clusters of citizens participate in the solution of problems through a multi-level continuous interaction. What Saunders and Azar (2002) describe as multi-track diplomacy and public peace process are intentional efforts in creating dialogue. People-to-people exchanges are at the core of these confidence-building measures, as they ensure that participants of such programs become more familiar with one another, look past official narratives, and develop their own understanding of conflicts.

The initiatives that assign agency to the public are also called public diplomacy, which according to Brian Hocking (2007) is diplomacy *by* rather than *of* the public. This new face of diplomatic practice has emerged with the advancement of civil society networks, which conceive citizens as active participants in diplomatic practice rather than passive recipients of information. Diplomacy by the public often utilizes cultural tools as a way to engage with foreign audiences and foster mutual understanding between people of different cultures (Schneider, 2007). The exchange of ideas, information, and art aims to establish long-term relationships and facilitate mutual understanding (Arsenault & Cowan, 2008; Cull, 2008; Leonard et al., 2002).

I suggest that non-state actors, even unofficial cultural exchanges, have a fundamental agency role in encouraging a conversation between societies. The relationship between Turkey and Israel is an example of how such unofficial non-state actors can facilitate a cultural bridge between two societies. Turkey and Israel have been at odds particularly since the 2010 Mavi Marmara flotilla incident. The relations between the two countries have been largely defined by the contours of the Arab–Israeli conflict and Turkey's persistent support for Hamas up until recent reconciliation efforts with Israel. When official diplomacy fails, non-state actors may take on the role of representatives who sustain the cultural, if not the political, ties between societies. Turkey was the first predominantly Muslim state to recognize Israel as an independent state and has had high-level security cooperation with Israel, particularly in the 1990s. Aside from the Turkish-Jewish community in Turkey and Israel, the Mizrahi community in Israel, given their historical ties to the former Ottoman territories, such as Iraq and Syria, present a potential for bridging the political divide.

These multiple factors are opportunities for dialogue and conversation, and there are numerous non-state actors actively seeking improved relations. The Turkey–Israel Business Council (DEIK) and the Turkish–Israeli Civil Society Platform (TICSF) are two initiatives that focus on culture, business, and networking. They encourage collaboration between

Turkish and Israeli counterparts in various areas. In addition, several organizations in Turkey have leverage in improving relations between the two countries, such as the Turkish Chief Rabbinate Foundation, the Sephardic Center of Istanbul, the Quincentennial Foundation and the Şalom newspaper. They are natural stakeholders in the enrichment of societal relations between Turkey and Israel. Idahdut Yotsey Turkiya (TurkIsrael), a Turkish Jewish community organization based in Israel, is also integral to these cross-cultural exchanges, as it represents a bridge between the two cultures. Some of the aforementioned non-state actors do not only relate to both cultures; they are also critical in educating the broader Turkish society about issues related to Turkish Jewish heritage, Israel, and the Holocaust. In this regard, they are also important civil society actors in educating Turkish society about its own multicultural heritage, while sustaining cultural ties within the Turkish Jewish community. In addition to the efforts of these actors to bridge the diplomatic gap, there has been a plethora of cultural exchanges between the two countries, in particular musical exchanges. In what many call the lost decade of Turkish–Israeli relations, musical collaborations between Israeli and Turkish artists have continued steadily. Some of these initiatives were made possible by the facilitation of the above-mentioned non-state actors and some took place serendipitously.

Where diplomacy fails, music heals

According to the renowned Israeli conductor-pianist, Daniel Barenboim, the cofounder of the famous West–Eastern Divan Orchestra, "When playing music, it is possible to achieve a unique sense of peace." In fact, Barenboim and the late Edward Said's vision of utilizing music to build bridges between cultures can serve as a pathway to build new communication frameworks. Particularly peoples of adversarial states can benefit from engaging with one another by way of civil society through culture, arts, sports, and music (Wiseman, 2010). The West–Eastern Divan Orchestra is a unique program that is dedicated to the empowerment of young musicians from the Middle East and North Africa. It focuses on engaging Arabs and Israelis to foster mutual understanding through culture.

Music can be utilized in multiple ways by states and non-state entities ranging from promoting peace and empathy to spreading animosity (Laurence, 2008; Urbain, 2008). Music has historically been used as a means of propaganda and political communication. National anthems like La Marseillaise, John Lennon's role in the American antiwar movement, military marches, and the German composer, Richard Wagner, whose music is tarnished by his anti-Semitism, are all examples of how music can indeed be political. In a similar vein, the United States employed music as a cultural tool to introduce American values and culture to international audiences during the Cold War (Cull, 2008). Although these examples are fairly different, they demonstrate that music and politics are interconnected.

As the Barenboim–Said vision of cultural engagement represents, music can also be a vehicle to understand and communicate with the other. There are various music programs specifically funded by states to facilitate dialogue. These music diplomacy initiatives help to educate their publics about the other by ensuring exposure to each other's culture. For example, the State Department-funded One Beat Program brings together emerging musical leaders from around the world to collaboratively create original work and to develop a global network of civically engaged musical initiatives. Many music diplomacy initiatives focusing on peace building, such as One Beat, are often limited to the participants. Thus, music diplomacy for the purposes of peace building can have limited impact and encounter obstacles in engaging the mainstream due to a lack of domestic and international political support. When music finds its way to the masses through concerts or collaboration, it becomes a valuable tool to facilitate cultural exchange to the larger segments of society. Although I am not trying to exaggerate the role of civil society, individuals, and celebrities in facilitating dialogue, I also do not want to underestimate their potential—whether purposely designed to do so or not—in building cultural bridges. One way or the other, music does provide exposure to the other culture.

Culture holds valuable potential in ensuring that societies communicate with each other despite the current nature of the political conflict between them. The music exchanges between Turkey and Israel are usually between their civil societies and, as such, can be categorized as unofficial and unintentional for diplomatic purposes. Cultural proximity between Turkey and Israel plays an important role in initiating musical diplomacy. Therefore, I think it's important to first discuss the localized Sephardic musical contributions, which by extension support understanding between cultures. The Sephardic Jewish heritage has a robust legacy within the Ottoman culture and serves as a natural pathway between Turkey and Israel. Eastern maqams—musical tunes—that exist in Sephardic Jewish liturgy called *maftirims* are unique examples of this cultural and musical interconnectedness (Demir, 2017; Şaul, 2015). Turkish cantor Aaron Kohen released his first album "Maftirimler" in 2001, which was the first effort to present this Sufi Jewish tradition; it was followed by Kudsi Ergüner Ensemble Birun's workshop in Venice in 2015. The Eastern Sufi-inspired liturgical tradition has been more recently arranged in the Western musical tradition by Turkish pianist Ayşe Taşpınar Gatenyo and composer Hakan Ali Toker for an album focusing on the maftirims. In 2022, Turkey's Yunus Emre Institute commissioned a new orchestration of one of the maftirims to Grammy Award-winning composer Erberk Eryılmaz which was later performed in the United States by the Los Angeles Jewish Symphony in a collaboration of Turkish and various Jewish musicians.

In addition, Ottoman Jewish composers are integral to Turkish classical music (Türk Sanat Müziği). Composer, poet, and cantor İzak Algazi, oud virtuoso Avram Hayat Levi, and tanbur virtuoso İsak Frekso Romano are famous Ottoman Jewish musicians who have contributed to Turkish music. Their tunes are widely enjoyed by Turkish classical music aficionados even to this day.

It is also important to mention more popular Turkish Jewish musical engagements as I believe they supplement the broader Turkish–Israeli musical exchanges. Although not all of them are directly connected to Israel, they could help establish a bond between communities by introducing elements of Jewish culture into Turkey. As a result, the audience could potentially have a better awareness of the complex fabric of Israeli society and culture. Sephardic Jewish romansas and kantikas in Ladino (Judeo-Espanol) are popular ballads, with occasional influences from Turkish, Greek, and Italian (Şaul, 2015). These folk songs have been passed on from one generation to another. Although Sephardic kantikas and romansas are relatively unknown to the broader Turkish community, Sefarad, a mid-2000s ethnic music band, introduced this musical heritage to the masses. The very trendy ethnic boy band of its era popularized the melodies of Ladino songs such as Avram Avinu, El Encalador, and Pasharo d'Ermozura. So much so that when their album came out, these folk songs were transformed into tunes played at Turkish night clubs. Another Ladino music band is world famous Los Pasharos Sepharadis which is an Istanbul-based Sephardic vocal and instrumental group whose four members have been working together since 1978. They have produced six albums that are considered milestones in Ladino music (Şarhon, 2011). Los Pasharos Sepharadis collaborated with famous Turkish musician Sezen Aksu in her Türkiye Şarkıları (Songs from Turkey) album and concert. Los Pasharos Sepharadis band usually performs abroad but their music is available online. The children's choir Estreyikas de Estambol led by İzzet Bana released two albums of Ladino music and they perform at special events, such as International Ladino Day.

Renan Koen is a renowned pianist, composer, soprano, and music therapist who is also an educator on Holocaust awareness. She carried out a Holocaust project on Terezin composers in 2015, which included a concert and an album. As a result of this project, the compositions of Terezin composers were performed in Turkey for the first time. Koen has also been conducting Positive Resistance through Holocaust Reality workshops, a project that provides Holocaust education and inspires young people to say no to violence. Koen's project is a major step toward Holocaust awareness, since formal Holocaust education is not a part of the school curriculum. These musical traditions predominantly reach upper middle class Turkish citizens in urban cities. Perhaps the most popular Ladino song to reach masses in Turkey is musician Ferhat Göçer's cover of "La Rosa Enflorece/Los Bilbilicos," a fifteenth-century Sephardic song. His Turkish rendition "Yastayım" topped Turkish music charts for months, gaining vast popularity. Nonetheless, most Turkish listeners are not aware that the song in its original format is sung by Sephardic Jews at the Shabbat and High Holiday dinners (Elitsoy, 2018).

Linet, an Israeli singer with her heritage in Turkey, released her first album in Turkey in 1995, and since then has been one of the most well-known musicians performing Turkish classical music. Her fluent knowledge of Hebrew, Turkish, English, Spanish, and French, as well as her understanding of Turkish culture, makes Linet a cultural ambassador between Turkey and Israel. She frequently appears on Turkish television and is a very popular musician.

In addition to more localized Sephardic Jewish musical heritage, there are numerous examples demonstrating that the civil society of Turkey and Israel have employed music to bolster mutual understanding. "The sound of music doesn't have any passport ... It does not recognize any border or religion," says Yinon Muallem, an Istanbul based Israeli composer and percussionist. Muallem is one of the most important artists when it comes to Turkish-Israeli musical exchanges and with that recognition he serves as the cultural attaché at the Israeli consulate general in Istanbul (Tokyay, 2012). Muallem has performed in Turkey with leading Turkish musicians, such as Tekfen Philharmonic, Şirin Pancaroğlu, and Ömer Faruk Tekbilek (Demir, 2017; Tokyay, 2012). Muallem is known as the musician who builds bridges between cultures and describes himself as multicultural. His musical style is influenced by Ottoman sounds with elements of Turkish and Jewish music. He synthesizes Hebrew poetry, Ladino, and Sufi music which makes the sound appealing to Turkish audiences (Hugi, 2013).

Perhaps one of the most well-known Israeli musicians in Turkey is Yasmin Levy, an Israeli singer-composer who has roots in Turkey. Levy, who often performs in Ladino, holds concerts in İstanbul as well as other parts of Turkey. Levy also covered Firuze, a 1980s Turkish pop classic. She performed duets with Turkish musicians, including İbrahim Tatlıses, Kubat, Ömer Faruk Tekbilek, Halil Sezai, and Koray Avcı (Elitsoy, 2018). One of the most memorable moments of musical exchange was Yasmin Levy's concert at the recently renovated Grand Synagogue of Edirne in 2019. The concert drew ample media attention to one of the largest synagogues in all of Europe. Israeli musician and songwriter Mor Karbasi has also gained a following in Turkey with her cantigas and romances. Following in the footsteps of other music divas in the Ladino language, Karbasi too has a vast repertoire in Ladino.

Israel's popular heavy metal band Orphaned Land is another example of musical exchange between Turkey and Israel. Their unique style of harmonizing metal with Eastern melodies has helped them gain a following in Turkey. Their songs are inspired by Abrahamic religions and their texts. They received a peace prize from the Istanbul Commerce University in 2010 for their efforts in peace building between Jews and Muslims (Demir, 2017; Tokyay, 2012). One of their songs "All in One" even has a Turkish version out. In attempts to boost cultural ties between Israel and Turkey, the Orphaned Land also donated all proceeds from the sales of a 2011 concert to the victims of the earthquake in Van, Turkey. They have also collaborated with leading Turkish rock musician Erkin Koray (Demir, 2017). Other Israeli musicians such as Riff Cohen, Dudu Tassa, Mark Eliyahu, and Itamar Erez have all regularly performed in Turkish cities, particularly in Istanbul, Ankara, and Izmir (Demir, 2017; Elitsoy, 2018).

How Turkish music looks on the Israeli side is fairly different than how Israeli and Sephardic Jewish musical heritage is presented in Turkey. It is not difficult to come across Turkish music in Israel, particularly in mixed neighborhoods, Turkish Jewish homes, and the homes of Mizrahi Jews. Given the cultural proximity of the two countries, some Turkish musicians are well known in Israel. Many of these musicians are in the arabesque genre, familiar to those Israelis who enjoy Middle Eastern melodies. Turkish musicians like İbrahim Tatlıses, Orhan Gencebay, Bülent Ersoy, and Ebru Gündeş are just a few musicians known in Israel. Their music can be heard in taxis, hotels, and restaurants; some are even covered in Hebrew.

İbrahim Tatlıses, known as the "Emperor of Arabesque," is quite popular throughout the Middle East. He performed in a sold-out concert in 2005 in Eilat in which he collaborated with Israeli musician Sarit Hadad and performed in Jerusalem in 2022. A recent winner of Israel's "The Voice," Sapir Saban, who has roots in Turkey, performed a famous song by Ibrahim Tatlises, putting a Turkish arabesque song on the map for all Israelis. This has inspired a collaboration between Sapir Saban and Turkish singer Mehmet Daş in performing a "Homage to Turkish Arabesque" concert. An event curated by the Jerusalem East-West Orchestra led by Tom Cohen, this concert also became very popular in Turkey via YouTube. Saban and Daş sang various popular İbrahim Tatlıses songs. Tom Cohen calls his sound Andalusian music or the Judeo-Arab tradition, which resonates with many Turks and Israelis.

In 2013, internationally acclaimed Turkish vocalist Sabahat Akkiraz performed at the Jerusalem International Oud Festival. At the time of her performance, she was also a member from the Republican People's

Party of the serving parliament, which makes her participation even more significant (Demir, 2017; Ziffer, 2012). Also, for the first time, in 2016, two simultaneous concerts were held in Tel Aviv and Istanbul. The concert series, called Sound Ports Festival Tel Aviv-Istanbul, is a unique musical event that aims to build bridges between the two cultural capitals of the Middle East. The music and arts festival is the first of its kind to take place simultaneously with the collaboration of numerous Turkish and Israeli artists. The festival involves artists from the two countries in an effort to connect the Turkish and Israeli cultures through art that celebrates the diversity of these cultures.

Cem Mansur, the world renowned Turkish conductor, led three concerts at the New Haifa Symphony in 2012. The concerts were attended by thousands of Israeli citizens and proved that music can unite people, even during periods of adversity (Hugi, 2013). Also, Ömer Faruk Tekbilek, a famous Turkish musician/composer, who plays ney, kaval, zurna, oud, and baglama, first performed in Israel in 2003. Since then he frequently gives concerts in Israeli cities and has worked with Yasmin Levy on his recent album. And Özcan Deniz, a famous Turkish singer and actor, is currently known in Israel for his role as Faruk in *The Bride of Istanbul* (*Istanbullu Gelin*). Following the initial success of the series in Israel, Özcan Deniz and Asli Enver, the two lead actors of the show, gained hundreds of thousands of fans across Israel. Özcan Deniz performed in a highly publicized concert in Tel Aviv in 2019, to which tens of thousands of women flocked.

Music adaptations are also very important in Turkish–Israeli musical exchanges. For an average Turkish citizen, the Yiddish folk tune "Az Der Rebe Elimelech" is very familiar in its 1972 Turkish adaptation "Memleketim." Although with very different lyrics, Memleketim is a staple of contemporary Turkish patriotic songs. In the 1970s, musical adaptations between Turkey and Israel were quite common. Turkish musicians adopted a number of Israeli songs of the era, including "Veshuv Itchem" by Ilanit, "Im Nin Alu" by Ofra Haza, and "Bim Bam Bom" by Ilan and Ilanit, all of which were hits. Israeli musicians too adopted songs of popular artists like Zeki Müren and Orhan Gencebay. These exchanges again were a result of cultural proximity as well as the infiltration of arabesque in Turkey and Mizrahi music into Israel (Binicewitz, 2021). Unlike the festival style, exchanges like these adaptations have the potential to reach masses of people who may not know where this music comes from.

Conclusion

Cultural initiatives do not always render the desired results or bring peace between peoples. Rather, what they do is spark an interest in the other culture and this may lead to building bridges. To be sure, isolated artistic approaches do not resolve conflicts, but as supportive approaches to official diplomacy, they provide a space for people to find common issues of interest, collaborate on future projects, and foster dialogue. The function of non-state actors in this regard serves as a transformative source in opening up the public sphere for discussions on relations and in fostering democratization. Furthermore, it demonstrates the agency role of celebrities in facilitating broader discussions within the public sphere.

Turkish–Israeli relations, of course, are far more complex than cultural exchanges can resolve but at the same time the disagreement between the two countries is certainly not comparable to violent ethnic conflicts. Rather, the relations are tense, with conflicting political identities especially when it comes to Israel's relations with Palestinians. A normalization of ties on the political level will require some sort of reconciliation on the public level and an in-depth exploration of heritage for that engagement to be long lasting. In order to reach all layers of society, grassroots cultural engagement that facilitates mutual understanding is essential.

Improving Turkish–Israeli relations requires both societal and political engagement. While diplomacy is working on improving bilateral relations, the societal level cannot be ignored. Music as an art form, an element of culture, is a vehicle to build bridges and unite people on the societal level. There have been many cross-cultural musical exchanges taking place in Turkey and Israel in various formats; however, Israel still remains an unknown regional neighbor for Turkey. The vast collection of music within a shared Turkish–Israeli heritage, including that of the Sephardic Jewish tradition, remains widely unknown, especially in Turkey, but it can be seen as a powerful untapped asset in helping to improve relations on the societal level. Additionally, *maftirims* are an untapped potential for both Turkey and Israel to explore their shared heritage. The maftirim tradition and arabesque music can be a natural audience for Israel, which has an ever-growing Mizrahi demographic.

The execution and impact of music diplomacy projects, in particular, depend on and contribute to a positive political climate. Turkey's past reconciliation efforts with Greece and Armenia point to the importance of political will setting the groundwork for cultural exchanges. Together with the encouragement of the high-level politics, the public sphere in Turkey has been more welcoming dialogue with estranged neighbors. Thus, the recent efforts to normalize ties between Turkey and Israel could further open up cultural channels for a better understanding between Turks and Israelis as neighbors in the Mediterranean.

References

Arsenault, A., & Cowan, G. (2008). Moving from monologue to dialogue to collaboration: The three layers of public diplomacy. *Annals of the American Academy of Political and Social Science*, 616(1): 10–30.

Azar, E. (2002). Protracted social conflicts and second track diplomacy. In: J. L. Davies & E. Kaufman (Eds.), *Second Track Citizens Diplomacy: Concepts and Techniques for Conflict Transformation* (pp. 5–30). Lanham, MD: Rowman & Littlefield.

Berridge, G. R. (2015). *Diplomacy: Theory and Practice*. Basingstoke, UK: Palgrave Macmillan.

Binicewitz, K. (2021). Ladies on records. https://ladiesonrecords.com (last accessed August 9, 2022).

Cull, N. J. (2008). Public diplomacy: Taxonomies and histories. *Annals of the American Academy of Political and Social Science*, 616(1): 31–53.

Davidson, W. D., & Montville, J. M. (1981). Foreign policy according to Freud. *Foreign Affairs*, 45: 145–157.

Demir, M. (2017). Music as a cultural diplomacy between Israel and Turkey (2008–2016). *Idil Journal of Art and Language*, 6(32): 1225–1240.

Elitsoy, Z. A. (2018). Can music act as a diplomatic tool in Turkish–Israeli rapprochement? *Turkeyscope: Insights on Turkish Affairs*. https://dayan.org/content/can-music-act-diplomatic-tool-turkish-israeli-rapprochement (last accessed August 9, 2022).

Fisher, G. H. (1972). *Public Diplomacy and the Behavioral Sciences*. Bloomington, IN: Indiana University Press.

Hocking, B. (2007). Rethinking the new public diplomacy. In: J. Melissen (Ed.), *The New Public Diplomacy: Soft Power in International Relations* (pp. 28–43). New York: Palgrave Macmillan.

Hugi, J. (2013, May 28). Musical bridges between Israel and Turkey. *Al-Monitor.* https://al-monitor.com/originals/2013/05/the-musician-who-bridges-between-israel-and-turkey.html (last accessed August 9, 2022).

Jarman, N. (2009). Policing the peace community-based peacebuilding and political transition. In: J. J. Popiolkowski & N. J. Cull (Eds.), *Public Diplomacy, Cultural Interventions and the Peace Process in Northern Ireland: Track Two to Peace?* (pp. 5–18). Los Angeles, CA: Figueroa.

Kelman, H. C., & Fisher, R. C. (2003). Conflict analysis and reconciliation. In: D. O. Sears, L. Huddy, & R. Jervis (Eds.), *Oxford Handbook of Political Psychology* (pp. 315–353). New York: Oxford University Press.

Laurence, F. (2008). Music and empathy. In: O. Urbain (Ed.), *Music and Conflict Transformation: Harmonies and Dissonances in Geopolitics* (pp. 13–25). London: I. B. Tauris.

Leonard, M., Stead, C., & Sweming, C. (2002). *Public Diplomacy*. London: The Foreign Policy Centre.

Montville, J. V. (1991). The arrow and the olive branch. In: J. Demetrios, J. V. Montville, & V. D. Volkan (Eds.), *The Psychodynamics of International Relationships Vol. II* (pp. 161–175). Lanham, MD: Lexington.

Şarhon, K. G. (2011). Ladino in Turkey: The situation today as reflected by the Ladino Database Project. *European Judaism*, 44(1): 62–71.

Şaul, L. (2015). Sefarad Şarkilarininin Tarihçesi, Oluşumu Ve Yapisi (History, formation and structure of Sephardic songs). *Ege Üniversitesi Devlet Türk Musikisi Konservatuvarı Dergisi*, 2015(7): 111–119.

Saunders, H. H. (2001). *A Public Peace Process: Sustained Dialogue to Transform Racial and Ethnic Conflicts*. Basingstoke, UK: Palgrave Macmillan.

Saunders, H. H. (2005). *Politics Is About Relationships*. Basingstoke, UK: Palgrave Macmillan.

Saunders, H. H. (2014). The relational paradigm and sustained dialogue. In: A. Arsenault, A. Fisher, & R. S. Zaharna (Eds.), *Relational, Networked, and Collaborative Approaches to Public Diplomacy: The Connective Mindshift* (pp. 132–143). New York: Routledge.

Schneider, C. P. (2007). Culture communicates: US diplomacy that works. In: J. Melissen (Ed.), *The New Public Diplomacy: Soft Power in International Relations* (pp. 147–168). Basingstoke, UK: Palgrave Macmillan.

Tokyay, M. (2012, February 27). Turkey and Israel keep bonds alive through music. *The Jerusalem Post*. https://jpost.com/Diplomacy-and-Politics/Turkey-and-Israel-keep-bonds-alive-through-music (last accessed August 9, 2022).

Urbain, O. (2008). Introduction. In: O. Urbain (Ed.), *Music and Conflict Transformation: Harmonies and Dissonances in Geopolitics* (pp. 1–9). London: I. B. Tauris.

Wiseman, G. (2010). Engaging the enemy: An essential norm for sustainable US diplomacy. In: C. M. Constantinou & J. D. Derian (Eds.), *Sustainable Diplomacies* (pp. 213–234). Basingstoke, UK: Palgrave Macmillan.

Ziffer, B. (2012, August 31). Musical diplomacy between Turkey and Israel. *Haaretz*. http://haaretz.com/israel-news/musical-diplomacy-between-turkey-and-israel-1.461992 (last accessed October 9, 2022).

CHAPTER 12

Multiple layers of laws and legal structures: a challenge to rendering justice and a source of identity crisis

Hiba Husseini

In any comparative study of laws and legal systems, Palestine represents an exceptional case, given its unique history. The legal system and structures in Palestine are complex, reflecting a plethora of legal heritage imposed by the foreign regimes that have ruled over Palestine throughout its history: customary practices and traditions passed on from one generation to the next; then the codification of such practices into rules and written laws; Jewish and Christian and Moslem Sharia norms and principles; followed by the formal introduction of laws during the Ottoman rule period stretching from 1550–1917; British Mandate laws from 1917–48; Egyptian and Jordanian laws applied in the Gaza Strip and the West Bank respectively from 1948–67; and Israeli laws and military orders from 1967–94 applied in the West Bank and the Gaza Strip.

With the advent of the Palestinian Government in 1994, a unification and harmonization process of laws started, only to be challenged from 2007 to the present by the national intra-Palestinian split between the Gaza Strip and the West Bank. The de facto government in the Gaza Strip suspended the harmonization and started to introduce new laws and regulations that are different from those applicable in the West Bank and Jerusalem. What is true of the laws is also true of the judiciary, the courts, and legal institutions. Accordingly, the justice system in Palestine is complex and often leads to conflicting applications of the law; even legal precedent is conflicted. However, while there are too many layers in some areas of the law, in other areas there are lacunae. Customary practices and informal alternative dispute resolution run parallel to the formal legal system and the judiciary.

All of these laws have been imposed by nations that ruled Palestine with the aim of advancing their own political agendas. The result is that there is now no "national" Palestinian legislation, serving Palestinian national interests, reflecting Palestinian national policies, and addressing the needs and interests of Palestinian individuals. Instead, those who have ruled Palestine over time acted in the service of their own policies, which aimed at furthering their interests at the cost of those subjected to their rule.

One consequence of having layers of laws imposed by different ruling nations is the territorial divisions that resulted. This has led to changing the names of the geographical spaces in which Palestinians live, or associating the name politically with whoever is controlling the land. It was Palestine during the Ottoman Empire and during the British Mandate from 1917–48, then the West Bank and Gaza Strip during the Jordanian/Egyptian rule from 1948–67, and has been the Occupied Palestinian Territories since 1967. In 1948, part of historic Palestine became part of the newly founded state of Israel.

Today, East Jerusalem is occupied Palestinian territory and regarded as the capital of the future state of Palestine; but, for Israelis, it, along with West Jerusalem, is the eternal capital of the state of Israel. As a case in point, in 1980, Israel formally annexed East Jerusalem and extended its legal jurisdiction over it and its residents, applying its laws in a selective and discriminatory fashion, with the aim of constraining and limiting Palestinian presence in the city. Further, Israel continues to maintain the upper hand in controlling the sea, air, and external land borders and the movement between the West Bank and the Gaza Strip, as well as within the West Bank. There are also territorial divisions within the West Bank: Areas A, B, and C, as designated in Article XI of the Oslo II agreement.

(Subsequent agreements have also referred to these three areas, including: Washington Declaration, July 25, 1994; Agreement on Preparatory Transfer of Powers and Responsibilities Between Israel and the PLO,

August 29, 1994; Protocol on Further Transfer of Powers and Responsibilities signed in Cairo on August 27, 1995; Interim Agreement on the West Bank and the Gaza Strip (Oslo II), September 28, 1995; Protocol Concerning the Redeployment in Hebron, January 15/January 17, 1997; Wye River Memorandum, October 23, 1998; Sharm El-Sheikh Memorandum on Implementation of Outstanding Commitments of Agreements Signed and the Resumption of Permanent Status Negotiations, September 4, 1999; and the Agreement on Movement and Access, November 15, 2005. The list of major summits or negotiations not leading to a final agreement includes: Madrid Peace Conference, October 30–November 1, 1991; Secret Talks in Stockholm, summer 2000; Camp David Summit, July 11–25, 2000; The Clinton Parameters, December 19–23, 2000; Taba Summit, January 21–27, 2001; Arab Peace Initiative, endorsed at Arab Summit Conference in Beirut on March 28, 2002; The Roadmap for Peace, April 30, 2003; Geneva Initiative, October 12, 2003; Annapolis Conference, November 27, 2007; George Mitchell-Led Talks, starting on September 2, 2010; and John Kerry-Led Talks, starting on July 29, 2013.)

Movement and access are defined in each of these areas. In Area C, Israel applies a mixture of Jordanian law and Israeli military orders. All of this affects residency permits, day-to-day activity, and business activity (as outlined in Article IX of Annex I, titled Protocol Concerning Redeployment and Security Arrangements of the Israeli-Palestinian Interim Agreement on the West Bank and the Gaza Strip). When Hamas and Fatah split in 2007, yet another name was created, this time by Israel, the international community, and Palestinians themselves: a Hamas Government in the Gaza Strip and Fatah Government in the West Bank.

As a result of these various legal regimes, territorial divisions, and different names, the sense of belonging for the Palestinian people has been deeply injured, a feeling further exacerbated by the fragmentation and lack of contiguity of Palestinian lands. In turn, this has contributed to a profound identity crisis and has deeply affected the Palestinian social fabric. Palestinians from the West Bank feel alienated from those in the Gaza Strip and vice versa; and Palestinians from East Jerusalem feel alienated from both the West Bankers and the Gazans. Moreover, after Israel was created in 1948 and part of historic Palestine became known as the state of Israel, some Palestinians remained in or returned to this area.

These Palestinian citizens of Israel, who are known as "Arab Israelis" to other Israelis (Israel does not recognize them as "Palestinians") or "1948 Palestinians" to other Palestinians, feel alienated from their Israeli compatriots and, to a lesser degree, from Palestinians in the West Bank and Gaza. Likewise, Palestinian refugees in Arab countries and the Palestinian diaspora are alienated from those in the Occupied Territories. (At the end of 2019, the number of Palestinian refugees in Arab countries was 5.986 million; in non-Arab countries 727,000; the Palestinian diaspora totaled 6.713 million; Palestinians in the West Bank totaled 3.020 million; and Palestinians in the Gaza Strip totaled 2.019 million. Source: http://pcbs.gov.ps/Downloads/book2497.pdf.)

But there are two sides to the coin of Palestinian identity, alienation being the most negative aspect. There is also a positive, collective sense of identity, very strongly experienced in response to the occupation. A future challenge may well be how to transform this reactive sense of positive identity into something proactive and independent of the oppressive other.

Legal quandaries

The historical background of the Palestinian people has created many legal quandaries. A mélange of historic layers of laws and regulations currently operate in concert. This blend of laws borrows from an ancient heritage and various traditions of jurisprudence, philosophy and theory, norms, reasoning, and precedent, emanating from old Byzantine and canon law, the Napoleonic code, Ottoman civil laws, Anglo-Saxon common law, principles of Sharia law, and more recently from Continental laws "Arabized" in the entire Arab world, though with different nuances. This has opened the door to having sets of laws in conflict with each other, and has led to considerable debate about the legal system to be developed for Palestine.

All of these legal traditions have had a profound influence on rendering justice and have led to confused and unfair application of the law with often contradictory rulings. This, in turn, has made the legal system too complex to reform. This is a challenge not only for legal scholars, law students, lawyers, judges, and lawmakers, but most importantly for Palestinian nationals, whose rights can be preempted or trampled because of this lack of clarity. Thus the justice system itself is rendered uncertain and unreliable, and too often fails to provide legal "standing" to a person whose personal sense of "standing" has been so diminished by oppression.

Legal education has also been a reflection of this assorted, complex, and challenging background, because it has adversely affected the education system's ability to provide clarity. This is especially true because teaching law in Palestine is relatively nascent. There was no legal education offered in Palestine from 1948–94. The Palestinian Law Institute, established in Jerusalem in 1922, offered legal education for some years until it closed at the end of the British Mandate, as Anne Bourland discussed in her 1997 paper on "The Teaching of Law in Palestine." Otherwise, the study of law was possible only for those who could afford to study abroad, either in neighboring or other Arab countries (Jordan, Syria, Lebanon, Iraq, Egypt, Algeria, Morocco, and Tunisia), in Europe, especially England and France, and more recently, the US and Canada. Only in 1994 was the first Palestinian-run law school established, at Al-Quds University.

As can be imagined, each of these educational jurisdictions has a different training system and study methodology. It is often not clear what legal skills and knowledge students receive and what research and analytical skills they acquire. Furthermore, it's unclear whether whatever skills students acquire are up to the task of dealing with the complex legal issues in an emerging system like Palestine's. Students, later to become practitioners, are generally not familiar with the peculiarities of the historic legal traditions and layers of law in Palestine, which make the Palestinian legal system much harder to navigate than other systems. Once law schools were established in Palestine, the challenge became how to design courses to tackle legal education, both at the substantive and procedural levels and in a uniform way, given that there was essentially "no autonomous and unified Palestinian law to teach," in Bourland's words. A direct consequence of this is that legal scholarship and practice became difficult to pursue and apply in a coherent and consistent manner. Instead of being forward looking and prescriptive, legal scholarship has become either stale or merely descriptive.

To add to the difficulty for legal training (and, of course, for citizens), it is not uncommon that court rulings, even at the Supreme Court level, can be substantively contradictory, making the setting of precedent difficult. Recently, for example, the Supreme Court rendered two different rulings on the same legal question: there is a vague provision in the Labor Law regarding prior notification to the Ministry of Labor of the termination of an employee's employment status, but does the Labor Law require such a prior notification or not? Similarly, because differences in the educational backgrounds of judges impact the way they interpret the law, Palestinian lawyers may opt for choosing the court that will treat their clients' claims more favorably. This resembles forum shopping but happens within the same jurisdiction rather than in situations where several courts have concurrent jurisdiction over the same claims. For example, motions for expedited orders are heavily based on the discretion of judges. One judge may consider a matter to have imminent adverse implications, thus triggering the need for an expedited order, while another may decide otherwise. Attorneys make every effort to appear before one, not the other, knowing how they would rule.

Another significant consequence to this confusing and chaotic legal legacy is the lawmaking process itself. Except for a short-lived period between 1962 and 1965, when the first legislative council in Palestine was instituted under Egyptian rule in Gaza (which only had a mandate over the Gaza Strip and was not very active due to political unrest), Palestine had no legislative process for the introduction, review, and adoption of legislation. This remained the case until the advent of the Palestinian Government and the establishment of the Legislative Council in 1996, as a result of the Oslo Accords. Aside from these two brief periods, Palestine has never gone through a full legislative process of review, consultation, and debate. In other words, lawmaking lacked the legal characteristics and process transparency afforded to most systems where democratic rule governs.

More recently came another period full of promise. In 1996, a national legislative council was elected in a democratic election. The Legislative Council assumed its role and functions and embarked on a massive undertaking of adopting laws, unifying and harmonizing the West Bank and Gaza laws. They also established through legislation the first Supreme Court presiding over appeals from Gaza and the West Bank. This was a short-lived achievement, lasting from 1996–2007, only to be marred by the political schism between Fatah and Hamas following the

Palestinian Legislative Council elections in 2006. These elections failed to form a unified government for a multitude of reasons. Chief among them were three: first, Israel and the international community had long deemed Hamas a "terrorist" organization; second, Fatah refused to join a national unity government with Hamas; and third, Hamas failed to agree on key ministerial posts and security related arrangements in the Gaza Strip.

As a result, Hamas took de facto control over the Gaza Strip while Fatah maintained control over the West Bank. This has led to the establishment of two different "governments" in each part of the Palestinian Territories, and has left the Palestinian Legislative Council in a state of paralysis, leading to its suspension in 2007, and later its dissolution in 2018—all at the very early stage of the harmonization, modernization, and updating of the laws. So much of the legal authority and law remain antiquated and inapplicable, leaving significant areas of the law in a state of uncertainty. Here again, Palestinian nationals find themselves caught in time and unable to trust the legal system or its outcomes.

No checks or balances

Since the Palestinian legislature was suspended, and then dissolved, lawmaking in the West Bank is solely within the power of the president, who issues laws by decree (executive orders), relying on a provision (Article 43) in 2003 Basic Law (Palestine's Interim Constitution) granting the president such power "in cases of necessity ... and when the Legislative Council is not in session". Moreover, the Council of Ministers in Ramallah has also been issuing rules and regulations in large volume, sometimes in contravention of established laws or superseding them when they should be subordinated to them. The Council thereby ignores the hierarchy of laws or the substance of the law. The president has signed 260 decrees into law, according to the Palestinian National Authority (PNA), exceeding his national emergency powers and making those powers the "new normal."

In Gaza, the Hamas government has continued to convene a legislative council, and has issued laws and regulations with limited territorial applicability to Gaza only. This has contributed to further legal segmentation between the different Palestinian territories, has deepened the legal complexity already in place, and has rendered legal harmonization between the West Bank and the Gaza Strip less likely. Through its legislature, the Hamas government has issued more than 160 laws, as recorded on the Palestinian Legislative Council's (PLC) website (further analysis of this has been made by Mahmoud Alawneh et al. in their 2014 paper, "The Impact of Political Division on the Rule of Law Principle in the Gaza Strip"). Further, the Hamas government has established its own Supreme Court. So now Palestine has two Supreme Courts, one in the West Bank and the other in Gaza.

The challenges encountered in the legal system are reflected in the separation of powers among the three branches of government, especially the judiciary. Legislative elections were scheduled to take place in May 2021, which would have been the first elections since 2006. However, President Mahmoud Abbas postponed them amid a dispute over voting and the participation of Jerusalemites in the election. In the absence of a well-functioning legislature, the checks and balances, especially over the powers of the executives, are seriously restricted. The judicial authority has not been immune to the consequences of the inconsistent Palestinian legal system, the unstable political situation, and the challenges triggered by the internal political split. There is currently a bifurcation in judicial authority—two judicial councils and two attorneys general: one in the West Bank and the other in the Gaza Strip. This draws judicial authority into the political division as it becomes yet another tool for executive authority to tap into as it seeks to keep a tight grip on all powers.

Interference by the executive branch in the judiciary seriously harms the principles of judicial independence, impartiality, and the rule of law. It undermines public confidence in the judiciary's integrity and institutional performance, and makes judicial power less reliable in providing prompt, efficient, and impartial justice to the Palestinian people. The appointment of judges is too often based on nepotism, and thus judges are not well qualified, having reached the judiciary without rigorous years of experience and training. There are many further examples of executive interference into the judiciary, including: the appointment of chairs of the High Judicial Council (HJC); requesting HJC chairs to sign a resignation letter before they are appointed; the establishment of the Presidential Committee for the Development of the Justice Sector;

the dissolution of the permanent HJC; the formation of a transitional HJC; the forced transfer of several judges to retirement against their will; and the secondment of judges to non-judicial government jobs while preserving their judicial capacity and privileges.

Further, enforcement of judicial decisions is often compromised and delayed. For example, the Supreme Court of Justice reversed a government decision to terminate employment of public school teachers on political grounds (for example, Case No. 209/2009) but it was not enforced for two years after the decision (Council of Ministers Decision No. 1/5/17 of 2014). Sometimes, court rulings are not enforced at all. For instance, an order issued by the Supreme Court expressly requiring the Secretary General of the Palestinian Council of Ministers to provide the court with a copy of Council meeting minutes was met with an apologetic reply and a refusal to provide the requested document for reasons of confidentiality (see Supreme Court of Justice Order dated 28/2/2010 in Case No. 24/2010). These examples are a few of many that indicate how the system of legal redress too often fails to provide justice because the executive branch abuses its power. It is as though the history of the exercise of power over Palestine continues within its own government, thereby undermining the development of institutional structures whose reliable functioning would help the Palestinian people emerge from that traumatic history.

Let us look at another example of the unanticipated consequences of fragmented power in Palestine. In 1929, the British Mandate introduced a Companies Law in Palestine, prior to which the Ottoman civil code, known as the *Mejelle*, applied. The Companies Law, layered on top of the *Mejelle*, remained applicable in Palestine until the Jordanian/Egyptian rule, when the West Bank was split from the Gaza Strip, and different Companies Laws were thereafter applied in each jurisdiction: by Egypt, the Companies Law of 1929 in Gaza; by Jordan the Jordanian Company Law of 1964 in the West Bank. Israel kept both laws in force. Then came an attempt to unify West Bank and Gaza laws by the Palestinian Government in 1996. After extensive review and debate, a unified and harmonized draft was submitted to the Legislation Council in 2008. But then Fatah and Hamas split. Hamas adopted the 2008 draft for Gaza, but the Fatah government in the West Bank did not. The substantive discrepancies between these two laws have considerable financial implications for companies' behavior, shareholder rights, corporate structure, governance and reporting, and investment opportunities, among other things. The same analysis applies to criminal law, torts and civil wrongs, taxation laws, court procedures, and evidence, all of which differ between the West Bank and the Gaza Strip.

With regard to real property rights, the West Bank has more than twenty-seven different laws governing land rights and transactions, making it difficult and complex for all concerned, from judges to lawyers to owners and buyers/sellers to understand the rules that apply. By contrast, the Gaza Strip has one uniform law, which dates back to the Ottoman rule period (1858). In the West Bank, the twenty-seven laws start with the Ottoman version, but with modifications introduced by the British during the Palestine Mandate, followed by more amendments by the Jordanians during their period of rule. More significant were changes made by Israel during the occupation period, which continue to impact land rights in Area C (constituting over 60 percent of the West Bank) to this day. All land-related transactions are now under full control of the Israeli authorities, and those land rights are seriously impacted by Israeli politics, policies, and facts on the ground, including the expansion of Israeli settlements. Law upon law upon law, leading to diffusion of authority and opening another door to the exercise of power.

Land and water

Indeed, Israel's control of the West Bank gave it a free hand to confiscate land in the name of security and to expand the settlement buildup. Today, it continues to expand its territory systematically and to transfer land from Palestinians to Israeli settlers. A case in point is what is happening as of the time of this writing in Jerusalem, particularly in the Sheikh Jarrah neighborhood (the author is a resident of the neighborhood). Four Palestinian families are facing forced eviction from their homes in an attempt to hand over the properties to Israeli settlers. This is leading to major clashes between Palestinian and Israeli residents of the entire city, not just the neighborhood, causing serious instability. The settlements, deemed illegal under international law, along with a separation wall, form a ring around the entire occupied part of Jerusalem, sealing it off from the rest of the West Bank. Further, Israel engaged in systematic planning for the buildup and expansion of the settlements in the West Bank, which is tantamount to confiscation of land and natural resources, especially water. This also deprives Palestinians of access to their agricultural lands, which for centuries constituted their livelihood. Without access to water and land, agricultural production and agrobusiness has declined, such that it is now a nonproductive sector of the economy. Thus, this use of Israeli power is certainly a challenge to some Palestinians at the level of basic subsistence, but it is also an identity challenge—an assault on a centuries old way of life for many and on a sense of one's country's integrity.

With respect to water, Palestinians do not receive their equitable share, which together with confiscation of occupied land is a breach of international law. Without control over natural resources (especially water), Palestinians have no option except to buy their water from Israeli companies at high prices, while Israel makes available more water to its illegal settlements. Israel also adopts discriminatory measures to deprive Palestinians of their right to access and control water resources. For instance, on the one hand, Israel restricts Palestinians' right to drill new wells or even to pump or deepen existing ones, but it approves, without delay, wells for Israeli settlements and allows their drilling deeper into the aquifer. Israeli settlements also benefit from a massive Israeli network of roads and related infrastructure. Settlers have free access to this system but Palestinians have restrictions on movement through a cobweb of security checkpoints. To achieve settlement objectives, Israel issues military orders or makes ad hoc security orders for each confiscation of land, whether it be public or private (for more on these orders, see https://bit.ly/3biaTZJ, https://bit.ly/33cTFIx, and https://bit.ly/2RiJT50, accessible only in Arabic, last accessed on May 4, 2021). These orders can be issued without notice and often no legal redress is afforded to Palestinians. As a consequence, unanticipated or strategic, the confiscation of land and resources limits the contiguity and economic viability of the West Bank.

Another law that "legitimizes" the confiscation of Palestinian lands by Israel is the Absentees' Property Law (1951). This law places properties belonging to Palestinians who are not physically present—labeled "absentees"—under Israeli control. Such "absenteeism" was a consequence of 1948 and 1967 when Israel either displaced Palestinians or prevented them from returning home, before stripping them of the land. Today, especially in East Jerusalem, this law is still frequently used by Israel to take possession of lands belonging to Palestinian refugees forced to flee their homes during the 1948 War (the Nakba). The law makes it difficult, if not impossible, to obtain licenses to build (issued by Israel) or to complete property transactions. It is applied automatically to property considered "absentee property," often leading to significant delay in the owners' finding out that their property has been lost. Usually, Palestinians don't learn that their property is now under Israel's control until they try to initiate a sale/transfer transaction or else to seek a construction permit. Therefore, Israel on the one hand issues discriminatory laws to take land and on the other cuts Palestinians off from those laws.

The law's application was extended to property held by Palestinians in East Jerusalem following the 1967 War (see: https://bit.ly/3eVh9r2, last accessed on May 4, 2021). Its reach is broad. Most privately owned land in Palestine is held in common (i.e., in private family ownership); under this law, if one member is deemed "absent"—even though the others are physically present—the Absentee Property Law established a function for a custodian who holds the "absentee" shares in custody on behalf of the absentee. In effect and in practice, the property is taken by the custodian because it can never be returned to the absentee. This is tantamount to stripping ownership from the family. This legal entanglement concerning land rights is very critical for Palestinians. After all, land is at the heart of the Palestinian–Israeli conflict. Israel strips the rights of Palestinians to land ownership by way of a law that itself violates international law.

A living example is the Separation Wall. Israel, citing security reasons, began building the Wall in 2002, but on Palestinian land. Seemingly enacting Israel's land grab policy, the Wall incorporates Israeli settlements on the "Israeli" side. To do this geographically, large tracts of land belonging to Palestinians had to be carved out and seized, cutting many Palestinians off from their livelihood and preventing access to education, social services, and natural resources, especially water. In effect, the Wall separates Palestinians from Palestinians at the same time as it separates Israelis from Palestinians. The very presence of the

Separation Wall as well as of Israeli settlements in the Occupied Territories is a source of instability and resentment and a trigger for clashes between the Palestinian population and the armed settlers. The settlements also have a serious impact on the socioeconomic and humanitarian conditions of the Palestinians, who suffer continued harassment and humiliation on top of economic loss.

Occupation

All this is happening under the overarching spectrum of occupation of the entire Palestinian territory, with its severe impact on every facet of life. The shadow of the occupation does not leave Palestinians. Coping becomes strained and manifests itself in various problematic behaviors or positions, some of which are self-harming, like the ideological split between Fatah and Hamas. The entire national project of independence and ending the occupation has fallen victim to this self-inflicted injury. Israel and some of its proponents in the international community have used the split within Palestine—which can be seen as a self-destructive response to occupation—to continue the occupation, by labeling Hamas a terrorist organization and boycotting talks with it.

The trauma of occupation is deep and manifests itself in defiant actions, both by individuals and groups, like Fatah and Hamas. Palestinians themselves undermine the rule of law in response to Israel's disrespecting it—especially international law, norms, and conventions—when it comes to Palestine. Today, psychological barriers are increasing, and the emotional separation is deepening between Palestinians. This is not only true between West Bank and Gaza Strip Palestinians; East Jerusalem Palestinians also feel alienated from their fellow Palestinians, as do Palestinian refugees in the Arab world, especially Lebanon, Jordan, and Syria. The layer of Israeli laws and military orders is one that Palestinians have to abide by, despite their being discriminatory and prejudicial, and therein lies a significant mental and emotional dimension to the occupation. No greater trauma befalls Palestinians than those who have to demolish their own homes by themselves because Israel military orders were issued to that effect.

The Oslo Accords, meant ideally to resolve this profound conflict about land, added to the legal complexity by producing more than eleven accords, protocols, and plans. The agreement created another layer of legal constructs that impacts Palestinian lives and rights, and that each Palestinian has to learn to accept, even though they contradict the very notion of freedom and basic human rights. Let us take a few short examples. The Civil Register (births and deaths) is administrated by the Palestinian government (one in Gaza and one in the West Bank); however, the issuance of identification cards (which start at age sixteen) is subject to the approval of the Israeli authorities, as per Article 28 of Annex III titled Protocol Concerning Civil Affairs of the Israeli–Palestinian Interim Agreement on the West Bank and the Gaza Strip. The same is true of the Palestinian passport. Moving one's place of residency within the West Bank or from Gaza to the West Bank is subject to the approval of the Israeli authorities. There are a number of cases where Israel has refused to recognize the Palestinian registration of a birth; and so at age sixteen, the person cannot receive Israeli approval for the issuance of the identification card nor receive a passport for travel. Thus, this individual cannot move through checkpoints and is effectively "stateless."

With respect to trade and imports, all goods have to pass through Israeli borders and are subject to Israeli security clearance. This, in turn, leads to delays, a very high transactional cost, and payment of demurrage. Palestinian import tariffs are based on the rates prevailing in Israel, which for Palestine are very high. The same is true of value added tax (VAT). In effect, the economic and monetary policies of Israel dictate the rates applicable in Palestine—a financial burden far exceeding the capacity of a nascent economy totally dependent on international aid. Both the tariff and VAT arrangements are laid out in the Israeli–Palestinian Interim Agreement on the West Bank and the Gaza Strip, which was due to apply for only a transitional period not exceeding five years from the date of signing in 1995. But the "Interim" Agreement remains applicable to this day, to the detriment of Palestinians' needs and rights.

The challenge

Palestinians are trapped in layers of legal constructs totally out of their control, which together create a legal regime difficult to decipher and trust. So legal manipulation is rampant. People feel that a "devilish" lawyer is their only chance to avoid having their rights trampled upon. In response to chronic helplessness and frustration, Palestinians are, in a sense, invited to counter a chaotic and often corrupt system by joining in the corruption themselves, further diminishing the personal integrity necessary to sustain the integrity of the overarching cause.

Thus, a major challenge in Palestine is establishing a trustworthy and predictable legal system based on a consistent set of laws and their consistent application and interpretation: this in contrast to a system based on conflicting or politically driven policies/agendas, be they intra-Palestinian or inter Israeli–Palestinian. The multiple legal regimes and the unreliable judicial system currently in place have had a profound psychological impact on anyone seeking to assert a "right" or enforce an obligation. Indeed, how can rights be redressed when they are subject to so many overlapping interpretations? Palestinians may well opt out of participating in the legal system because the "system" they are compelled to interact with is hopelessly confusing, duplicative, unstable, and unreliable. Whimsical, capricious, and even abusive rulings (favoring parties in the litigation because of connections or other subjective considerations) are issued, and all this unfair adjudication of rights is justified under the guise and cover of the multilayered laws.

No wonder that the individual and group identities of Palestinians manifest as trauma. It stems from a long history of being ruled and occupied by different nations imposing their respective laws, whims, and practices—all serving to undermine Palestinian group identity and negate its national aspirations. The intra-Palestinian schism between the Palestinian center represented by Fatah and the right represented by Hamas continues this long history of enforced fragmentation. Those Palestinians on the left are either left alone, trying to understand what is happening, or so sidelined that they suffer their own trauma of isolation and feeling like an outsider in one's own homeland.

As a consequence, Palestinians, both as individuals and as a group, feel insecure, victimized, and underprivileged. The justice system to them is one of hardship. The sense of injustice they experienced as an occupied people led to their having no trust at all in the judiciary during the official Israeli occupation years (1967 to 1994). This mistrust, of course, lingers on today because the occupation has not ended, even if it seems to have taken a different shape. It is the invisible hand that still operates very strongly to curtail rights, liberties, and the dream of statehood. In the absence of a fair solution to the Israeli–Palestinian conflict and an intra-Palestinian reconciliation, trauma will persist and healing is not foreseeable. No wonder there are multiple layers to the legal construct, given that the core source of trauma has never been addressed and remains a major psychological barrier to reaching peace, justice, and the rule of law. Unless that core source—the occupation and its history in Palestine—is addressed, trauma will continue to manifest itself in different shapes and forms in the long term and will have ever worsening consequences politically, socially, and on every other aspect of daily life.

Since my graduation from the Georgetown Law Center in 1992, and my participation as a legal advisor to the Palestinian Team in the Israeli–Palestinian Negotiations, starting in 1994 to the present, while at the same time as a practicing attorney-at-law, heading the only female-led law firm in Palestine starting in 1997, I have initiated and created many legal development initiatives, having to do with both laws and institutions. My desire to work on the growth of the law stems from the fact that Palestine's reputation among its citizens and globally would be greatly served by its becoming a rule-based society with reliable and trustworthy systems, especially since it relies on international law as a premise to ending the Israeli occupation. In that regard, being a fellow of the International Dialogue Initiative (IDI) has brought yet another dimension to my long commitment to Palestine: the opportunity to understand the group identity of Palestinians traumatized by a long history of being ruled and occupied by different nations, all of which imposed their respective laws, whims, and practices and all of which undermined our group identity and negated our national aspirations. As such, Palestinians continue to experience instability in an unpredictable political and legal system, causing them ongoing anxieties and deepening trauma.

Reference

Alawneh, M., Hammad, A., & Barghouti, R. (2014). *Law and Politics in the Gaza Strip: The Impact of the Palestinian Internal Political Division on the Rule of Law.* The Institute of Law, Birzeit University: 15–56.

CHAPTER 13

Religious identity and shared trauma: the First Crusade

Ford Rowan

When I was a young man—long before I envisioned becoming an attorney (along with Hiba Husseini and David Fromm, one of the three Georgetown law graduates in this volume)—I heard horrifying accounts about the trauma in my family. My grandmother told me dreadful stories of the Trail of Tears. She was a Choctaw, one of the tribes forcibly removed from their ancestral land by President Andrew Jackson in the 1830s. She recounted how her parents and uncles and aunts were herded on foot from the tribe's land in Mississippi to reservations in Oklahoma. I heard tales of injury and death on the Trail of Tears.

I did not realize until after my grandmother died at age ninety-six that she was not an eyewitness. She was born about half a century *after* the Trail of Tears. She had inherited the trauma—and its continuing manifestation—and it was a major factor in her decision to move off the Choctaw reservation where she was born, get a college education (she was the first person to graduate from college in my family), and get elected as a tax assessor in Wharton County, Texas. She advised me "to never let anyone know you are a Choctaw." I assume she was warning that my tribal identity could lead to discrimination and exclusion.

This was my first experience of what Vamık Volkan, one of the founders of the IDI, calls the transgenerational transmission of trauma (2006). Trauma haunts America whenever pain is handed down from one generation to another. One of the reasons it did not have a traumatic impact in my own life is that I am mostly white—the result of intermarriage of white colonists from Europe with Choctaw brides and of the openness of the tribe to intermarriage.

Fast forward to the early 1960s and the civil rights protests in the US: I am a young news reporter, and I am covering the integration of the University of Mississippi by the first black student, James Meredith. I will never forget the violence of the white student riots as Meredith was admitted with the help of federal marshals. What I did not learn until four decades later is that Meredith and I are members of the same tribe, the Choctaws. His ancestors were black slaves who escaped from slavery in New Orleans, were welcomed by the tribe, and intermarried. My ancestors included white colonists who married Choctaw brides. I learned how Meredith's ancestor, Chief Sam Cobb, had refused to sign the Treaty of Dancing Rabbit Creek, which sent most of the Choctaws onto the Trail of Tears to Oklahoma. My ancestor, Chief Greenwood Leflore, did sign the removal treaty, causing the forced exodus to Oklahoma. Meredith's ancestors hid in the woods in Mississippi to escape the Trail of Tears (Meredith, 1995).

There are many other trails of tears in Western history, and the travails of refugees fleeing oppression or otherwise forced from their homes are broadcast widely even now. But one trail—from Europe to the Middle East in the eleventh century—led to centuries of tears in the relationship among the Abrahamic religions. The fight between Christians, Muslims, and Jews was over the Holy Land. Christians called it a Crusade.

As a person of faith who has worked for interfaith social justice, racial reconciliation, criminal justice reform, and reducing the psychological barriers to peace, I want to understand how three religions that preach peace can inflict such violent destruction on other people of faith. That brought me to examine what may be the foundational conflict in East-West relations. Many Americans think of the Crusades as ancient history. But for people now living in the Middle East, the Crusades still seem very much alive and profoundly unwell.

Indeed, a few days after the 9/11 attacks on the World Trade Center and the Pentagon, President George W. Bush described America's impending military response as "this crusade, this war on terrorism," the purpose of which was to "rid the world of evil-doers" (Waldman & Pope, 2001). After the 9/11 attacks, I focused some of my work on how religious violence undermined the emphasis on peace propounded in all three of the Abrahamic religions. I studied at the Ecumenical Institute of St. Mary's Seminary in Baltimore and began online courses in history at the Harvard extension school, eventually finishing twenty courses and a thesis on religious violence. Some of what I learned is recounted below (Rowan, 2019).

The First Crusade and the "Just War"

Psychological concepts of large group identity, distrust of other ethnic groups, the appeal of martyrdom, and other emotional dynamics all provide insights into what motivated thousands of people to join the First Crusade (1096–99) and to take up arms, walk more than a thousand miles, and fight numerous battles—all in an effort to conquer Jerusalem. To understand the persistent pain in the Mideast, one must consider how violence was rationalized before and during the Crusades, leading to a series of traumatic events that have influenced behaviors and attitudes across generations. Psychological insights may well increase our understanding of how those who feel that their ancestors were victims can themselves become victimizers and oppressors. And lessons from past violence can inform contemporary efforts at peacemaking and interfaith cooperation.

Judaism, Christianity, and Islam were all born in bloodshed, as victims, aggressors, or both. The Hebrews escaped slavery and had to fight to win the Promised Land. Christians were persecuted after Jesus's execution by the Romans. From the beginning, Mohammad had to fight for the survival and growth of his faith. Sometimes, fighting seemed a family affair, with one part of a clan fighting the other over who was in charge of its "home" or founding ideology. Given the birth pains of all three religions, a fight over the Holy Land was not an anomaly. But intra-faith tensions were as much to blame as conflict among the three traditions. The Crusades evolved not simply from a Christian reaction to Muslim expansion generally and occupation of Jerusalem specifically. They also grew from tensions within Christian society—a society not too far removed from the tribal violence of the Dark Ages—and disagreements between Greek Orthodox and Roman Catholics. Jihad, often described as the Muslim response to the Crusades, initially resulted from fractures within Islam itself, especially the Sunni-Shia split.

Intra-faith violence has occurred throughout history; for example, when the chief priests of the Jews persecuted early followers of an observant Jew named Jesus of Nazareth. The first Christians also argued among themselves, but quickly became the victims of violent persecution by the Romans. Many zealots wanted Jesus to be a military savior, a role he refused (Kimball, 2020) both implicitly and explicitly, in his teachings, eschewing violence as a solution to conflict. But some early Christians purged other followers of Christ whom they denounced as heretics—a trend continuing in horrific form during the Inquisition following the Protestant Reformation. In the early centuries, Latin Christians crusaded against Greek Orthodox Christians, and, indeed, the first victims of Crusader violence were Jews, not Muslims.

While all three faiths resorted to violence, they also disavowed forced conversions. This meant that, until the Crusades, most people lived according to their own religious mores and traditions. One oft-cited example of this is the "peaceful coexistence" of Muslims, Christians, and Jews under Islamic rule of the Iberian Peninsula from the eighth to the fifteenth centuries. Given Christ's teachings, violence was a theological problem for Christianity. Indeed, "Christianity and war were incompatible," according to John Ferguson (1978, p. 103). The strong pacifist belief at the heart of Christianity was exemplified by Jesus who urged his followers to "love your enemies, bless them that curse you, do good to them that hate you" (Matthew 5:44). Nonetheless, in the late fourth century, Saint Augustine developed a formula that, under certain circumstances, permitted violence—primarily to protect the innocent in what came to be called a "Just War."

Among the acceptable conditions for permissible warfare was the recovery of property that had been wrongfully seized—a rationale that was later applied to Islamic control of the Holy Land (Claster, 2009, p. xviii). Because Jesus had preached that victims should "turn the other cheek," Augustine argued that *individuals* could not use self-defense as an excuse to fight force with force, but a *government* could command individual soldiers to fight aggressors. His example was the Roman Empire, which, by the time he was writing, was a Christian nation. Augustine did not approve of killing another person in order to avoid being killed oneself, but he made an exception for soldiers or public officials acting for the sake of others and society (Burt, 1999).

As a consequence, the Church allowed armed resistance for those serving in an army but disapproved of, or ignored, self-defense taken by individual victims who were not serving the government or the Church. James O'Donnell (2005) noted Augustine's "muddled moderation that led to his acceptance of the notion of 'just war'" (p. 154). John Ferguson (1978) argued that the Just War doctrine supports those in power, whether in government or in the Church; violence against the powerful was, by Augustine's definition, unjust. In effect, there was no clear way to determine if a war was just; it was just if the one in authority declared it to be just (Kimball, 2020).

Both Christianity and Islam justified violent resistance to aggression. Each faith exhorted its faithful to take up arms against enemies, but the rationales for justifying offensive military operations varied. Combat to repel an advancing enemy was a practical response, but territorial expansion and conquest required more explanation. Three factors—religious teaching, such as St. Augustine's; greed for territory, fame, and wealth; and past traumatic experience—must have combined as reasons for 200 years of conflict between Islam and Christianity during the era of the Crusades. Both faiths sought guidance in holy texts, both faiths coveted territory, and both must have been dealing with their collective histories and with the tragedies they had set in motion. One legacy of the Crusades is that it indeed altered the rationales for warfare for both Muslims and Christians, rationales which persist today. But while new rationales for war may have freed individuals from restraints of conscience, does that fully explain why thousands of people responded positively to their leaders' calls, developed a burning passion for war, and became willing to travel hundreds of miles to fight a foreign foe? The numbers are impressive. About 40,000 people marched in the First Crusade and approximately 100,000 people from across Europe joined the battles in subsequent Crusades (Madden, 2014). *How did this happen and why?*

Medieval propaganda leading to atrocity

One clue is provided by Robert the Monk, who told about the appeal that Pope Urban made in 1095 at the Council of Clermont (reprinted in Munro, 1895). In a dramatic address, Urban talked about Muslims this way: They were "an accursed race." Holy sites were "defiled with their uncleanness." They "devastated [Christians] with sword, pillage and fire." Urban said Muslims had enslaved Christians, destroyed churches, turned churches into mosques, desecrated altars … the list of alleged atrocities goes on. He had both spiritual and economic messages. Those who joined in liberating the Holy Land would be forgiven their sins and—as an extra incentive—they could "take the land from that wicked people and make it your own." The pope told his followers that those who liberated the Holy Land would possess a land "flowing with milk and honey" (https://sourcebooks.fordham.edu/source/urban2-5vers.asp).

Pope Urban's speech was "one of the most incendiary speeches in the history of the world, [one] that gathered up the squabbling, discontented masses of western Europe and galvanized them into action" (Fidler, 2017, p. 290). His speech dehumanized Muslims, and it seemed to promise to those gathered a new, more unified and even exalted group identity. The pope's lurid and entirely imaginary tale of atrocities against Christian pilgrims—an early example of either misinformation or disinformation—tapped into "enormous latent energies" in Western Europe, Fidler argues (p. 290). Norman Cohn (1970) notes that something was already at work in the pope's audience, something that he connected with and fed: "emotions of overwhelming power," triggering tears and trembling, and leading to "the idea of murder as a form of worship, the idea that religion sanctions murder" (p. 61).

Although the eventual targets of the pilgrims on the First Crusade were Muslims, the first actual victims were not. Along the way to the Holy Land, the Crusaders encountered their first victims—Jews living peacefully in Christian lands. An account by Albert of Aachen comments that "I know not whether by a judgment of the Lord or by some error of mind, [the Crusaders] rose in a spirit of cruelty against the Jewish people scattered throughout these cities and slaughtered them without mercy." They said it was their "duty against the enemies of the Christian faith." Albert concludes that the pilgrims slaughtered the Jews "through greed of money" rather than for God (quoted in Susan Edgington, 2013, pp. 110–111). While Albert's conclusion focuses on lower, rather than higher, motives, his noting the "spirit of cruelty" does indeed testify to "emotions of overwhelming power."

One "error of mind" may have been that the Crusaders—fueled by such intense emotions—may not have had the ability or the self-restraint to discern any differences between Jews and Muslims; instead they were all lumped together as enemies of Christ (Krug, 1987). Christians eventually killed thousands of Muslims, and bodies "lay in pools of blood on the doorsteps of their homes or alongside the mosques"; the fate of the Jews "was no less atrocious," with temples barricaded and then torched with many burned inside (Maalouf, 1984, p. xiv). Other victims of the Crusaders were Eastern Orthodox clerics. Orthodox and Roman Catholicism had grown apart over many years, but the final split occurred earlier in 1054, only a few decades before the First Crusade. The Roman Catholic Church claimed supremacy over all of Christendom, and the Crusades gave the pope an opportunity to assert that claim with military force.

The Crusades must have been hugely traumatic for Muslims (Cook, 2005), though it is difficult to apply modern definitions of psychological states to medieval peoples. But we can indeed imagine that overwhelming experiences generally connected with trauma—experiences of massive horror, terror, sudden loss, betrayal—must have left lasting marks on the Crusaders' victims. Eyewitness accounts, including those of Archbishop William of the Crusader kingdom established in Tyre, described mass slaughter, the bloodthirstiness of the Crusaders, and widespread massacre upon the conquest of cities. All of this destruction and pillaging followed long sieges of urban centers that had already resulted in mass starvation. In some places, the Crusaders were even said to have engaged in cannibalism. Stories like these led to centuries of terror, distrust, and hatred between Muslims and Christians. In the end, "jihadism which until then had been little more than a colorful slogan, took on new life and meaning" for Muslims (Gerges, 2006, p. 193).

These atrocities eventually galvanized Muslims to repel the Crusaders. Their leaders quoted the Qur'an to embolden warriors. Muslims were told they had a duty to submit to God (Qur'an Surah 3.102), to fear and obey God (64.16), to strive and fight in the service of God (9.41).

Surah 2.216 says "Enjoined on you is fighting and this you abhor. You may dislike a thing, yet it may be good for you." The next verse adds that it is a sin to fail to resist oppression because enemy "oppression is worse than killing." Surah 22.39 states: "Permission is granted those who fight because they were oppressed." The faithful should "slay the idolaters wheresoever you find them" (Surah 9.5). Those who die in the service of God will be admitted into paradise (Surah 3.169). One who fails to resist the enemy commits a mortal sin that "will bring the wrath of God on himself and have hell as an abode" (Surah 8.16). In the index to his translation of the Qur'an, Muhammad Asad (2003) lists twenty-six passages that describe "fighting in God's cause." Some of these rationales and exhortations can be heard in jihadist movements to this day.

The evidence is overwhelming: the Crusades poisoned relations between Christians and Muslims and hastened the development of militant jihad in Islam. The final defeat of the Crusaders in the Holy Land occurred in 1291, but "in Europe residues of the Crusades persisted for years to come" (Ansary, 2009, p. 199). Persecutions of sects considered heretical were "whipped up by the Pope," and in Iberia, the Christian Reconquista of territory the Muslims had conquered in the eighth century, which was a sort of crusade in itself, continued until 1492 when the Muslims were finally defeated. One main consequence on the Muslim side was a "belt of anti-Christian hostility that stretched from Egypt to Azerbaijan" (Ansary, 2009, p. 199).

The mindset of the Crusaders and the Book of Revelation

Religious differences and territorial disputes may not have been the only triggers for violence. The living conditions, emotional states, tribal conflicts, and level of psychological development in European ethnic groups must have played an important role in preparing fertile ground for theological statements as motivators during the Crusades. Religious justifications—particularly related to the pope's desire to reclaim Jerusalem and protect the Eastern Church from Muslim aggression—were not a pretext, but these goals alone seemed unlikely to have stirred so many to take up arms. Pope Urban II was able to "channel the raw brute energy" that motivated the crowd listening to his call to action at Clermont (Foss, 2011, p. 29). But what was the nature of that energy?

And how much did the disordered internal state of European groups lead to their using an external foe to galvanize unified action and forge a collective large-group identity? Foss notes that "Mohammad was seen as Anti-Christ," so exhortations by Catholic leaders struck a chord about a strong and exalted large group identity, fueling hatred of Muslims who were stigmatized as completely "other" (Foss, 2011, p. 18) and offering potential Crusaders a positive, even holy, sense of themselves.

Historians have shown a new interest in understanding the mindset of the Crusaders. One approach has been to examine the letters of those who participated in or closely watched the Crusades. Ordman (2013) notes that there indeed was joy among holy warriors that many enemies were killed, but that they also grieved over the deaths of their horses. The death of a comrade produced great sorrow, but also rejoicing that his soul was now with the angels. After bloody victories, warriors sometimes forgot to defend their positions, there were visits by pagan dancing girls, and festive celebrations were held. Ordman concludes that those clerics who wrote about the warriors were seeking to prove that their motives for fighting were linked with concepts of justice and spiritual purity. But she also notes the gruesome victory celebrations while helping us understand how fighters felt and how they justified the violence they committed. Indeed she shows that the Crusaders were not simply a primitive people; they were quite capable of empathy, but for horses and comrades rather than the enemy Other.

These practices are reinforced by scriptural references to ancient conflicts and a desire to "purify the religious community." Even Christians who believe in pacifism, Mark Juergensmeyer (2000) notes, have traditions where "martial images abound in the rhetoric and symbolism of the faith." (pp. 156–157). Indeed, military imagery and metaphors are used in more than twenty-five places in the New Testament. And, in the century following the First Crusade, the code of chivalry developed, which represented a loose integration of military practice, noble conduct, and spiritual values. This development—in the direction of greater civilization and embodied by the idea of knighthood—was stirring in European societies from the time of Charlemagne. Its utter breakdown during the Crusades attests to its fragility among the masses and also to its being used—by Pope Urban, for example—to license and even sanctify violence toward the Other.

The first wave of Christian pilgrims in the Crusades included a people's army composed mainly of poor and desperate peasants who engaged in mob violence long before they got near any Muslims. While some (Rude, 1985) have argued that the violence represented rational self-interest because desperately poor people sought material goods to improve their living standards, the "frenzied, hysterical" group dimension (Ireland, 1907, p. 322) is inescapable. The violence of the Crusades shows us that individual sanity may exist alongside what looks like group insanity, fueled by religious fervor and apocalyptic imagery.

The chivalrous claim by Christian leadership that the Lord of Hosts was the Crusades' founder was lifted from the Book of Revelation, particularly Chapter 19, which was then misused to justify the Crusades against infidels. In fact, Revelation describes the final battle between good and evil, the apocalypse. Its rider on a white horse "is called Faithful and True, and in righteousness he judges and makes war" and the "armies of heaven" follow him (Rev. 19:11–14). Verse 15 says that he "will rule with a rod of iron" to execute the "fury of the wrath of God the Almighty." With such statements, it is easy to see how those who heard this message would envision themselves as warriors for a vengeful God doing battle with infidels occupying the Holy Land.

However, there is only one weapon mentioned in Revelation as being carried by the rider: "From his mouth comes a sharp sword with which to strike down the nations" (Rev. 19:15). The text "has nothing to say in support of human actions of violence," and judgment "is carried out by a judicial word, not by physical violence" (Witherington, 2003, p. 259). That weapon is the Word of God. This view is echoed by Michael Gorman (2011): "Revelation should be understood as portraying *symbolically* what God does *actually* with a divine performative utterance, an effective word not unlike the word that spoke creation into existence" (p. 152). In Revelation, humans are not sent into battle; rather, "Revelation conveys a spirituality and ethic of nonviolence" (p. 183, italics in the original).

But "Sacred texts in the wrong hands can be dangerous things, especially apocalyptic texts," says Witherington (2003, p. 259). Historian Jay Rubenstein (2011) says the First Crusaders did indeed carry an apocalyptic mindset, adding that as "Christian armies marched east, they witnessed miracles, they bathed in rivers of blood" (p. xii) and many believed they were entering the Last Days. Indeed, in 1095, there was a meteor shower over Western Europe, and in 1096, an eclipse of the moon, which then turned red. Many interpreted these as prophetic signs, after which the recruitment of warriors increased. That same year there was another eclipse and an aurora. In 1097, a comet blazed through the night. In 1098, a great light brightened the night sky and then there was an eclipse of the sun.

It is not difficult to see how, within an apocalyptic mindset, clever or fanatical leaders could build on the superstitions, presuppositions, and emotions of their followers to encourage and in fact direct them into battle. The peasants in what was called the People's Crusade were the ones who wreaked the most destruction, murdering Jews and Muslims in great numbers. Some believed that this havoc was a necessary preliminary to the Second Coming of Christ (Cohn, 2019). Such was the thinking that resulted in horrific massacres. Such *is* the thinking—or perhaps failure of thinking in favor of the mob's frenzied impulses—that is characteristic of societal regression and transgenerational trauma.

Trauma and religion

There is growing evidence that experiencing trauma can shatter a person's worldview. If an individual's core beliefs are destroyed, severe symptoms of PTSD can result. Elana Newman and her colleagues found that PTSD symptoms were less severe if an individual's "construct of the world" was not seriously disrupted, but in the event of such disruption, "maladaptive belief structures and negative affective states" were fostered. Traumatic events can trigger profound feelings of vulnerability, undermining survivors' beliefs about the self, the world, and the future. "There is also emerging consensus that healthy adaptation following severe stressors requires both an adaptive integration of the event into one's belief system and the process of negative emotions" (Newman et al., 1997, pp. 197–198).

In their research, they underline affective states that can reshape a worldview, including chronic states of helplessness, rage, terror, loss, grief, regret, shame, guilt, and diffuse pain. They also note that benign expectations about the dangerousness of the world or about the predictability, fairness, and trustworthiness of other people may be shattered by trauma. Trauma also profoundly affects self-worth, potentially leading to feelings of self-reproach, alienation, a diminished capacity to love, and a diminished sense of personal legitimacy (Newman et al., 1997, p. 200). Complex PTSD with extreme stress proved to be extremely disruptive to the core beliefs of sufferers and led to substantive changes in their basic cognitive-affective organization. This research dovetails with recent research on "moral injury" as a key element in some traumatic breakdowns (Litz, 2014; Shay, 2014).

The moral dimension of a person's deepest beliefs links the study of trauma to religion, and indeed, recent psychological studies of the role of religion in trauma suggest that a person's belief system is an important factor in how stress is experienced. There is evidence to support Sinclair's view that the "most corrosive impact of horrific emotional trauma is to be found in the spiritual fabric of persons" (quoted in McBride & Armstrong, 1995, p. 6). Trauma disrupts the connectedness associated with spirituality, particularly when there is a loss of faith in order and continuity. Consider the experience of Elie Wiesel, traumatized in a Nazi concentration camp, whose response to seeing innocent children burning alive was to feel murdered by God. Trauma renders the sufferer a deeply "wounded self" (Bradshaw, 1988).

A review of empirical research into the relationship between religion and traumatic stress indicates significant linkages. Chen and Koenig reviewed eleven studies in 2006 and concluded that all but one of the peer-reviewed studies reported significant associations between measures of PTSD and spirituality. Interestingly, some showed an inverse association (higher spirituality correlated with lower measures of symptoms) and some showed a positive association (higher scores on PTSD symptoms correlated with higher scores on religion/spirituality). That the correlation of spirituality and symptomatology went in opposite directions might suggest that, in many cases, religious belief is a protective factor against severe trauma, but in others, trauma destroys a person's belief system. Another meta-analysis by Weaver and colleagues (1996) examined more than fifty published studies and demonstrated a positive correlation between religious commitment and mental health. What is not clear is what happens when trauma destroys religious commitment or when that commitment is exploited to commit violence.

The First Crusade is a story of religious commitment used to perpetrate trauma, and of that group's then suffering trauma as the victims retaliate. Both have contributed to the continuing enmity between faith groups as the violence done to the Other is passed down across generations.

Last words

The conflicted relationship between Muslims and Christians, which led to the First Crusade, was the result of the Church's response to Islamic conquest of the Eastern lands, based in part on stories of Muslim atrocities passed down from Christian leaders to their followers and from Christian parents to their children. At the same time, Christian atrocities became part of the collective memory of Muslims in those conquered lands. Over the long term, both would become victims and victimizers.

When Muslims lost control of Jerusalem to the Crusaders, trauma on the ground also became a traumatic loss to their large-group identity. The later loss of Jerusalem, and centuries later of Constantinople, to the Muslims were similar blows to Christian large-group identity. The 1096 message of Pope Urban must have resonated powerfully with Christians because they heard his appeal as a plea for the faithful to not only avenge the loss of the Holy Land but also to restore the Church's and their own large-group identity. A "collective mental representation of an event [with] drastic common losses," where the faithful felt "victimized by another group" must have triggered humiliation, profound damage to the Christian collective self-image, and the violent desire for repair (Volkan, 2006, p. 48).

Can this pattern of conflict be broken? One way to mitigate the repeated triggering of traumatic revenge may be to understand those rare situations of reconciliation by, for example, studying some of the successes of the civil rights movement in the United States. As we have seen, religion can be enlisted in the service of massive conflict, but it can also help to resolve conflict, as, for example, in the Truth and Reconciliation process in South Africa, and in conflicts between gangs in American prisons (Rowan, 2018).

James Meredith, whom we met at the beginning of this chapter, was widely acclaimed (and widely denounced) because he was a black man seeking admission to an all-white university. In reality, he was a mixed-race man, a member of the same tribe that I can claim as my ancestors. He had more in common with poor whites in his home state than many other more affluent whites who grew up as racists. Viewing the brotherhood and sisterhood of humans is one way to start finding common ground, and to help people toward this way of viewing one another is the essence of genuine religious leadership.

In December 2021, one of those great religious leaders passed away. Archbishop Desmond Tutu led his country in the fight against apartheid and then in the painful effort toward reconciliation. During his visit to the United States several years ago, I asked Archbishop Tutu about the Truth and Reconciliation program he had championed in South Africa, a process widely viewed as having prevented mass violence, despite some serious setbacks. In our conversation, Tutu said that truth was key to avoiding massive bloodshed. Reconciliation, he acknowledged, would take a lot longer, especially given that truth was purchased with amnesty for white officials who testified publicly about their crimes against humanity. Whites had to then listen to the laments of black victims.

The foundation of Tutu's effort was built on speaking the truth—both of egregious actions and of horrific trauma—face to face. In this process, the defense of dehumanization, which allows for the perpetration of such violence, comes up against the actual humanity of its victims.

When I first met Tutu, I was interested in how the oppressive system in South Africa was similar to (or different from) the oppressive system in the American South. Race was the dividing line for group identities in both places. But Archbishop Tutu shared a worldview called Ubuntu, which appealed for the peaceful cohabitation of people of different identities. Ubuntu was central to Tutu's own sense of identity and community. Ubuntu recognizes the wrongs people do to each other, but the goal is not revenge; rather, it's the healing of the relationship.

Covid-19 forced me to cancel a recent trip to visit Archbishop Tutu in South Africa, one on which I hoped to ask him what he thought we should do about the current state of race relations in his country and mine. After he died, I dreamed that I was with him; in my dream, Greenwood Leflore and Sam Cobb were there too. I asked my question and eagerly awaited Tutu's response. But the alarm clock went off, and I woke up thinking I would never be able to get the direct answer from Tutu. Then, I realized Tutu had already given it, in what he did with his whole life. Facing the truth was essential. Retribution was a dead end. Dialogues help with reconciliation. Desmond Tutu was under no illusions that it would be easy, but—nearly a millennium after the religion-driven violence of the First Crusade—he showed us a way.

References

Ansary, T. (2009). *Destiny Disrupted: A History of the World through Islamic Eyes*. New York: Public Affairs.

Asad, M. (2003). *The Message of the Qur'an*. Bristol, UK: Book Foundation.

Bradshaw, J. (1988). *Healing the Shame that Binds You*. Deerfield Beach, FL: Health Communication.

Burt, D. X. (1999). *Friendship and Society: An Introduction to Augustine's Practical Philosophy*. Grand Rapids, MI: Eerdmans.

Chen, Y. Y., & Koenig, H. G. (2006). Traumatic stress and religion: Is there a relationship? A review of empirical findings. *Journal of Religion and Health*, 45: 375–378.

Claster, J. N. (2009). *Sacred Violence: The European Crusades to the Middle East*. Toronto, Canada: University of Toronto Press.

Cohn, N. (1970). *The Pursuit of the Millennium*. New York: Oxford University Press.

Cohn, N. (2019, March 1). Apocalypticism explained: The Crusades. *PBS Frontline*. https://pbs.org/wgbh/pages/frontline/show/ apocalypse/explanation/crusades.html (last accessed April 11, 2021).

Cook, D. (2005). *Understanding Jihad*. Berkeley, CA: University of California Press.

Edgington, S. B. (2013). *Albert of Aachen's History of the Journey to Jerusalem. Volume 1: Books 1–6. The First Crusade, 1095–1099*. New York: Routledge.

Ferguson, J. (1978). *War and Peace in the World's Religions*. New York: Oxford University Press.

Fidler, R. (2017). *Ghost Empire: A Journey to Legendary Constantinople*. New York: Penguin.

Foss, M. (2011). *People of the First Crusade: The Truth About the Christian-Muslim War Revealed*. New York: Arcade.

Gerges, F. (2006). *Journey of the Jihadist: Inside Muslim Militancy.* New York: Harcourt.

Gorman, M. J. (2011). *Reading Revelation Responsibly: Uncivil Worship and Witness Following the Lamb into the New Creation.* Eugene, OR: Cascade.

Ireland, W. (1907). On the psychology of the Crusades II. *British Journal of Psychiatry, 53*: 322–341.

Juergensmeyer, M. (2000). *Terror in the Mind of God: The Global Rise of Religious Violence.* Berkeley, CA: University of California Press.

Kimball, C. (2020). *When Religion Becomes Evil.* New York: HarperCollins.

Krug, D. (1987). Review of the First Crusade and the idea of crusading by Jonathan Riley-Smith. *Church History, 56*(4): 520–521.

Litz, B. (2014). Clinical heuristics and strategies for service members and veterans with war-related PTSD. *Psychoanalytic Psychology, 31*(2): 192–205.

Maalouf, A. (1984). *The Crusades through Arab Eyes.* J. Rothschild (Trans.). New York: Schocken.

Madden, T. F. (2014). *The Concise History of the Crusades.* Lanham, MD: Rowman & Littlefield.

McBride, J. L., & Armstrong, G. (1995). The spiritual dynamics of chronic post traumatic stress disorder. *Journal of Religion and Health, 34*(1): 5–16.

Meredith, J. (1995). *Mississippi: A Volume of Eleven Books.* Jackson, MS: Meredith.

Munro, D. N. (1895). *Urban and the Crusaders, Vol. 1:2.* Philadelphia, PA: University of Pennsylvania Press.

Newman, E., Riggs, D. S., & Roth, S. (1977). Thematic resolution, PTSD, and complex PTSD: The relationship between meaning and trauma-related diagnoses. *Journal of Traumatic Stress, 3*: 197–213.

O'Donnell, J. J. (2005). *Augustine: A New Biography.* New York: Harper Perennial.

Ordman, J. (2013). Feeling like a holy warrior: Western authors' attributions of emotions as proof of motives for violence among Christian actors in military conflicts: Tenth through early twelfth centuries. PhD dissertation, Loyola University Chicago. proquest.com.ezpprod1.hul.harvard.edu/docview/146437751 (last accessed April 11, 2021).

Rowan, F. (2018). Forgiveness and healing in prison. *Interpretation: A Journal of Bible and Theology, 72*: 293–303.

Rowan, F. (2019). Reimagined history: Trauma as provocation for the First Crusade. http://nrs.harvard.edu/urn-3:HUL.InstRepos:42004230 (last accessed April 11, 2021).

Rubenstein, J. (2011). *Armies of Heaven: The First Crusade and the Quest for Apocalypse*. New York: Basic Books.

Rubenstein, J. (2014). *Writing the Early Crusades: Text, Transmission and Memory*. Rochester, NY: Boydell.

Rude, G. (1985). *The Crowd in History: A Study of Popular Disturbances in France and England*. London: Lawrence & Wishart.

Shay, J. (2014). Moral injury. *Psychoanalytic Psychology, 31*(2): 182–191.

Volkan, V. D. (2006). *Killing in the Name of Identity: A Study of Bloody Conflicts*. Charlottesville, VA: Pitchstone.

Waldman, P., & Pope, H. (2001, September 21). "Crusade" reference reinforces fears war on terrorism is against Muslims. *The Wall Street Journal*. https://wsj.com/articles/SB1001020294332922160 (last accessed April 11, 2021).

Weaver, A. J., Koenig, H. G., & Ochberg, F. (1996). Posttraumatic stress, mental health professionals and the clergy: A need for collaboration, training and research. *Journal of Traumatic Stress, 9*: 852.

Witherington III, B. (2003). *Revelation*. New York: Cambridge University Press.

CHAPTER 14

IDI thinking in one Georgetown lawyer working in one small pocket of the legal community

David G. Fromm

I have spent the majority of my two-plus decades since graduating from Georgetown University's Law Center engaged in the practice of civil litigation—that is, whittling away at my finite number of days in pursuit of the legal adjudication of private disputes, usually involving some perceived violation of contractual obligations or norms of mutual behavior. Why? Well, the money, of course. But, also, because helping people to resolve disputes—to free themselves from some seemingly intractable problem so that they can proceed and contribute—can feel, in the best of times, like a worthwhile way to spend one's life.

Civil litigation is dispute resolution, though not in the sense that that term is typically used. The term "dispute resolution" encompasses a variety of methods whereby disputants end their battles. Most of these methods, and the ones most implied by the phrase "dispute resolution," are alternatives to civil litigation—arbitration, mediation, restorative justice, self-help, and the like. In civil litigation, disputes "resolve" either through court rulings or, far more often, by settlement between the parties when the costs and uncertainties of pursuing the case become too much to bear. Civil litigation itself involves the "zealous advocacy" of one's clients' interests by their attorneys, trying to "win" a formal lawsuit, usually at the expense of the opposing party.

Sometimes this work can be rewarding, even thrilling, in a competitive sense. Sometimes lawyers engage in a sort of theatre of gravitas, seizing the high road while belittling their opponents' positions. Judges cut through this theatre, ruling for or against positions, and sometimes it even feels like justice is served. More often, at the day-to-day level, it can feel like being one of a thousand small cogs in the massive machines of law and commerce. I suspect that this may be true for lawyers engaged in other legal fields beyond civil litigation—transactional attorneys, for example, wading through their due diligence and board books. The knights of bankruptcy. Maybe even criminal lawyers, whose cases implicate more than just the allocation of funds.

Recently I've been thinking about how lawyers understand themselves and their projects—cases, transactions, prosecutions, representations—vis-à-vis their clients, opposing counsel, the system, and the public; how lawyers see their work strategically, as part of a system of regulation. But also thinking about how clients—the public, citizens—see the necessary, if un-wished-for, work of lawyers. This thinking, fueled in part by a mid-career pivot toward pro bono legal representation and more traditional dispute resolution work, has been influenced by my work with the International Dialogue Initiative, a private, international, multidisciplinary group that studies the psychopolitical aspects of conflict. The IDI's holistic, analytical approach to large group trauma places that trauma, and the conflicts it creates, within a larger context and mirrors in some ways the foundation of my own legal education.

At Georgetown, as at many US law schools, the primary first year curriculum focused on discrete areas of law, including torts, contracts, constitutional law, and property, the specific "need-to-know" building blocks of any legal education. Georgetown, however, also offered an alternative curriculum, one which placed less emphasis on those building blocks and more emphasis on the regulatory and philosophical marble from which they were hewn. This alternative curriculum focused not just on what a lawyer does but on what the purpose of that work is, why a lawyer does it. It proposed legal regimes as overlapping frameworks grounded in the regulation of resources and behavior, in constant development, governing the lives of citizens. I don't know if this is particularly original but it seems to me that many of my Georgetown law classmates who self-selected this curriculum went on to non-traditional legal careers, which perhaps means something.

Motivated by both intellectual and financial insecurity, I pursued a more traditional legal career at first and joined a large Boston law firm as an associate attorney, a position for which I was not particularly suited but one that did help pay back most of my loans while providing an education in corporate America, anxiety, and billing. At the firm (and at subsequent firms), a not-insubstantial amount of time was spent on client management—explaining to the client what certain charges meant and why they were necessary, what to expect tactically and strategically in litigation, what the likelihood of success was, and what success might look like (these latter points offered very diplomatically). We associates spent little time discussing the clients' position within a matrix regulating resources and behavior—and why would we? That would have added to the bill. Corporate clients, as a rule, have the bottom line in mind.

But it isn't just the well-heeled corporate clients of large law firms who must navigate these matrices, it's individuals and defendants and families and prisoners. All of them are compelled to interact with systems that are unfamiliar, full of strange rules and language and symbols, that nonetheless purport to exert control over them. Moreover, many of these systems exist within one another—that is, for example, a local system to resolve domestic disputes may exist within a courthouse resource system which exists within a county bar system which exists within a system of state laws, which in turn exists within a larger Constitutional framework, these systems forming a sort of Matryoshka of individual regulation. One reason, perhaps, that many corporate clients do not need to locate themselves within a regulatory system and can instead focus on the bottom line is that they are already aware of their places within the regulatory system—indeed in many instances these corporate clients have helped shape the system itself.

For individuals, locating oneself within the regulatory scheme is often different. I have seen this especially in my recent work with underprivileged clients. I volunteer for the local bar association in my county and spend one day a week available to individuals who come into the clinic at the courthouse to ask questions about a legal issue they believe they have. Many of these clients present with consumer debt problems—they have defaulted on a credit card bill, the credit card company has sold the debt to a collection agency and the collection agency has sued the client. The clients—whose fiscal condition is often tenuous, which is how they got into their credit predicament in the first place—receive a summons and complaint in the mail with a letter informing them that they must respond within twenty days, or a default judgment will be entered against them. To many of the clients, these (often form) letters, written in the legalese of the courts, may as well be written in Sumerian. Rather than welcoming the clients into a hallowed system of jurisprudence, where disputes can be addressed and wrongs righted peaceably, these letters act as a closed, impenetrable gate put up in front of the recipients. Confronted by this gate, the recipients will ignore it, default on the complaint, a judgment will be entered against them, the judgment will accrue interest, liens will be filed, credit reports will be picked to pieces, wages may be garnished, the system will churn on. Nobody will get paid.

One example may suffice: at the legal clinic, creditor-debtor actions are so common that the clinic provides a form for debtors to file in response to receipt of a complaint. This form, which is a two-page document with three pages of instructions, is also available on the internet—it can be located with a simple Google search—in a printer-friendly, ready-to-file format. The form acts as an answer to a creditor's complaint and provides a list of potential defenses and counterclaims, some of which might be dispositive of the case—if, for instance, the debtor is above a certain age or has only a protected source of income or if the creditor has engaged in chicanery. If a debtor fills out and files the form as an answer, at the very least they will not default on the complaint.

For a lawyer, a form like this can simplify things significantly, decreasing time and expense. But for a non-lawyer it is still incredibly daunting. Which boxes must be checked? Which defenses have a reasonable basis and what if I miss one? What am I *joining* by filing this document? What will be asked of me next? Some clients, enormously ambivalent about the process, take the form home with them and never file it, opting out of participation. Others check every box on the form, initiating a counteraction they have no interest in (and often no grounds for) pursuing, but which will nonetheless clutter the court's docket, which is its own form of opting out.

Other clients come into the legal clinic because a dispute with a neighbor has gone sideways. A contractor is fully paid and almost done but no longer shows up. A landlord has changed the locks. A gun license has been denied. A restraining order is required. A restraining order is overbroad. A restraining order is based on fraud. A restraining order is blocking the client from taking the short route to work. These clients—like the large-firm corporate clients—are not that interested in their place within a regulatory matrix. They just want to know what to do with the novella they've gotten from the collection agency. They just want their gun back. They read the law—correctly—as a system of restraint placed upon them.

How does IDI thinking come into play here? Well, best first to define what we mean by IDI thinking. When I am asked to describe "IDI thinking"—or when I attempt to describe it to myself—I often turn to the formulation articulated by IDI member Dr. Ed Shapiro after the IDI's 17th Meeting in the autumn of 2019. In a post available on the IDI website, Dr. Shapiro wrote:

> International conflict is marked by powerful feelings, often poorly understood, across cultural and ethnic boundaries. These feelings emerge around security concerns, economic needs, religious tensions and traumatic pasts, and regularly lead to impasse. [...] We have increasingly recognized, through the work of Vamık Volkan, that each large group (ethnic, national, religious) carries with it an organizing "identity," created through the transmission of narratives, symbols, and the residue of chosen trauma and glories. This identity can readily be reactivated by political leaders, leading to wishes for revenge and retribution. But what aspects of such trauma are carried by individuals—and how can those aspects help us understand the large group?

Here I might add, as an aside, that the concept of "international law," at least as a counterbalance to international conflict, is problematic in some ways—in particular because, for most populations, legal regimes are viewed as positive creations, that is, "posited" by the citizens of a defined jurisdiction. Jurisdiction is a threshold consideration for the regulation of behavior. It answers the question: "What gives you the right to control me?" It is perhaps one thing for a "citizen" to confront a domestic regulatory regime they distrust and quite another for an individual to confront a regulatory regime imposed by some amorphous international "authority" they do not recognize as controlling.

But do the underprivileged groups—and, setting aside relative privilege, the non-litigious groups—I see in my pro bono work (and previously saw in my corporate work) recognize the authority of the legal systems they encounter? Are they in many ways a "large group" whose "organizing identity" manifests, perhaps subconsciously, as outside of, but subject to, the regulatory system of law? Typically, we think of large groups as sharing some identity—ethnic, religious, national—but the sorts of people I see in my work might be seen as sharing the identity of the disenfranchised, or perhaps of the "regulated." Perhaps they share a sense of powerlessness in the face of authority, or of humiliation at the hands of some regulating agent. One might even posit that large parts of American society see themselves as an "out-group" when it comes to their perceptions about who is in charge. (What else explains the gun fetish in the United States better than a desire to assert power and independence via a firearm? Indeed, in my work some of the most frustrated clients are the ones who are confronting the denial of their handgun permits.)

I won't attempt to generalize too much about possible traumas inflicted by this regulatory system on underprivileged groups (for a discussion of the identity-forming effects of group trauma and humiliation, see for example, John Alderdice's 2012 speech to the United Nations and/or Vamık Volkan's 2020 work on large group identity, cited below), but courtrooms and complaints (and even we lawyers in our suits) are certainly powerful symbols. Symbols of what? Of regulation, perhaps. Or of fairness or unfairness. Almost certainly of control, and therefore of power.

For many members of these groups, the idea of being sued by a "predatory" debt collection agency for a debt whose balance has ballooned in mysterious ways may activate a defensive impulse to withdraw, to ignore the summons, and to "default" out of reluctance to be regulated in ways they don't understand or connect to. For some members of these groups, the notion of an impenetrable regulatory agency denying their "God-given" right to carry a firearm may feel like an assault by one large group—"the government"—on members of another large group—"the governed"—complete with symbols and narratives and chosen glory fantasies. The ex-husband whose parental role is subject to a court-ordered restriction may retreat into an obstreperous pique in the same way a corporate defendant obligated to answer interrogatories under oath might. "I have not consented to this regulation," they might say, staring down a byzantine set of rules and requirements. "I reject it."

With my pro bono clients, I often begin my consultation with a quick sketch of the legal system—the differences between the civil and criminal systems, the process of a lawsuit, the likelihood that most people will play an active role in a lawsuit at some point in their lives, the certainty that our system of self-regulation is already playing a passive role in all our lives. Many of these individuals present as part of the "out-group," the one for whom a system of regulation is confusing at best and punitive and untrustworthy at worst, and during our consultation I seek to help these individuals locate themselves within the in-group, within the system of which they are of course already a part. Some of these individuals come to our consultations with impressions of the legal system formed from popular media, impressions of courtrooms and bailiffs and confrontations, when reality is usually much more mundane.

We talk about the language of this system—their role as a plaintiff or defendant, the idea of a dispute "at issue," the role of lawyers and courts and judgment. We do not have time for a first-year law school course on the overlapping systems of regulation—our consults are usually only a half-hour long (if that)—but we do talk about why these systems of regulation exist and the sorts of social behaviors they promote and discourage. We aim to demystify, at least to a degree, the system these individuals find themselves compelled to confront.

Rarely, but occasionally, the client at the legal clinic will leave with an understanding of the system with which they are engaging, a system that has after all been operating all around them for their entire life, and with the understanding that they are not part of an "out-group"; rather, their participation is as essential to the system's efficient functioning as the lawyers and courts and language they implicitly distrust. They will see this system as one in which their rights are respected, their claims heard, their transgressions accounted for, and their future clarified. Having been oriented within a necessary system of regulation, they will know what to do next. That knowledge, in my limited experience, can bring comfort and perhaps even peace of mind.

In the IDI, we take note of large group psychology and the ways that such psychology manifests in conflict, in group dynamics, and in individual behavior. These phenomena often play a role in international disputes but also, and far more frequently, they appear in intra-group negotiations over how the group will regulate itself, what rules will govern. A legal system is one such system. I find that my work as an attorney is immeasurably improved for being attuned to this psychology of large group identity and the effects it has on individual members of these groups, and I attribute that awareness to Georgetown's alternative, holistic legal education and the IDI's attention to symbols, narratives, and trauma.

References

Alderdice, J. (2012, September 13). *Speech to the United Nations General Assembly*. New York.

Volkan, V. D. (2020). *Large-Group Psychology: Racism, Societal Division, Narcissistic Leaders and Who We Are Now*. Bicester, UK: Phoenix.

Part III

Methodology

CHAPTER 15

International conflict is within individuals: a reflection

Edward R. Shapiro

International conflict is marked by powerful feelings, often poorly understood, across cultural and ethnic differences. These feelings emerge around security concerns, economic needs, religious tensions, and traumatic pasts and regularly lead to impasse. The International Dialogue Initiative brings together a small group of psychoanalysts, political scientists, politicians, lawyers, historians, economists, and other leaders from a range of nationalities, generations, and ethnic groups to study human experience through the lens of differing disciplines to maximize psychological understanding. We focus on the psycho-historical origins of conflict and the possibility of gaining perspective on unmanageable feelings. We have increasingly recognized, through the work of Vamık Volkan (2006, 2020), that each large group (ethnic, national, religious) carries with it an organizing "identity," created through the transmission of narratives, symbols, and the residue of chosen trauma and glories. This can readily be reactivated by political leaders, leading to wishes for revenge and retribution. But what aspects of such trauma are carried by individuals—and how can this kind of representation help us understand the large group?

Our families shape us, and we shape them. When we leave the family, we carry aspects of them with us. We emerge with values and ideals that are shaped by and transmitted through family interaction and development. Though we may not be aware of it, we become *representatives*: of the family, of our ethnicity, and of our multigenerational history. Other people recognize this, and they respond to us in ways we may not see; they shape us further as representatives of our family's missions. Over time, we increasingly perceive the world through those lenses. Even when we are not aware of it, we represent to others these elements of our identity. Some of the internalized history becomes evident through painful affects—sadness, anger, hesitation, anxiety, fear—visible and enacted through subtle cues. These generate affective reactions in others; attention to that process can illuminate group interaction between representatives of different cultures.

Given IDI's commitment to deepening international dialogue and studying conflict, the group attends to painful feelings as they emerge in individual reports and notes the group's process during our meetings as potentially reflective of international tensions. In this brief communication, I will illustrate this method through the use of two cases.

Case 1

In an opening discussion about the way Germany has borne the full burden of guilt and responsibility for World War II and its atrocities, a British negotiator in our group notes that the Americans and the British also carry some responsibility for carrying out terrible things during the war. He tells the story of a heroic Polish woman who spied for the Allies, taking enormous risks and saving many lives. After the war, the British refused to give her a passport. She was later murdered in a British hotel. He uses this story to suggest that the burden of guilt might more appropriately be shared if it were understood more complexly, rather than located in stereotyped and polarized delineations of German "perpetrators," Jewish "victims," and Allied "heroes." Following this discussion, we turned to our first case.

A young Polish psychologist presents a group intervention she has organized in her country about "reflective citizenship." Since many World War II concentration camps were located in Poland, the Polish people are blamed for them, though they were run by the Nazis. Her citizenship intervention invites Poles to consider what aspects of the war actually "belong" to Poland.

The IDI group asks how this social commitment evolved in her own life. She hesitates to respond, indicating that she doesn't like to think about her past because, when she does, she weeps. She then reports the following:

> Her grandmother lived through World War II, and her mother was born right after the war when Warsaw was totally destroyed. Overwhelmed by managing postwar survival and in her attempt to soften the traumas of the war for her developing family, she did not speak to her young daughter (the presenter's mother) about the terrible things that happened. Her grandchild, our presenter, reports that her favorite childhood book, given to her by her beloved grandmother and kept behind her bed, contained stories with details about the soap that was made from the fat of Jewish corpses. Grandmother also told her stories about the war that frightened her, and in school she watched horrifying documentaries. She often woke up screaming at night. No adult helped her with these feelings or put these stories and films in perspective.

This is an example of the transgenerational transmission of trauma, placed into a child without conscious awareness. In the first generation, the war experience was unbearable and not able to be symbolized. A generation later, it could be represented through books and images but not yet faced; the child was unconsciously invited to carry the unbearable affect. As an adult, our presenter's ability to tolerate these war images ended when she had her own children (the next generation); looking through her children's eyes brought back her childhood feelings. She discovered that she could no longer watch such movies; she now limits herself to seeing romantic comedies. An IDI member asks her what might allow her to look again at such movies and she answers, with tears, "I might be able to do it if some others watched them with me and held my hand." This deeply moved IDI members and they associated to the earlier discussion about sharing the guilt of war.

This Polish grandmother, a war survivor, had unconsciously located her denied and overwhelming feelings of terror, guilt, and anger in her granddaughter, who could not manage them alone, a mirror of her own experience. The group considered the possibility that the story might reveal a parallel in the behavior of nations, who have simplistically parceled out war guilt without "holding the hand" of those nations who have been invited to carry it all, preserving "heroism" for the victors in a way that inhibits international integration and perspective. Though Germany seems to have found ways to manage the burden of war guilt, Japan has not.

The IDI group then continued its discussion about the cultural and historical differences that explain this outcome, raising the question about where else in the world this phenomenon might be happening?

When historical memory is experienced as a presence that has never made its way into words, it is transmitted through affect and bodily communication to the next generation (Davoine & Gaudillière, 2004; Volkan, 2006, 2020). If individuals silently carry in their experience a map of generational and national trauma, under what circumstances—and with what kind of help—can they offer their perspective to those working at conflict negotiation?

Case 2

A discussion between an aging senior Israeli former official and a British negotiator comes to a stop around an exploration of the current Palestinian conflict. Our Palestinian member reports on the current disengagement of Palestinians, their dissatisfaction with their own leaders, and their increasing long-term sense of helplessness. The older Israeli states, however, that things are much better between the two cultures in Israel because the economic situation for Palestinians has so much improved. In his view, Palestinians have consolidated their political parties and can have an impact on the formation of the government, though they will not be able to take up leadership roles in Israeli society because of the structure of "The Jewish State."

The British negotiator notes that open dissent from the impoverished and disenfranchised can more easily be managed by government than the dissent that begins to emerge once the group is better off and less marginalized. With beginning economic and political power comes stronger demands about equal participation. The implied challenge embedded in this statement to the ongoing existence of the "Jewish" state evokes such an angry and defensive response in the older Israeli that the conversation stops. But quietly, a younger Israeli member reports on his own conflict between wanting to sustain a Jewish state and wanting to be forgiven for wanting it.

This is an example of an impasse in political discussion. The passion about historical trauma carried by the older Israeli (who had experienced it) is more muted when offered by the younger Israeli, at more distance from the events. But still, the group does not dare to push the discussion. In the moment, the traumatic histories of Israelis and Palestinians are on the table, with representatives from both sides, but even in this intimate group of colleagues, the discussion cannot deepen.

The tension has been evoked by the recognition that it is more difficult to hold off the power of marginalized groups when their economic and political power is stronger. Without naming the connection, the group turns to a parallel problem in another nation.

> Political polarization around race in America has taken a new turn in America with the presidencies of Donald Trump and Joe Biden. With significant, though still limited improvement in the economic and political progress of African Americans, their voices have become more powerful. The conversation turns to the current power operations of the white majority, many of whom feel that the identity of America is being threatened by the increasing voice of black Americans. This insight leads to the group's ability to explore (in displacement) the question that could not be raised with the Israelis. What would it take in any nation for the dominant voices of the more powerful players to put their own strongly held beliefs and sources of power on the table for review to get beyond impasse?

Discussion

These two examples represent the range of opportunities the group's discussion offers. But the method for effective engagement requires attention to some technical considerations. The first is how to help presenters recognize that their psychological conflicts are not to be understood as individual psychopathology to be opened up for "psychotherapy" from the group. The presenters are not asking to be in the role of "patient" and psychologically trained IDI members are not taking up roles as "therapists." Instead, the group has negotiated a recognition that each of us can be understood as a representative—both conscious and unconscious—of our nations, our ethnicities, our multigenerational pasts. The troubles we carry around with us derive from our environments and represent aspects of social conflict that we have unwittingly been invited to carry on behalf of others.

For example, if I am a third-generation postwar Polish woman and my grandmother who survived the war has repressed the horror and is too traumatized by the immediate postwar management of the struggle to make sense of it, she is unavailable to help me understand our history. If she cannot recognize the adult protection her grandchild needs because no one protected her and she unwittingly passes on the horror onto me and, if it is unmediated by my mother who is part of a shared family denial, I will be terrorized as a child by a range of powerful feelings I don't understand. But when I am an adult, I might be able to begin to see what I need from others to put that trauma in some perspective. I will begin to recognize my need for others who have differentially managed the trauma of postwar anxiety and guilt to put my own experience in perspective.

Is this discussion usable as a metaphor for a three-generational transmission of trauma? Is it a beginning recognition of the consequences of simplistic formulations about perpetrators and victims, and the need for more complex international management of war trauma? The presenter's case was about her adaptive creation of learning opportunities for "reflective citizenship." Can coming to terms with these experiences and putting a voice to them mobilize more effectively the citizenship role? Speaking these memories appeared to allow the presenter to take up leadership, an authority that she had not previously exercised in the group.

The second technical challenge is to help individual IDI members begin to recognize that their national experiences—and the group's process—can be used as metaphors for the range of global conflicts.

For example, the passionate (and seemingly unmovable) commitment to a Jewish state ("Never again!"), though derived from a unique experience of the Holocaust, was used to begin to understand the anxiety, resistance, and power politics mobilized by other seemingly unipolar national majorities in the face of the impending "threat" of integrating difference, for example, the anxiety of the white majority in America about the challenge of immigration, the anxiety in Jordan about the sizable Palestinian population, etc.

Once similar dynamics are recognized across cultures and nations, there is an opportunity to go deeper within each culture to tease out the unique cultural histories, the significance of particular "chosen trauma" and the symbolic connections that make each culture unique.

Summary concepts

- Individuals, small groups, organizations and nations are all open systems. Each is configured with an internal world, an external world, and a boundary function that mediates between the two (Erikson, 1968; Modell, 1984).
- Open systems are linked through the communication of feelings (Modell, 1984).
- For individuals, that boundary function mediates between the internal views of the self and the views of others. For groups and organizations, the mission is the boundary.
- Individuals are representatives of their culture, gender, race, ethnicity, multigenerational history, whether they are aware of it or not. They carry signs of these identities that others can perceive and relate to (Shapiro, 2020, 2021).
- Painful experience, when put into words, can illuminate aspects of personal and social history. Integration of multiple role identities within an individual increases the potential for engagement as a citizen. For groups and organizations (and nations), differences can become useful if subordinated and integrated with a mission (Shapiro, 2020, 2021).
- A group's affective responses can illuminate hidden meanings and pathways for understanding related to the topic under discussion.

References

Davoine, F., & Gaudillière, J. (2004). *History beyond Trauma*. New York: Other Press.

Erikson, E. H. (1950). *Childhood and Society*. New York: W. W. Norton

Erikson, E. H. (1968). *Identity, Youth, and Crisis*. New York: W. W. Norton.

Modell, A. (1984). *Psychoanalysis in a New Context*. New York: International Universities Press.

Shapiro, E. R. (2020). *Finding a Place to Stand: Developing Self-Reflective Institutions, Leaders and Citizens*. Bicester, UK: Phoenix.

Shapiro, E. R. (2021). Why do I have to do this? Institutions, integrity, and citizenship. *Organisational and Social Dynamics*, *21*: 197–211.

Volkan, V. D. (2006). *Killing in the Name of Identity: A Study of Bloody Conflicts*. Charlottesville, VA: Pitchstone.

Volkan, V. D. (2020). *Large-Group Psychology: Racism, Societal Divisions, Narcissistic Leaders, and Who We Are Now*. Bicester, UK: Phoenix.

CHAPTER 16

The Sandwich Model: applying the power of small and large groups to conflict resolution

Robi Friedman

There is no bigger challenge than dealing with conflicts between subgroups of a society or between nations. The aim of our times may be to convince enemies to stop fighting, to create a secure environment where we stop investing in arms and instead invest in creative and productive societies. Professionals who deal with conflict are trying to understand the best ways to mediate between sides.

We can conceive of two general approaches to conflict resolution between nations, which do not oppose each other, but rather are complementary. One is to work with the leaders of the conflicting sides, and the other is working with the people involved in the conflict (see also Volkan's "Tree Model" (2020)). In both cases, work in groups is needed in order to actually come closer to each other, to grow through some process of reciprocal acknowledgments and to negotiate a new coexistence. Professional group workers are direly needed in order to hold and contain such meetings.

I suggest that without both aspects of working together in groups, the best negotiations will only achieve a stop to the fighting. While achieving even momentary peace is always a great outcome, without the presence of both leaders and individuals in this process, real peace may not truly be established for generations. Politicians and lawyers are much better at dividing and splitting nations and communities; seldom will they help bring them closer. Even the most successful negotiation will not truly bring enemies together; often they do the opposite. Romeo and Juliet would have benefited from a successful group process and a deeper, more meaningful dialogue about their families' differences, rivalry, and hateful narratives. Without face-to-face meetings, the distance felt between fighting parties—Jews and Palestinians in Israel, Catholics and Protestants in Northern Ireland, and Greek and Turkish Cypriots, as well as hundreds of other conflicts around the world—leads to splitting painful emotions between large groups (Volkan, 2020) and prevents the healing process. I propose that the best and optimal face-to-face meetings for psycho-political purposes are large and median groups.

As an addendum, I suggest looking at standing social and national conflicts as a kind of mental illness, which we might call "relations disorders" (Friedman, 2019). This perspective on pathology centers on understanding that the disturbance is usually not located in one person or one nation, but between them, in their relationship. Keeping this "social" perspective on relations disorders in mind means that the healing of these disorders must be done by curing the relationships, and this means dialogue between the conflicting sides. Conceptualizing a situation as reflecting a "rejection relations disorder," for example, may help us understand how, in the face of the continuous threat of expulsion, the suffering caused to both enemies and one's own people includes pathological processes that loosen controls over violence. Simultaneously, emotions that help a group contain violence, like shame, guilt, and empathy, are inhibited.

After visiting the Balkans in the decades following their 1990s bloodbath, we conflict workers witnessed the emotional situations manifested in a post-conflict area: whole societies that could not think or reason in difficult situations because of anger and hate, the desire for revenge, the avoidance of coexistence and cooperation, tendencies toward separatism, and transgenerational narratives that perpetuated hate and mutual suspicion. And this is true outside of the Balkans as well. A few years ago, in an intimate group where Norwegians, Danes, and Swedes felt secure enough to speak openly, one Norwegian participant shared the main existential message he received "with his mother's milk": hate the Swedes and kill the Germans. This was more than half a century after World War II. Is this surprising? It only surprises those who think that speaking "politically correctly" truly represents how people feel.

As I am writing, we are having meetings in "median groups" (up to thirty-five participants) between local Jews and Palestinians of our mixed cities, like Jaffa, Lydda, and Haifa, in the wake of recent violence and conflict. These meetings were initiated by professionals after the violence which erupted in the summer of 2021, triggered by conflicts in East Jerusalem. In these sessions, surprised citizens from both sides raised their voices, their surprise being only from lack of communication with their neighbors. Jews seemed appalled by the deep resentments in the Palestinian population, who feel chronically excluded and often rejected. The Palestinians were surprised by the degree of ignorance, denial, and blindness of their distant Jewish neighbors. After a session or two, it became clear to all sides that, if they had talked before, much of the anger, which was acted out in destructive, terroristic activities (like lynchings or Molotov bombs), would not have occurred. These group discussions truly made very clear how important and impactful such face-to-face conversations are.

Back to the first path of conflict resolution: working with leaders involved in the conflict. Sometimes, for one reason or another, prominent enemies will come together in order to negotiate an agreement, in hopes of stopping the destruction and the conflict. Ideally, these leading forces should have enough influence on the fighting forces and on legislators, and be well enough connected to their people that positive change can occur. In the Tree Model (Volkan, 2020), a whole evaluation process is described in order to understand if the conflict can be approached and how this might happen. I want to add also the importance of accompanying professional group workers, who are especially able to hold and contain the highly volatile emotions in the relations. This process contains at least two professional aspects: one is the ability to digest high levels of hatred, which themselves are the result of experienced or feared traumas and of promised glories. The other aspect is the holding of such a process within the right setting. Many activities like politics, sports, or high risk business, which must cope continuously with emergency situations, seem to strive for immediate results and have low tolerance for longer processes. Unfortunately, conflict resolution cannot be done in one short stroke. A professional group worker understands and forms a setting in which the highly explosive traumas and glories can be elaborated step by step.

This is also why simply negotiating an agreement, no matter how clever and well designed and no matter how great the lawyers, is never enough. The need for nations and communities to digest the agreement and translate it into coexistence takes "dialogue time," meaning the investment in meetings, as will be presented as the Sandwich Model (a temporary and affectionate name). Taking the Northern Ireland conflict as only one prominent conflict: after a series of meetings, a small group of people from many sides (Unionists, Republicans, and representatives from Ireland, the UK, and other countries) negotiated the "Good Friday Agreement." I have a great deal of respect for the ability to finalize such an agreement, no matter how incomplete or imperfect it may seem. As an Israeli, I am envious of this agreement when I compare it to the Oslo agreements, which I also respect. Having had inside knowledge of the Oslo process, I know it succeeded well enough as a negotiation, but unfortunately it did not prevail as an agreed proposition to all fighting sides in Israel. Implementing the negotiated results of the Oslo process into the political and social reality of the region became impossible, emphasizing and juxtaposing the relative success of the Northern Ireland process. But even in Northern Ireland, if judging by taxi drivers and walls, the Montagues and Capulets of Romeo and Juliet's Belfast families do not seem even close to coexisting, despite their wishful thinking.

The group Sandwich Model: the use of a mix between small and large groups as a social curative and developmental space

Individuals talking in dyads and in small groups seem to easily make progress in an accepting dialogue with different "partners" and even with the enemy. But those of us who have worked for years in conflict resolution using these formats have been deeply disappointed by these processes, which, at first glance, seem to be successful. The moment the dialogue ends, very little of the mediation process seemed to carry a continuing influence on the political and social atmosphere in the enemy camps. It took us many years to accept it and understand why. Changes in participants of dyadic or small group dialogues do not hold because the community and the society are much more influential than any individual. Societies do not trust changes stemming from the individual or small groups, and do not let themselves be influenced by it. I want to limit myself here for two reasons: one is that in a society, in Volkan's "large group" of a nation or tribe (2020), the individual is expected to be selfless, norm abiding, and not deviant, and he should certainly not be influenced by the state of the enemy's psyche. The second, unconscious reason is that in everyone's "unthought known" (Bollas, 1987), the small group is the heir of the family. As such, the main relational principle it carries is the fantasy that no one will be rejected from the family. For very primal reasons, every family holds a "promise of no rejection" (Friedman, 2018). Thus, because the small group accepts everything, even the suffering or motivations of enemies, the small group is dismissed by the larger society and its potential influence curtailed. In the setting known to many of us as "the median group" (twelve to forty participants) or the large group (from forty to hundreds), the promise of non-rejection does not hold: these groups increasingly represent society and have the ability to reject any participant who is not accepted as a representative of the norms or leadership.

The Sandwich Model is designed to cope with conflictual situations in disturbed communities. Participation in the large group, this massive face to face meeting, has proven itself to have a unique potential, transforming hate into nonviolent coexistence. As the common citizen is not used to the often violent dialogue that occurs in large groups and often appears threatened by it in the beginning, the large group is "sandwiched," or inserted, between two smaller group sessions. The Sandwich Model combines the familiarity of a small group setting with the experience of what a large group setting—of hundreds of participants—is like, even when it is conducted with an innovative, soft, group analytic approach. Exclusion and rejection dynamics are handled in benign, optimal ways through this combination of small and large groups.

The Sandwich Model is Face*look*, in contrast to Face*book* and its dynamics. There is ample evidence in schools and other communities that Facebook and other virtual designs, which enable large groups to "meet" virtually, seem only to offer the ability to make "friends" and get closer to those one is already in some way close to. But actually they seem to reinforce enmity and feelings of detachment from many others. The inherent distance between people on the internet, as a general rule, makes attacking one another easier. But in a face-to-face meeting, such as those in the Sandwich Model, a developmental space is created which provides an opportunity to encounter extremism by reintroducing violence-inhibiting mechanisms like guilt, shame, and empathy. Working in the large group pushes individuals toward finding a voice and the right tone, in the presence of a potentially threatening mass and the massive authority it seems to carry. Meeting these challenges in the large group enhances a person's citizenship.

The Sandwich Model is designed to cope with conflictual situations and disturbed communities. It combines the relative security of small groups with the social character of large groups. Using the opportunities large groups can offer—a setting which offers maximum face-to-face encounters—participants can, if rightly conducted by staff, establish a unique social dialogue. Such powerful verbal and nonverbal experiences expose participants to the views of others, as well as enabling the ability to voice one's own view. The large-group interaction, which promises a more lasting change, is prepared by a small group session and its leader, which will later accompany the group into the large group and its second small group meeting. The relation with the authority also helps anxious participants find some security.

Voicing conflicts in the large group, with its completely different atmosphere, may well provide a unique opportunity to find one's own authority in a less secure social group, which is an important developmental step for an individual. Moving back from the large group to the small group, the Sandwich Model provides a further opportunity to understand and cope with the social dynamics of splitting and hating. Selfless attitudes, together with societal and authoritarian dominance, can be elaborated. The Sandwich Model may be the optimal method for holding a potentially transformative dialogue on extremism and fanaticism.

Application

The model has been applied to both professional and lay groups in conflicts: in Ukraine during the fighting in the eastern part of the country (but before the Russian invasion in 2022), in Northern Ireland, with politicians and leaders of the civil society, and in German-Jewish dialogues. I have also applied this model in schools and in villages. We have worked with this model in a kibbutz where, for a decade, one part of the kibbutz refused to speak to another. We have succeeded in many places in starting and increasing the dialogue. Participants learned to step away from long monologues toward dialogues, from lecturing to "tweeting," which usually improves communication. Participants' minimum age might be lower than one might think—right now, my experience is with individuals as young as fifteen years of age.

There are other similar forms of interventions used to negotiate in conflict situations or in societies as an exercise in democracy. The best known is the Reflective Citizen method (Mojović, 2016), which is now applied in places other than where it originated in Serbia. The large group is also the center stage for communication. The difference with the Sandwich Model is that, in RC, the small groups are self-conducted and a session of "social dreaming" (Lawrence, 1991) is part of the process. The question of self-conducted groups has two aspects: first, self-conduction may require that the group already has less enmity—both in terms of quantity and quality—in its members; otherwise it may be uncontainable without the help of conductors. The large group will be dealing with powerful emotions and differences, so the small group must be able to hold and elaborate these feelings. On the other side is the question of conductor availability; some interventions might take place far away from an organization, like a group analytic institute, which can provide professional leadership. So self-conduction, if done well, may be necessary.

An example

When the dozen conductors arrived in the village, about 100 participants were waiting for us. The invitation to intervene followed conflicts in this village, which had started to deteriorate into physical destruction of property. Attacking a person was becoming an option. The dispute, which could not be solved by laws and rulings, was over the application of political ideology on the inclusion of former enemies to buy land and build in the village. The invitation to the conductors was suggested to the village's council by an inhabitant who had participated in a former conflict resolution group. The council left the professional organization of the intervention to me, and invited the villagers through a letter with explanations, partly designed by me. The conductors' team consisted of volunteers members from the Israel Institute of Group Analysis.

In the introduction (fifteen minutes), the Sandwich Model, its advantages and difficulties, was explained to participants. They were encouraged to commit to a "working alliance" with the program. The mix between small and large groups was described, together with the aims of the large groups and the challenges of participating in it. The overall aim of the dialogue was emphasized.

Small groups, which lasted about an hour, helped the participants to find their voices and a kind of preliminary openness to diverging opinions. After that a large group meeting consisting of eleven groups, which lasted about an hour and ten minutes, was formed with their conductors. In this large group, many of the community's sociopolitical positions were voiced in a very personal, emotional tone. The encouragement to "tweet" instead of monologuing was actually modeled by younger participants about sixteen years of age. This experience aroused both very strong feelings together with the awareness of differing and similar views, and the danger of acting out angry and opposing feelings. After a twenty minute pause, a short small group session, which lasted about thirty minutes, was tasked with calming those who felt threatened by the large group. It also provided an additional space to voice unspoken issues. A fifteen minute closing session finished the intervention.

Groups were led by highly professional conductors. The participants in this event found that the group analytic approach to their large group proved that it was not necessary to become violent. This provided the community with a good motivation to continue the process. This process, which usually starts at eighteen hours and continues for three or more hours, should be repeated for three evenings, ideally no more than two weeks apart, for the best results. However, we have had good results with pauses of many months if the organization is unable to keep a tighter schedule.

Later, the vast majority of the participants of the Sandwich Model intervention wrote favorable feedback. While many at first were overwhelmed by the massive "groupishness" of the evening and especially by the large group—an experience heretofore unknown to the general population—many wrote about their new awareness of the community's conflicts and rifts. The developmental process ignited by the Sandwich Model continued in the days and weeks that followed, although I think it often takes months to understand the power of such intervention. The most important feedback was that violence did not return for at least the following year.

Epilogue

The Sandwich Model requires optimal organizational abilities in order to bring people together and to administer the three meeting process. The Sandwich Model, and other similar approaches to the solution of conflicts, build a post-conflict frame, which conducts, holds, and contains a group process, and, in so doing, demonstrates the potential advantage of using a mix of small and large groups in governmental and private organizations, schools and universities, and with the general population.

References

Bollas, C. (1987). The unthought known: Early considerations. In: *The Shadow of the Object* (pp. 277–283). London: Free Association.

Friedman, R. (2018). Beyond rejection, glory and the Soldier's Matrix: The heart of my group analysis. *Group Analysis, 51*(4): 1–17.

Friedman, R. (2019). *Dreamtelling, Relations and Large Groups: New Developments in Group Analysis.* London: Routledge.

Lawrence, W. G. (1991). Won from the void and formless infinite: Experiences of social dreaming. *Free Associations, 2:* 259–294.

Mojović, M. (2016). Serbian reflective citizens' matrix flourishing in leaking containers: Response to the 40th Foulkes Lecture. *Group Analysis, 49*(4): 370–384.

Volkan, V. D. (2020). *Large-Group Psychology: Racism, Societal Divisions, Narcissistic Leaders, and Who We Are Now.* Bicester, UK: Phoenix.

CHAPTER 17

Traveling through time: a group intervention in Northern Ireland

M. Gerard Fromm

A few years ago, several members of the International Dialogue Initiative were invited to design and facilitate a set of meetings to address an outbreak of violence in Belfast, the capital of Northern Ireland. Over the course of thirty years, sectarian violence between Protestants and Catholics—a period known as The Troubles—had led to more than 3,500 deaths. A lengthy, sometimes turbulent peace process culminated in the Good Friday Agreement of 1998, which, more or less, ended the fighting and established a power-sharing government. The agreement has held for two decades, though outbreaks of violence do occur periodically—this one over escalating tensions about the protocol for flying the Union flag. Given this terrible history, such a resurgence is always of great concern.

This particular retreat brought together high level representatives from all five of Northern Ireland's major political parties as well as civic leaders from various segments of society (senior police officers, the Gaelic Athletic Association, clergy, a business executive, and leaders of NGOs, including a representative of a victims' organization). Organized by an ecumenical group, the meeting was held over two days at a remote retreat house on the north coast. Five formal one and a half hour sessions took place over this time; retreat members, the ecumenical group, and the facilitating team shared meals and engaged informally outside the sessions. There were twenty-one invited participants and a team of five IDI facilitators, of which I was one. This chapter reports on the retreat's structure, the emotion-driven themes that emerged, and important process moments.

The agreed-upon task of the retreat was to explore and diagnose underlying *psychological obstacles* to a more peaceful and stable Northern Ireland. The IDI team's aim was not to focus on individual dynamics, except to the degree that they might represent the larger group and societal dynamic. Participants in this kind of meeting—because they are embedded in the identity of their groups and because the immediate group dynamic pushes for it—inevitably function as informal spokespersons for the groups they represent. By listening to personal stories and observing interactions among the participants, the team tried to understand, name, and describe various processes that occur in and between large groups in Northern Ireland: Catholics and Protestants, Unionists and Nationalists, and various political and community organizations. Our effort was to help participants go beyond political statements and talk openly about emotional issues that might be very difficult to speak about. In this way, we hoped to explore what was going on in the communities in conflict and how the emotional legacy of The Troubles was manifesting itself currently.

Bullets through time

"Bullets don't just travel through skin and bone. They travel through time." As noted in the Introduction, this statement was tattooed onto the shoulder of a young woman whose father was shot during The Troubles. It captures the emotional legacy of trauma, the way that the next generation and even subsequent generations must deal with what happened to people they loved and are deeply connected to. Sometimes this transmission leads to further violence, sometimes to mourning and reparative efforts. One way or the other, it's on the skin, so to speak; it's an inescapable part of a person's emotional life.

In Northern Ireland, real resolution of emotional difficulties has been difficult to achieve. There is considerable suspicion and a resigned weariness about reconciliation efforts. Some participants in the retreat wondered if this set of conversations would be genuinely useful or, as one participant put it on the first day of the gathering, "just going around in the cement mixer again." Spontaneous metaphors are revealing. "Going around in the cement mixer" seems fruitless indeed, but it also prevents a dangerous hardening. The use of this metaphor raises a question about this sort of peacemaking effort: Whether or not a given intervention proves valuable, is the continued work preventive in itself? Does it at least keep things in motion and some measure of hope alive?

The hand

The day before the retreat began, my IDI colleague, Dr. Robi Friedman, arrived and brought a small gift to the member of our team who had initiated the project, Lord John Alderdice. A citizen of Northern Ireland himself, Lord Alderdice had been deeply involved in the peace process for years (Alderdice, 2010) and, when the Good Friday Agreement was finally negotiated, he was elected the first Speaker of the Assembly. The gift was a porcelain hand making a sign of peace. That evening, Dr. Friedman and I encountered a different hand. As the sun was setting, we walked down the hill, along the coast and into the small town, where we visited a pub. We sat at the bar, ordered our pints, and chatted about the upcoming meeting. The atmosphere was jovial on the surface but edgy underneath. A man seemed to be singing loudly into his friend's ear. The young woman behind the bar looked at her regulars with resigned exasperation.

Then a young man—perhaps in his thirties—sitting next to my colleague abruptly introduced himself, welcomed us to the pub and asked where we were from. He seemed completely drunk, an impression confirmed by his garrulous speech and by his repeatedly thrusting his hand toward us for handshakes over the next half hour. We were taken aback not just by his raucous intrusion but by the fact that all of the fingers on his right hand had been cut off at the knuckle. This man seemed to have been the victim of an industrial accident. He was both very friendly to us but also very angry, and he seemed to want us to see what, from a psychoanalytic angle, was his castrated hand. As we walked back to the retreat house, my friend and I felt we had encountered something profoundly painful in Northern Ireland's current culture.

Leadership

In the formal meetings of the retreat, four members of the IDI facilitating team sat in a large circle with enough chairs for the other twenty-one invited participants. A fifth IDI facilitator sat with the small ecumenical group outside the circle. They remained silent during the discussions, taking up an observer role, perhaps representing, psychologically speaking, the Northern Ireland public in general. After each session, the IDI facilitator met with them separately, collected their impressions about what they had observed, and helped them understand the interventions of the facilitating team. The IDI facilitators also met privately after the sessions, evaluating what we had observed and learned, listening to reports of the observers' views, and making decisions about how to proceed during the next session. At the end of the last session, a summary of the facilitators' findings and the observers' perceptions were shared with everyone in the room for general discussion.

As the first meeting was about to begin, we learned that one participant had had to drop out and another would be arriving late. Thus there were two empty chairs in the large circle as we began, which happened to be the two chairs on either side of the lead facilitator, Dr. Vamık Volkan. This may seem like a strange coincidence, but, in my experience, when people enter a group—especially an emotionally charged one—they pay subtle attention to where they sit. What did it mean that no one sat next to the lead facilitator? One hypothesis would be that he represented authority, perhaps authority attributed to him as an accomplished person, but also the authority of someone who represented the risky task they were about to take up. Thus there may well have been some fear in the group's reactions to Dr. Volkan. Perhaps also, in such a bitterly contested larger environment, no one wanted to be seen as trying to curry favor with the person in authority by sitting next to him.

But this potential pairing dynamic—that is, the wish to gain advantage by forming a power couple with the person in authority—seemed present in an informal moment just before the session began. This moment too involved a hand. A young charismatic politician from one of the Nationalist parties—a party that wants Northern Ireland to unite with the larger Republic of Ireland—reached out to shake hands with Dr. Volkan, and said "Welcome to Ireland!" Not "Welcome to Northern Ireland." The struggle to have the person representing authority on one side and not the other seemed to have begun. In fact, the desperate search for a leader was the first major theme of the conversation. In various ways, people communicated an intense need for someone who had the power to contain and tame aggression, someone or something that could function as a stabilizing third structure. First, the police officers in the group were turned to. When the senior police representatives tried to explain *logically* how the Northern Ireland police institution worked—that it could not serve a partisan purpose nor, in an effort to manage such widespread aggression, turn the society into a police state—disappointment ensued. The officers felt "caught in the middle" in this group as they also felt themselves to be in the society.

Then the participants searched for other symbolic "leaders," such as religious institutions and even business organizations. The clergy in the room at times attempted to fill this role, sometimes movingly, other times with frustration. One clergyman's story of how he called on his community to reclaim their church square from militants was a concrete and, it turned out, successful example of a citizen's effort to claim the societal space. Then a business leader pleaded that the economy and education were crucial bridging issues, if only groups could get past their rage. Finally, someone petitioned for a "bill of rights." The facilitators spoke to the participants' preoccupation with finding a stabilizing "leader," an institution, a focus, in psychoanalytic terms, a "shared superego" to help contain frightening, potentially destructive feelings. Since the overall population was fragmented, no one leader in Northern Ireland was currently able to do that. No one was able to help this traumatized large group restore its basic trust in each other and in a way of living together.

Dr. Volkan's leadership, developed over his many years of working with groups in conflict (2013), was exercised both in the management of the event and, as we shall soon see, in his framing of certain emotional issues. Sessions started and ended on time. Dr. Volkan set out the task at the beginning, invited people to speak openly and personally about their problematic experiences, and asked the group for a critical authorization. "I ask you, with all due respect, to allow me to say 'Shut up!' if I feel someone is giving a speech," he said. This elicited laughter and easy consent from the group, but it was extremely important to the group's confidence that, at least in the microcosm of the retreat, someone would indeed manage aggression. And, managing it made it possible to talk about it specifically and directly. Another important intervention early on was Dr. Volkan's question to a man who reported having been in jail for a considerable period of time. "What were you in jail for?" Dr. Volkan asked. "Murder," the man said, in front of police officers, though he added that, from his point of view, he was a soldier who had killed in combat.

The group and the community

During the initial session, the women—none of whom were politicians—were completely silent. This eventually came to represent the silence of almost all of the non-political leadership, who seemed to be living out one person's idea that they were "spare parts." Again, an interesting metaphor; "spare parts" conveys a sense of being useless, but in fact, they are essential when something breaks down. On the other hand, the politician members of the group spoke easily, although in ways that sounded at first like party platforms. As a way of grounding themselves in their political identities and establishing security at the beginning of an anxiety-arousing discussion, this way of speaking made a certain kind of sense. But it was not a dialogue across representatives of different groups nor was it personal. The team noted that real dialogue across the political/non-political boundary was difficult, and so for a while the conversation was in a state, as one member put it, of "suspended animation," just as the politics of Northern Ireland were.

When this was noticed and understood, women among the participants were able to find their voices and to include the feelings they had kept silent about. One set of feelings erupted in response to a story one of the clergy told, a poignant story about having bought a new tie for a family celebration and then, to his shock, being greeted with a bitter question about whether he was ashamed to wear his collar. Initially, the group did not pick up on the obvious pain this man brought to the discussion. But when a facilitator noted the potential emotional obstacle of shame, another member burst into a rage: "How dare you speak about shame?" she said to the facilitator. "There is so much shame in all of us that, if we allowed ourselves to feel it, we would all kill ourselves."

This almost primal outburst highlighted two emotional obstacles to the group's and perhaps the community's moving forward. First, to speak the feelings made them real. It was as though the facilitator had not simply heard what the clergyman had just said about shame; he had made it real by speaking it. In this sense, he had inflicted it on the group. Second, having become real, the shame was now dangerous, dangerous to the very community essential to getting through these terrible feelings. "We would all kill ourselves" is a profound statement about the community-in-the-mind: that it simply would not survive the intense feelings of its members. These participants seemed to be saying that there was no holding environment for them, no collective capacity to contain together the shame of actions done to each other over so many years. Hence the longing for some third outside the community to serve this function.

Betrayal

Other intolerable feelings eventually came into the conversation: guilt for abandoning past injustices, wishes for retribution intermixed with, and sometimes identified with, demands for justice, and existential fear of the other group. To some degree, the emotional engagement around shame seemed to free members, especially among the non-political subgroup, to join the discussion, while those in political leadership seemed more invested, and perhaps more stuck, in their positions. Was this the result of how powerfully they were carrying their constituencies' pain, grievances, and difficulty grieving? Ironically, the phrase "political class" was used a number of times, a phrase that could suggest their being "above" the people. But did this distract all concerned from how embedded political leadership is in the most basic and stubborn feelings of the people? Is this one reason that it can be difficult to exercise real leadership in the face of constituents' resistance?

This brought up the nature of the loyalty to one's group. Actual feelings of loyalty to one's group was intermixed with fear of being seen as disloyal and seemed to bind members of the same group together, both in the meeting and probably in the society as well. As one member put it, "I'm part of a group that will be suspicious of you, so I'm morally bound to be suspicious." And, more frighteningly, should one be or appear to be disloyal, "the danger is from our own group." The history of The Troubles is full of lethal punishment for real or suspected disloyalty. This question of loyalty presents an enormous problem for political leaders, who are elected by a part of the community but must lead the whole community. In the context of violent rivalries, there is a major risk—to electability and perhaps to safety—in being seen as betraying one's own group. But real leadership sometimes requires what a colleague calls "virtuous betrayal" (Krantz, 2006), that is, a leader's taking decisions that may betray a narrow, emotional, and even self-defeating interest of a constituency in favor of a greater, encompassing good. One politician described how his bipartisan work on the damage sectarian fighting had done to children's education was met with a grandmother's rage that he would dare talk with the people who had killed her grandson. "My dilemma," he said, is: "I betray the past or I betray the future."

Grievance and grief

This grandmother's pain captures the distinction between grievance and grief. The legacy of The Troubles is full of deep grievances that, at a psychological level, function as a powerful defense against grief. Grievance looks toward a future in which revenge of some sort or at least some compensatory righting of a grievous wrong will occur. Grief, on the other hand, is about a loss that is now in the past. Whatever has been lost, usually a person, is irrecoverable. In one sense, there is no future, certainly for the lost loved one, but also, as it is felt by those left behind, for the grief-struck as well. The only real way forward is through mourning, but the trauma of sudden loss makes opening up the mourning process very difficult, especially for those who have suffered so many losses over so long a time.

As the sessions proceeded, we began to hear more personal stories, which were very moving. Because the group had begun to work with each other and with us, and because time was short, Dr. Volkan made a critical intervention:

I am sure that most you in this room and perhaps all of you experienced losses during The Troubles. You lost family members, friends, things that you deeply value. Psychologically, it is necessary that after important losses, people mourn. People die, things disappear, but their images, their "mental doubles" remain in our minds. We have an internal relationship with these mental doubles, which goes on until we say goodbye to them over time, until they become futureless, so to speak. If everything goes well such internal relationships slowly come to rest. But, in Northern Ireland such losses were linked to severe traumas and conflicts. So, my hunch is that such mental doubles are still very much around. What do they tell you?

Initially there was anger about this intervention because it invited the participants to open up very difficult emotions. At least two participants stated that they were not there "to be psychoanalyzed." They even suggested that the facilitator needed their permission before making this statement. Clearly, a frightening question had entered people's thoughts; if the community might kill itself because of shame, how could it survive the unbearable grief built up over so many years? Soon, however, the dynamics changed when one member dared to speak his own mind. "Are you kidding?" he said to the more resistant group members, "Ghosts are everywhere in Northern Ireland!"

Following this, participants began to talk about lost friends and relatives, and about what those "ghosts" were telling them, so to speak. They began to realize that, without going through and dealing with their complicated grief reactions, unspoken feelings remained alive in the mourner. At a group level, being stuck in a shared but warded-off mourning process forces traumatized communities to unconsciously hold on to other problematic emotions: survival guilt, wishes for revenge, shame for being friendly with the opposite side, guilt for abandoning past injustices, an unending list of grievances, and confusion about how to deal with victims. This discussion showed that even rational people must deal with "ghosts." Without the presence of a stabilizing "leader," this group (representing Northern Ireland's various communities) seemed to need outsiders (the facilitators) to help open and care for these "wounds." Now they were beginning to see how the intensity and pervasiveness of traumatic loss had become a profound emotional obstacle to peacemaking.

Another hand

One of the Nationalist leaders repeatedly stated how his party was extending its open hand to political opponents in order to "move forward," but that that gesture was always rejected. The facilitators noted that representatives of the Unionist parties—who want Northern Ireland to remain a part of the United Kingdom—were suspicious of these overtures. They felt that Nationalists had not really renounced what for the Unionists was an existentially threatening strategy, but had simply changed their tactics. Nationalists might give lip service to the reconciliation process but not really engage with it. The Nationalist side seemed unable to understand or alter this part of the dialogue. To them, the Unionists in the group seemed split among their various parties, unclear about their stance, silenced by their own colleagues, and not ready to meet the offer of an "open hand."

Did this stalemate represent what was happening with the majority of the silent electorate, who might themselves feel culturally and politically disempowered? Were Unionists worried about simply surviving (in contrast to the main Nationalist party's sense that it was thriving)? Were they worried about feeling abandoned by the British government, or something else? We did not have time to fully understand all of these issues. Nationalists did not seem curious about their opponents' refusal to join them and did not present their own genuine arguments for societal change. Nor was empathy for the other's experiences a part of the culture of communication between these groups; it was as though empathy risked betrayal of one's own side and humiliation by the other. Meanwhile, "the hand" once again emerged as a metaphor for working toward peace or refusing it.

In this context, Lord Alderdice found himself thinking about the mythic origins of Northern Ireland, and he brought to the facilitators' and the participants' attention the meaning of the Irish symbol, the Red Hand. According to mythology, the North had no rightful owner and was claimed by the two most powerful clans in the South. The clans' leaders agreed to a race between the fastest runner from each clan; whoever's hand first touched the land of the North would be its owner. As the two runners neared their goal, one saw that he was about to lose and so cut off his hand and threw it ahead onto the soil of the North. Thus, a claim was made and the battle started. The bloody "Red Hand of Ulster" is actually a ubiquitous symbol in Northern Ireland and emerged in the discussion as a powerful metaphor, capturing a deep, life-or-death sense of rivalry between two warring groups. The story—a story not only of rivalry but of bad faith agreements—and its being told in this moment, felt like a powerful intervention. An important historical and cultural context—a Genesis story really—had been discovered, one that cast grave doubts on what it means to work together.

The myth of the Red Hand of Ulster brought to our attention another "hidden" emotional factor that most likely plays a role in preventing a settling of The Troubles in Northern Ireland: a stubbornly enduring, conscious and unconscious culture of rivalry, which stirs the adrenaline even if its actual goals are mythic and its means of achieving them unfair. After the retreat, we learned more about how the symbol of the Red Hand is very much "alive" in Northern Ireland. It is part of the provincial and political flags of Ulster and Northern Ireland. Its image is deployed frequently by the Ulster Volunteer Force and other loyalist paramilitaries (including the Red Hand Commandos). The Gaelic Athletic Association uses it for one of its county teams. A Red Hand marks burial plots maintained by the National Graves Association, adorns stained-glass windows in Belfast's City Hall, and even advertises the services of Indian palmists. For decades, the Red Hand was the logo for the Northern Ireland Tourist Board, though it has since been replaced by a heart. As I have noted elsewhere (Fromm, 2022), people sometimes put right there on the mantelpiece, so to speak, a critical signifier of their trouble, which then becomes unconscious to them, the kind of secret, Adam Phillips (1996) says, that one can only tell oneself by telling someone else.

Respect

In the final session, a young Unionist, who to that point had been the only silent member of the group, said to a Nationalist: "You extend your hand, and say you want us to join you but, when we don't, you interpret that as our problem, rather than asking us *why* we don't join you." He was pointing out how real curiosity was missing from the Nationalist's approach, in favor of presumptions and defensive certainty. It was as though Nationalists felt they already knew the answers, so didn't need to ask the questions. Indeed it was generally true for the entire group that inquiry into why someone felt a certain way or hesitated about joining was largely missing, as though to genuinely explore issues across this highly charged political boundary was dangerous.

The Unionist then added, referring to a comment made earlier in that session: "And why do you want us to respect your dead? I respect my own dead; I don't need you to respect them." Then, one of the Nationalist members—to that point a jovial, collaborative sort of person—spoke with genuine feeling: "I'll tell you why. When I was growing up, people didn't even acknowledge that my mother and father and grandmother even existed, and when they did, they treated them like dirt. So, if they weren't respected in life, I want them respected in death." An NGO leader, formerly a senior police officer, responded, in a way that joined with the facilitators: "That's what they mean by the *ghosts of the past*." Then he said to the Nationalist: "I won't remember much of the political talk here, but *I will never forget what you just said*."

Words that are unforgettable—unforgettable because so profoundly and personally true—are one of the most important outcomes of any intervention into trauma. In the relatively short time of the retreat, we noted a number of hopeful progressions. Over the course of the five sessions, there was increasing emotional engagement throughout the membership, an increasing capacity to tolerate the expression of feeling, and increasing strength in the voices of the civic leadership. Related to this, there was more person-to-person talk, including, very importantly, the political leaders' speaking personally. After phases of resistance, members joined the facilitating team's consultation and opened up personal experiences of trauma and loss. Finally, new leadership emerged, as did important bridging issues and a number of hypotheses that might shed further light on the emotional dynamics of this conflicted but very appealing community.

The IDI facilitating team left the retreat feeling very grateful to the participants for the risks they had taken and for their growing trust in our capacity to contain and make sense of the strong feelings they had expressed. For various reasons, this was a one-time intervention, the outcomes of which, whatever they were, were carried back by individual members into their political and societal roles. We learned that there were some behind-the-scenes communications between a few participants that seemed to move in a constructive direction. While it was probably being planned long before the retreat, the Centre for Democracy and Peace-Building was founded in Belfast not long after the retreat. Led by two of the retreat's participants, the CDPB institutionalizes the larger task, of which the retreat was a part. It tries to find "entry points" within Northern Ireland's political and social dynamics for *actions* that might diminish the power of the psychological obstacles that emerged in the retreat. In doing so, it works to counter community fragmentation and despair. Traumatized societies are seriously at risk of collapsing back into traumatizing conflict. It is a testament to the Good Friday Agreement and to the perseverance of people, like those who organized and participated in this retreat, that so far this battered, tenacious, and profoundly alive group of people has managed to get on with the task of being a community.

References

Alderdice, J. (2010). Off the couch and round the conference table. In: A. Lemma & M. Patrick (Eds.), *Off the Couch: Contemporary Psychoanalytic Applications* (pp. 1–15). London: Routledge.

Fromm, M. G. (2022). *Traveling through Time: How Trauma Plays Itself Out in Families, Organizations and Society*. Bicester, UK: Phoenix.

Krantz, J. (2006). Leadership, betrayal and adaptation. *Human Relations*, 59(2): 221–240.

Phillips, A. (1996). *Terrors and Experts*. Cambridge, MA: Harvard University Press.

Volkan, V. D. (2013). *Enemies on the Couch: A Psychopolitical Journey through War and Peace*. Durham, NC: Pitchstone.

Index

Abbas, M., 218
Aberfan, Welsh village, 5
Absentees' Property Law (in Israel), 221
accordion phenomenon, 154
Acharya, A., 92
Akhtar, S., 187–188
Akkiraz, S., 204
Aksu, S., 202
Alawneh, M., 218
Albert of Aachen, 232
Alexievich, S., 82
Algazi, İ., 201
Allensbach Institute, 173
Al-Qaeda, 92
Alderdice, J., 21, 59, 250, 275, 282
Arendt, H., 81, 141
Arıboğan, D. Ü., xiii, 91
Armenian–Azeri conflict, 5
Armstrong, G., 238
Armstrong, N., 105
Arsenault, A., 198
Ansary, T., 234
anti-Semitism, 16, 149, 200, 232–233
Arab Spring, 62

Arsenault, A., 198
Asad, M., 234
Ash, T. G., 78
Assmann, A., 42
Augustine, 230–231
Aum Shinrikyo, 9, 84
Austen Riggs Center, xx
Avcı. K., 203
Azar, E., 97

Bana, İ., 202
Barber, B., 130
Bar On, D., 45
Barenboim, D., 199
Barenboim–Said vision of cultural engagement, 200
Baum, G., 137
Becker, D., 40
Berezin, M., 96
Berridge, G. R., 196
Biden, J., 109, 259
Binicewitz, K., 205
biological regeneration, 5
Black Death, 16

Black Lives Matter, 129
Blos, P., 188
Bode, S., 271
Bongardt, A., 108
Bollas, C., 12, 267
Booth, R., 169
border, 16, 55, 74, 79, 93, 107, 126, 157, 160, 182–183, 190, 203
　　psychological, 10–11
Bosse, H., 43
Bourland, A., 215
Bradshaw, J., 238
Bredella, L., 171
Brenner, I., 12
Brenner, Y., 173
Branch Davidians, 9
Burki, T., 107
Burt, D. X., 231
Bush, G. W., 119, 126, 128, 229
Butler, K., 108

Campbell, C., 99
Carey, A., 102
Carter, J., 18
Center for National Policy, 121
Center for the Study of Mind and Human Interaction, xx, 6, 13, 18, 58
Çevik, A., xiv, 181, 183–184, 187–188, 190–191
Çevik, S. B., xiv, 195
Ceyhun, B., 191
Chamberlain, N., 149
Chanturia, G., 4
Chen, Y. Y., 238
Chernobyl, 4–5, 10
Chirac, J., 169
Choctaws, 228
chosen glory, 151, 251
chosen trauma, xxii, 13–16, 42–46, 52–54, 62, 144, 151, 249, 255
Chow, K., 101
Christoslavism, 14
Chukhray, G., 148
Churchill, W., 149
civil litigation, xv, 245–246
civil wars, 140
Claster, J. N., 230

Cobb, S., 240
Cohen, R., 204
Cohen, T., 204
Cohn, N., 232, 237
Cold War, 36, 46, 74, 82
Colston, E., 170
Coltart, N., 25, 37
Connolly, K., 159
Cook, D., 233
Corera, G., 105
Cotter, C., 95
Coups, P., 86–87
Covid-19, 16, 21, 92, 94–96, 98, 100–102, 240
Covington, C., 140
Cowan, G., 198
Crusades, 227–237, 239, 241
Cull, N. J., 198, 200
cultural memory, 42–43, 45
Cyprus, 7, 9, 184–185
　　Cypriot Greeks, 9, 58, 264
　　Cypriot Turks, 9–10, 58, 264

Dakota Indians, 13
Dart Foundation, xxii
Darwin, C., 145, 153
Daş, M., 204
Dasgupta, R., 74
Davidson, W., 197
Davis, K. C., 95–97
Davoine, F., 61, 258
DeAngelis, T., 98
dehumanization, 25, 30, 33–38, 139
Demir, M., 201, 203–205
Deniz, Ö., 205
Derakhshan, H., 94
Diamond, S., 169
Diana, Princess of Wales, 4
Dickinson, P., 104
Didili, Z., 96
disease
　　Bolshevik, 95
　　British, 100
　　Chinese Pox, 100
　　Christian, 100
　　French Evil, 100
　　French Flu, 95
　　German Plague, 95

Irish, 100
Jewish, 100
Kirghiz, 95
Naples Soldiers, 95
Neapolitan, 100
origin and blame, 100
Persian Fire, 100
Polish, 100
Spanish, 100
Spanish Lady, 95
Turkish, 100
White Man's, 95
Duma, West Bank village, 63
Duterte, R., 73

earthquakes, 4–6, 204
Edgington, S., 233
Ee, S., 99
Einstein, A., 145
Ekim, S., 186
Elitsoy, Z. A., 202–204
Eliyahu, M., 204
Elmendorf, D., xviii
entitlement ideology, 14, 16
Enver, A., 205
Eppleh, N., 137
Epstein, H., 86
Erdheim, M., 44
Erdoğan, R. T., 191
Erez, I., 204
Erikson, E. H., xx–xxii, 8, 53, 58–59, 120, 128, 261
Ersoy, B., 204
Etkind, A., 135
externalization, 10, 185

Fadeyev, A., 140
Faimberg, H., 12
Farmer, P., 103
Fatah, 55, 213, 216–217, 219, 223, 225
Ferguson, J., 230–231
Ferguson, N., 131
Ferro, M., 146
Fidler, R., 232
Fisher, G. H., 197
Fisher, R. C., 197
Foss, M., 234–235
Foy, H., 82

Freedland, J., 158
Freud, A., 29–30, 36–37
Freud, S., 35–36, 39, 44–45, 145, 182
Friedman, R., 52, 57, 264, 267, 275
Friedman, T. L., 93
Frith, J., 100
Fromm, D. G., 227
Fromm, M. G., xx, 12, 57, 120, 128, 283
Frölich, M., 164
Fuerzas Armadas Revolucionarias de Colombia, 9
fundamentalism, xiii, 7, 31, 36, 130, 184

Gabriel, O., 158
Gagarin, Y., 107
Galbraith, J. K., 95
Garschagen, T., 166
Garza-Guerrero, A. C., 187
Gatenyo, A. T., 201
Gaudillière, J. M., 61, 258
Gelfand, M. J., 97
Gencebay, O., 204, 205
gender, xxiii, 56–57, 91, 104, 122, 129, 261
Gerges, F., 233
Gerson, M., 170
Gessen, M., 81
ghosts, 151, 281, 284
Gilligan, J., 29–30
Ginzburg, C., 109
Girard, R., 35–38
Giscard d'Estaing, V., 186
globalization, 21, 36, 76, 81, 92, 110, 121, 181–187, 189, 191
Gobodo-Madikizela, P., 168
Göçer, F., 202
Goebbels, J., 84
Golubovsky, A., xviii
Good Friday Agreement, 266, 273, 275, 285
Gorbachev, M., 82
Gore, A., 119
Gorman, M. J., 236
Graham, C., 77
Graham-Harrison, E., 107
Great Patriotic War, 138
grief, 111, 59, 64, 128, 136, 237, 280–281
Grinberg, L., 187–188

Grinberg, R., 187–188
group relations conferences, xxiii
The Guardian, 186
Gumb, L., 99
Gündeş, E., 204

Haass, R., 97
Hadad, S., 204
Hagelüken, A., 172
Halbfinger, D., 64
Hamas, 55, 198, 213, 216–218, 223, 225
Handke, P., 85
Haq, S., 4
Hariri, R., 4
Hartmann, H., 187
Havel, V., 153
Haza, O., 205
Herszenhorn, D., 108
Herzfeld, M., 14
Heuft, G., 41, 48
Hillebrandt, R., 40
Hiroshima Peace Memorial, 61
Hirsch, A., 170
Hirsch, M., 168
Hitler, A., 60, 83–84, 149, 151
Hocking, B., 198
Holocaust, 12, 15, 43, 45, 52, 64, 144, 148–149, 158, 161, 164, 168, 171–172, 199
Horowitz, D. L., 11
Horton, R., 102
Huber, F., 83
Hugi, J., 203, 205
Hui, Z., 102
Hussein, S., 7, 10, 188
Husseini, H., xvi, 211, 227

Ilan (musician), 205
Ilanit (singer), 205
identity
    American, 119–121, 123–124, 127–131
    Crow Indians', 86–87
    formation 120–121
    globalization and, 73–74
    immigrants and, 187–188
    individual, 8, 12

    large group, 3–4, 6, 8–14, 19–20, 44, 46, 53–56, 59, 184–185, 252, 255
    Nazi, 84
    Palestinian, 225
İlhan, R. S., 183
immigrants/immigration, 8, 72–79, 122, 140–141, 158, 167, 169–170, 172–174, 182, 187, 189–191
Inglehart, R., 79, 80, 138
Institutional Event, 56
International Dialogue Initiative, xix, xxii–xxv, 21–22, 52, 62, 63, 134, 137, 146, 226, 246, 249, 252, 256, 257–258, 260, 274, 276, 284
Iran, xxiii, 165, 184
Ireland, W., 236
Israel–Palestine conflict, 55, 211–226
Itzkowitz, N., 14

Jackson, A., 227
Jacobi, G., the Reverend, 83–84
Jarman, N., 197
Javakhishvili, J. D., 15
Jesus, 14, 26, 229–230
Johnson, B., 73, 183
Johnson, N., 100
Jokl, A., 168
Jost, J. T., 97
Juergensmeyer, M., 235
Julius, D. A., 187

Kalibas, S., 140
Kandil, C. Y., 101
Kashmiri Muslims, 4
Kellerhoff, S., 169
Kelman, H. C., 197
Kendrick, K. M., 170
Kennedy, J. F., 4, 46, 105
Kestenberg, J. S., 12
Khajehpour, B., xviii
Khomeini, R., 184
Khrushchev, N., 82
Kim, S. Y., 101
Kimball, C., 230–231
King, M. L., 4

INDEX

Kirişçi, K., 186
Kissinger, H. A., 92
Klein, M., 58–59, 60
Kliman, G., 4
Knipp, K., 169
Koen, R., 202
Koenig, H. G., 238
Kogan, I., 12, 39
Kohen, A., 201
Kohut, H., 59
Koray, E., 204
Kormann, J., 169
Kossert, A., 164
Kral, M., 85
Krantz, J., 280
Kropotkin, P., 145, 153
Krug, D., 233
Kubat, 203
Kühner, A., 40–41
Kunzig, R., 158

Lacan, J., 60
Laurence, F., 200
Lawrence, W. G., 57, 269
Lazar, Prince, 14–15
leaders, 6, 8, 18, 46, 53, 56, 59, 74, 99, 124, 129–130
  Christian, 235–237, 239
  narcissistic, 59–60, 80
  Northern Ireland, 280
Lear, J., 87
Leflore, G., 228, 240
legal quandaries (in Palestine), 214–217
Lemlij, M., 27
Lenin, V., 82
Lennon, J., 200
Leonard, M., 198
Leuzinger-Bohleber, M., 40
Levada, Y., 81–82
Levi, A. H., 201
Levy, Y., 203, 205
Lewis, J., 127
Lifton, R. J., 4, 34, 84–85
Lindner, J., 176
Linet, 202
Litz, B., 238

Liu, Y., 101
Loewenberg, P., 54
Lohl, J., 168

Maalouf, A., 233
Macias, A., 102
Macron, E., 96, 169
Madden, T. F., 231
Mahler, M., 46
Mahler, M. S., 188
Major, B., 99
Mansur, C., 205
Markides, K. C., 14
McAuliffe, C., 4
McBride, J. L., 238
McNeil, D. G., 100
Megali Idea, 14
Mejelle, 219
Meredith, J., 228, 239
Merhav, R., xvii
Merkel, A., 157, 159
Mihm, S., 100
Millennium Declaration (U.N.), 91
Milošević, S., 14–15
minor differences, 11
Modell, A., 261
Modi, N., 73
Mohammad, 229, 235
Mojović, M., 269
Molotov–Ribbentrop Pact, 149–150
Mongol-Tatar Yoke, 13
Montville, J., 197
Moré, A., 168
Mori, S., 41
Moses-Hrushovski, R., 4
mourning, 3, 11–12, 19, 43, 61, 136, 147, 150–151, 162, 274, 280–281
  immigrants', 187–188
  shared, large-group, 15, 18, 54, 150–151
Muallem, Y., 203
Muller, J.-W., 74–75
multi-track diplomacy, 197
Münchau, W., 77
Munro, D. N., 232
Müren, Z., 205
Mysorekar, S., 173

narcissism/narcissistic
  adolescent, 120
  American, 121, 126, 127, 129
  gain(s), 18, 44
  injury, 59
  investment in identity, 6, 14
  leaders, 59–60, 80
  of small differences, 154
Navalny, A., 139
The Nazi Doctors, 34
Nazis, 12, 15–16, 74, 84, 135, 141, 147, 149, 164, 169–170, 238, 257
  neo-, 9, 16, 173
Negahdar, F., xviii
Netanyahu, B., 63
Newman, E., 237–238
Nicias, 88
Nicolson, A., 67, 87–88
Niederland, W. C., 11
Northern Ireland, 25, 27, 34–35, 264, 266, 269
  International Dialogue Initiative intervention, xxv, 273, 277–285
Nye, J. S., 105–106

Obama, B., 46, 61, 77, 121, 128–129
Obolonsky, A. V., 135, 141
O'Brien, L. T., 99
Ochberg, F., xviii, 136–137, 147, 150
O'Donnell, J. J., 231
Ohlendorf, K., 173
Orbán, V., 73
Ordman, J., 235
Oslo Accords, 212–213, 223–224, 266

Palme, O., 4
Parkes, C. M., 5
Pancaroğlu, S., 203
Pegida (Patriotic Europeans Against the Islamization of the West), 78
perestroika, 137, 150
Peters, M., 171
Petter, O., 170
Phillips, A., 283
Phillips, T., 107

Pickrel, R., 102
Piketty, T., 76
Pilgrim, D., 173
Plato, 88
Poitras, C., 103
Poland, G., 107
Polakow-Suransky, S., 80
political polarization, 119, 124, 130, 259
Ponarin, E., 82
Pope, H., 229
Porter, R., 95
Potsdam Conference, 161
prestige policy, 104–105
propaganda, 84, 93, 102, 105–106, 108, 138, 200
  medieval, 232
Putin, V., 15, 73, 81, 82, 106

Rabin, Y., 4, 46, 58
racial segregation, 4, 16, 74, 122–123, 125, 141, 187, 228
Rasgon, A., 64
Raviv, A., 4
Red Hand of Ulster, 283
Reflective Citizen method, 269
refugees, xxii, 75, 77, 79, 157–160, 164–168, 173, 186, 188
religion, 18, 35–36, 38, 53–54, 76, 85, 153, 163, 186, 203, 228–229, 232, 237–241
Rifkind, G., 52
Robert the Monk, 232
Rodrik, D., 93
Romano, İ. F., 201
RosGuard, 138
Rothgerber, H., 97
Rowan, F., 229, 239
Rubenstein, J., 236
Rude, G., 236
Rüütel, R., 21

Saban, S., 204
Sadat, A., xix, 6, 46, 58
Said, E., 199
Sands, B., 35
Sandwich Model, 266–271

Şarhon, K. G., 202
Sarkar, S., 107
Şaul, L., 201
Saunders, H., 197
Sayar, K., 99
Schlapobersky, J., 47
Schlink, B., 159
Schneider, C. P., 198
Scholz, R., 40, 171
Schützenberger, A. A., 12
Šebek, M., 11
Sells, M. A., 14
Sendero Luminoso (Shining Path), 27
separation wall, 220, 222–223
September 11, 2001, 26, 121, 125–126
Sezai, H., 203
Shapiro, E. R., xvii, xx, 4, 119–121, 123, 128, 137, 249, 255, 261
Sharafutdinova, G., 82
Sharon, A., 57
Shay, J., 238
Sholokhov, M., 140
Silver, L., 101
Singer, T., 130
Sinn Fein, 35
Sitting Bull, 86–87
Snyder, T., 83
Soble, J., 61
Social Darwinist, 153
social dreaming, 269
soldier's matrix, 52
Solovyov, V., 142
Solzhenitsyn, A., 142
Sonntag, A., 105
Spanish Flu, 94–95
Stanley-Becker, I., 158
Stein, H. R., 185
Stalin, J., 82, 143, 150–151
Stalinism, 137–138
Stanley-Becker, I., 158
stigmatization, 91, 99–103
Stockholm Bloodbath, 43
Stockholm syndrome, 141
Stora, B., 169
Suistola, J., 9
suitable reservoirs, 184

Tähkä, V., 11
Tamil Tigers, 34
Tassa, D., 204
Tatlıses, İ., 203–204
Taylor, S., 97
Tekbilek, Ö. F., 203
Thatcher, M., 35, 149
terrorism, terrorists, 21, 26–27, 31–32, 35, 64, 74, 92, 97, 109, 121, 126–128, 183, 191, 229, 265
Ticho, G., 187
time collapse, 13, 19, 43–44, 47
Toker, H. A., 201
Tokyay, M., 203–204
Tooze, A., 107
Torres, F., 108
transgenerational transmissions, xx, 3, 11–13, 19, 228, 257, 264
track-one diplomacy, 196–197
track-two diplomacy, 197
Trail of Tears, 227–228
trauma
    chosen, xxii, 13–17, 42–48, 52–53, 58–59, 61, 94, 96–97, 144, 151, 228
    collective, historical, xxv, 3–7, 9–13, 17–18, 39, 47, 59, 62, 122, 144, 147–152, 258, 260
    individual, 134–137, 140–143
    post-traumatic society, 134–135, 140, 143
    undigested past, 3, 6–7, 15–16
Travin, D., 143
Treaty of Dancing Rabbit Creek, 228
Tree Model, 18, 20–21, 293, 265
Trump, D., 60, 73–74, 76, 81, 93, 95, 101–102, 108–109, 121, 127–129, 183, 259
Turkish migrants in Europe, 191
Tutsis, 139
Tutu, D., 17–18, 240–241

Urbain, O., 200
Urban, Pope, 232, 234–235, 239
Uretsky, E., 106

Vagnoni, G., 102
Volkan, V. D., xix–xx, xxi–xxii, 4–5, 7–16, 18, 20, 41, 43–44, 52–53, 58–60, 79, 84, 136, 144, 146, 154, 158–159, 184, 187, 228, 239, 249–250, 255, 258, 263–265, 267, 276–278, 280–281
von der Leyen, U., 108
Vysotsky, V., 140

Wade, R., 76–77
Waelder, R., 12
Wagner, R., 200
Wainer, D., 109
Waldman, P., 229
Wardi, D., 40
Wardle, C., 94
Weathon, S., 108
Weaver, A. J., 238
Welldon, E., 29
Welzer, H., 42–43
Wessely, A., 170
West-Eastern Divan Orchestra, 199
Westernophobia, 143

White, D. W., 108
white supremacists, 3, 9, 16
William, Archbishop of the Crusader kingdom, 233
Williams, R. M., 5
Wingrove, J., 109
Winnicott, D. W., 62
Wirth, H.-J., 41
Wiseman, G., 199
Witherington III, B., 236
Wolf, M., 75
Wolfenstein, M., 4
Wounded Knee, 13

Xi, J., 73
Xu, C., 101

Yeats, W. B., 25–26, 37
Yurchak, A., 151

Zeidler, M., 161
Zeuch-Wiese, I., 172
Ziffer, B., 205
Zimbardo, P. G., 105, 153